Mixed

HARVEST

STUDIES IN RURAL CULTURE   *Jack Temple Kirby, editor*

HAL S. BARRON

Mixed

HARVEST

The Second Great
Transformation in
the Rural North,
1870–1930

The University of North Carolina Press
Chapel Hill and London

Designed by Heidi Perov
Set in Garamond MT Digital
by G&S Typesetters

Manufactured in the United States of America

The paper in this book meets the guidelines for
permanence and durability of the Committee on
Production Guidelines for Book Longevity of the
Council on Library Resources.

Library of Congress Cataloging-in-Publication Data

Barron, Hal S.
     Mixed harvest : the second great transformation
in the rural North, 1870–1930 / by Hal S. Barron.
          p.   cm. — (Studies in rural culture)
     Includes bibliographical references (p.   ) and
index.
     ISBN 0-8078-2354-6 (cloth : alk. paper). —
ISBN 0-8078-4659-7 (pbk. : alk. paper)
     1. United States—Rural conditions.   2. Social
change—United States—History.   I. Series.
HN57.B334   1997
307.72'0973—dc21   96-51451
                                                      CIP

09   08   07   06   05   6   5   4   3   2

For my parents, Bernard W. and Judith T. Barron,
and my daughter, Maya Kobayashi Barron

CONTENTS

ILLUSTRATIONS

PREFACE

Rural life and rural history have been central to the definition of American society but are, today, far removed from most people's lives. In a certain sense, this book is about that very transition—the great change in U.S. history from a nation that was "born in the country," as Richard Hofstadter put it, to one that has "moved to the city." Rather than examining the urban side of that story or viewing the countryside from that point of view, however, I have tried to reconstruct the experiences and perspectives of those who remained on the other side of this historical trajectory. And, rather than revisiting the Populist revolt, which is the way most scholars approach agrarian society at the turn of the twentieth century, I attempt to shed light on more commonplace dimensions of rural life, which are also freighted with meaning and significance.

This is an account of resistance and accommodation and of change and continuity, which took place on battlefields large and small, public and private. At the national level, the issues at stake often received relatively little attention, but for the rural men and women who struggled with them, they were hotly contested and represented profound challenges to their sense of themselves and the place of their communities in a changing and often puzzling world. It is at this level, then, that their history continues to speak to us.

Such a task demands close attention to local history, but this book is not a history of any one community. Instead, I have cast my net over a broader region and through a wider range of sources in order to gather many local examples and case studies. The canvas that I have chosen is a large one, stretching from New England to the northern Great Plains, but not so large, I trust, as to lose sight of important specifics and details. It is a portrait that includes farmers and farm families as well as the townspeople who mediated between farm life and the larger society. And, I argue, the whole is greater than the sum of its parts, for the differences between communities were outweighed by the ubiquity of the tensions between small town and open country, the commonalities of the outside forces that they faced, and the similarities of their responses.

What emerges, I hope, is an understanding of a society and a culture that is both the same and different, both in relation to its own past and with respect to the larger world that increasingly made its presence felt.

This book and its author have received much help along the way. In particular, the National Endowment for the Humanities provided essential financial support. I first began the research for this book as an NEH Fellow at the Newberry Library, and I subsequently received a travel-to-collections grant, a summer stipend, and a senior fellowship at later stages of its development. It pains me deeply that the Endowment is under political attack and that future scholars may not be able to benefit from it as I have. I am also grateful for funding from a Huntington Library–Haynes Foundation fellowship, an AHA Beveridge grant, a Haynes Foundation summer research fellowship, and repeated faculty summer research awards from Harvey Mudd College.

It is imperative, too, that I acknowledge the very valuable assistance I have received from numerous research libraries and their staffs. The Newberry Library, with its treasure trove of obscure local histories and its Center for Family and Social History, was an ideal place to begin this project, and Richard Brown, John Jentz, and David Thackery made my stay there enjoyable as well as productive. The John Crerar Library and the Regenstein Library at the University of Chicago were also important resources, and I made fruitful research trips to the National Agricultural Library in Beltsville, Maryland, the Olin and Mann Libraries at Cornell University, the Wisconsin Historical Society, the Minnesota Historical Society, and the Regional History Center at Northern Illinois University. Montgomery Ward kindly provided me with a microfilm set of the company's early catalogues as well as other materials.

My home library, the Honnold-Mudd Library of the Claremont Colleges, is also home to a very patient and diligent interlibrary loan department and to reference librarians Adam Rosenkranz and Martha Smith, who introduced me to the wonders of computerized searches long before the World Wide Web cast its spell. My home away from home (actually only five minutes from where I live) has been the Huntington Library. I have done most of the writing for this book at my desk by the window in its main reading room. Lunchtime, usually alfresco, is a feast for the mind as well as the body, as many U.S. historians eventually make their way there for research and conversation. The permanent members of the Huntington community form a more constant source of support, especially Martin Ridge and Roy Ritchie, the past and present directors of research, and the able and helpful staff of Readers' Services.

A different version of the first chapter was published previously as "And the Crooked Shall Be Made Straight: Public Road Administration and the Decline of Localism in the Rural North, 1870–1930," in the *Journal of Social History* 26 (1992), and I thank the *Journal* for permission to include it here.

A number of colleagues have read parts of the manuscript in one form or another and have given me valuable criticism as well as much appreciated reassurance and encouragement: Steve Aron, Martha Banta, David Blanke, Peter Blodgett, David Brigham, Kathy Conzen, Clark Davis, Bill Deverell, Lynn Dumenil, Lowell Dyson, Dan Horowitz, Michael Kammen, Stu McConnell, Liz Raymond, and Greg Sharrow. Collectively, and over the past ten years, members of the Los Angeles Social History Study Group have read and commented on many, and in some cases all, of the chapters, and I would like to thank each of them: Roberto Calderon, Phil Ethington, Nancy Fitch, Doug Flamming, Jackie Greenberg, Darryl Holter, John Laslett, Margo McBane, Sandy Jacoby, Ruth Milkman, Gary Nash, Jan Reiff, Steve Ross, Alex Saxton, Dorothee Schneider, Victor Silverman, Bob Slayton, Frank Stricker, Devra Weber, and Leila Zenderland.

Al Bogue and Martin Ridge, each a master of the craft as well as a skilled editor, read the entire manuscript in its penultimate stage and provided me with many helpful suggestions. So, too, did Jack Kirby, who evaluated it for the University of North Carolina Press and welcomed it into his series. Thanks are due as well to Lewis Bateman, executive editor at UNC Press, and his colleagues for the skillful and considerate way they have shepherded my manuscript along. And, finally, I want to express much respect and appreciation for both the older generations of agricultural historians and the newer generations of rural historians, who have given me strong shoulders to stand on and good reason to be optimistic about the future of the field.

In an effort to evoke the theme of continuity in rural life, I have used an epigraph from the Old Testament at the beginning of each chapter. I acknowledge that continuity in my own life by dedicating this book to the two generations of my family who are closest to me: my parents, Bernard W. and Judith T. Barron, and my daughter, Maya Kobayashi Barron. My wife, Kathy Kobayashi, remains my most thorough and critical reader. Even more, she gives me the love and sense of balance that allow me to make my way.

They have sown wheat and have reaped thorns,

they have tired themselves out but profit nothing.

— JEREMIAH 12:13

Those who go out weeping, bearing the seed for sowing,

shall come home with shouts of joy, carrying their sheaves.

— PSALMS 126:6

Mixed

HARVEST

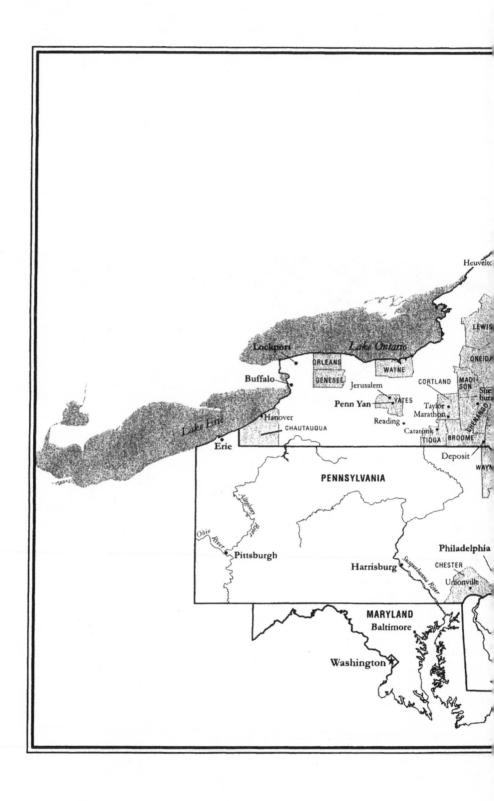

Lockport

Lake Ontario

ORLEANS

WAYNE

Buffalo

GENESEE

Jerusalem

CORTLAND

MADI-SON

Penn Yan

YATES

Taylor
Marathon

She-
bur

Hanover

Reading

CHAUTAUQUA

Lake Erie

Catatonk

Erie

TIOGA

BROOME

Deposit

PENNSYLVANIA

WAYN

Heuvelto

LEWIS

ONEID

Ohio River

Allegheny River

Pittsburgh

Harrisburg

Susquehanna River

Philadelphia

CHESTER

Unionville

MARYLAND
Baltimore

Washington

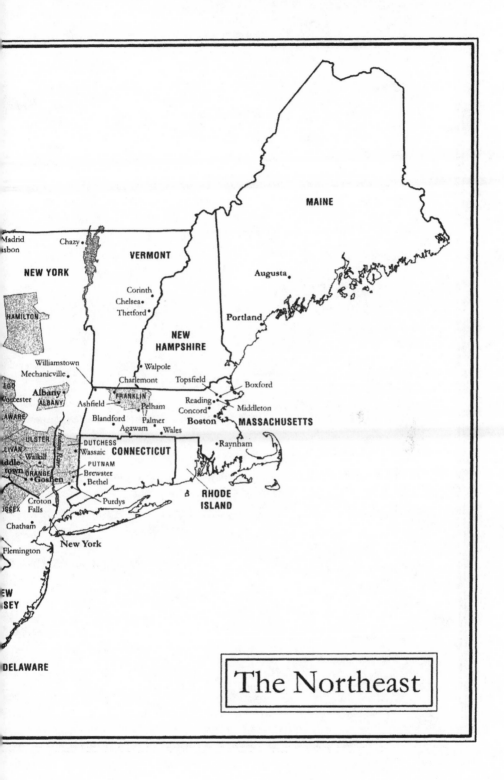

MAINE

Madrid
Lisbon
Chazy •

NEW YORK

VERMONT

Augusta •

Corinth
Chelsea •
Thetford •

HAMILTON

Portland •

NEW
HAMPSHIRE

Walpole •

Williamstown
Mechanicville •

EGO
Worcester

Charlemont
Topsfield •

Boxford •

FRANKLIN

Reading •
Middleton

Albany •
ALBANY

Ashfield •
Pelham
Concord •

AWARE

Blandford •
Palmer
Boston •

MASSACHUSETTS

Agawam •
Wales •

Raynham •

ULSTER
DUTCHESS

LIVAN
Wallkill •
Wassaic •
CONNECTICUT

ddle-
town
PUTNAM

RHODE
ISLAND

ORANGE
Brewster •

Goshen •
Bethel •

SSEX
Croton
Falls •
Purdys •

Chatham •

Flemington •
New York

EW
SEY

DELAWARE

The Northeast

NORTH DAKOTA

MINNESOTA

Duluth

Askov

• Grove Lake

Vasa Township

Minneapolis

Glencoe •

SOUTH DAKOTA

• Amiret
• Florence

Northfield
Faribault

St. Charles

NOBLES

Clark's Grove •

Yankton

• Hull

• Estherville

• Mason City

Rockwell • • Dougherty

• Hampton

HARDIN

SAC

• Gowrie

• Owasa

GRUN

NEBRASKA

Jefferson •

STORY

BOONE

• Blairstown

Des Moines •

• Ord

WARREN

Platte River

Nysted •

• Omaha

IOWA

Des Moines Riv

ADAMS

Missouri River

KANSAS

Topeka •

Kansas
City

Kansas City

Block •

Emporia •

MISSOURI

RENO

The Midwest

INTRODUCTION

Change, Continuity, and the
Transformations of Rural Life

Consider three incidents:

In 1901, Flemington, the county seat of Hunterdon County in rural New Jersey, macadamized its main road. This was an expensive process that involved the careful placement of different sizes of crushed stone to create a smooth and permanent surface, but under the New Jersey road law of 1891, those costs were shared by the state, the county, and local residents. New Jersey farmers, however, were not big supporters of this law, and those in Hunterdon County had little use for this project. According to their spokesman, the editor of a local paper, much of the demand for the new roads came from urban bicyclists, and public funds were better spent on improving old dirt roads rather than on constructing new stone ones. Turn-of-the-century farmers also had little use for the new automobiles that were beginning to appear on country roads, which at that time were luxury vehicles intended primarily for wealthy townspeople and city dwellers. Thus, when increasing automobile traffic quickly destroyed the surface of the new macadam road, its opponents were jubilant.[1]

Responding to a contest sponsored by local merchants during the 1910s, a rural Kansas woman hoped to win $50 for collecting the greatest number of mail-order catalogues. She gathered three hundred of them from relatives, neighbors, and friends scattered over three counties and gave assurances that they would be returned after the contest was over. However, when the local merchants burned the catalogues in the public square (and she failed to win any prizes), she wrote to Montgomery Ward and asked them to please send her three hundred new books at her expense so that she could make good on her promise to return them to their original owners. Ward's did this gladly.[2]

In 1916, organized dairymen in upstate New York withheld their milk from the market in order to gain an advantage over the powerful New York City dealers and corporations that they sold to. Although the strike enjoyed widespread support, a few dairy farmers continued shipping their milk, but it was often dumped by their striking neighbors. The son-in-law of a local milk dealer blamed his wife's cousin, who was one of the strike's leaders, for dumping his milk, and the striking farmer felt betrayed that his cousin would think that he was responsible. So even though the two families had been very close, the accusation left a rift that never healed. As the striker's daughter recalled about milk dumping more generally: "This was really war and everybody felt badly—you know—they didn't like to look at each other after this had happened. They were ashamed of it. On the other hand they felt that they had to fight for this way of life."[3]

Each of these incidents, none of them particularly momentous, illustrates different rural reactions to the restructuring of U.S. society that began during the last quarter of the nineteenth century. Starting with the emergence and consolidation of large-scale businesses that operated on a national as opposed to a local level, this process continued into the twentieth century as new classes of managers and professionals attempted to refashion other aspects of American life along similar lines. At the same time, the growing centrality of cities and the rise of a consumer culture threatened to erode traditional sources of authority and diminish the social and cultural primacy of local communities. These changes recast the United States into a centralized and national society at the expense of what Robert Wiebe has termed the "island community"; taken together, they represented a second great transformation of American society equal to the initial spread of industrial capitalism earlier in the century.

The above examples illustrate a variety of responses to this second great transformation. Farmers resisted attempts to improve local roads, which reflected the agendas of townspeople, professional engineers, and members of an urban "new middle class," and they resented greater state interference in what had been the province of local government. Yet, rural northerners willingly became integrated into a burgeoning consumer economy, largely through the catalogue houses, even though this posed an economic threat to local merchants and eclipsed the importance of their communities as arbiters of taste and values. And, as farmers confronted an agricultural marketplace that was increasingly dominated by new monopolistic and oligopolistic corporations, they, too, organized in new ways and struggled with a fundamentally different understanding of their place in American society and of the role of their local communities.

None of these reactions, however, needs to be couched in terms of the proverbial conflict between "traditional" and "modern" that is so often invoked in discussions of agrarian life. Northern farmers and rural society during the late nineteenth and early twentieth centuries will not be explained by either ideal type or by assuming a clear progression from one to the other. Rather, historical understanding is more nuanced and is to be found between and beyond these categories and by following finer threads of analysis that lead in different and, at times, opposing directions.

This is the perspective adopted in this book, and it is particularly appropriate for the older, established rural areas of the Northeast and the Midwest and the decades at the beginning of the twentieth century that form its subject. By the 1910s, rural society in New England, the Middle Atlantic, the Old Northwest, and, increasingly, the northern prairies and plains was long past the tensions that had accompanied settlement and the upheavals brought on by the initial transition to a market economy earlier in the nineteenth century. And, as the foregoing examples suggest, negotiations with the second great transformation of American society often took place in more prosaic ways, which have been overshadowed by the more dramatic episodes of rural history that scholars have devoted so much attention to. Rather than offering an explanation of Populism, then, this book attempts, in part, to understand how the rural North developed after the agrarian crusade and how those changes both built on and departed from earlier sensibilities. Thus, when Helen Bull Vandervort remembers her father and others feeling that they "had to fight for this way of life" in 1916, we ask, What was that way of life, where did it come from, and where did it lead to in the wake of the second great transformation in the northern countryside?

The notion of a second great transformation, which was characterized by the centralization of the economy, the expansion of state power and professional expertise, and the rise of an urban consumer culture, reflects an important historical reinterpretation of the United States during the twentieth century. One strain of this historiography stresses the emergence and influence of large-scale organizations. According to this so-called organizational synthesis, which is heavily influenced by the work of business historian Alfred D. Chandler, the rise of big business was less a morality play propelled by the avarice of a few robber barons than the story of thousands of new managers with new operational procedures rationalizing production and marketing in order to maximize efficiency. Others, most notably Robert Wiebe, have extended this paradigm and portray Progressive reform as the product of a "new middle class" of professionals, which sought to impose order on a distended American society by reconfiguring social institutions and government in accordance with their own professional priorities and values.[4]

More recent scholarship has explored change in different arenas. Political scientists and historical sociologists have attempted to "bring the state back in" as an independent historical actor, arguing that the internal dynamics of state building as well as its organizational characteristics were themselves important forces in the definition of twentieth-century American society. In a different vein, cultural historians have stressed the effects of corporations on American attitudes and values during this period and have delineated the emergence of a "culture of desire" that was driven by consumer capitalism.[5]

Upon further consideration, however, it seems that this second great transformation was neither as monolithic nor as comprehensive as originally portrayed. This rereading is especially obvious when people, in addition to the corporations and the state, are "brought back in." Olivier Zunz, who explored the belly of the beast by reconstructing the experiences of middle managers and other white-collar employees, finds a great deal of variation and flux in the development of a singular corporate culture even though, he argues, that new corporate culture did ultimately establish hegemony. Lizabeth Cohen's analysis, meanwhile, illustrates how working-class Chicagoans during the 1920s were able to adapt and incorporate the products of consumer capitalism according to their own agendas rather than the other way around. Indeed, in the estimation of one recent reconsideration of Wiebe's *Search for Order*, it is the very absence of human actors that gives his synthesis its clarity and allows him to impose his own interpretive order on historical events.[6]

Rural society, in particular, poses something of an enigma for understanding the second great transformation. On the one hand, the countryside is often singled out for its opposition to the new order and for its resistance to change. The Populist revolt of the 1890s, which still provides the lens through which most historians examine the rural experience during this period, represented, in the works of many scholars, a critique of corporate power and an alternative vision of a cooperative commonwealth that was informed by older Jeffersonian precepts. In the wake of the movement's defeat, however, rural opposition devolved into the antiurban, antimodern, and nativist attitudes characteristic of the "Tribal Twenties." Wiebe himself notes this rural exception to the new order in his conclusion: "a great many in the countryside had also escaped the bureaucratic web," he writes, subscribing instead to "an enduring rural localism, premised upon the infinite applicability of the old village values."[7]

Other views of the countryside during this period, however, stress change and convergence with national and nationalizing trends, either in accordance with or in spite of the preferences of rural people. In his history of the connections between Chicago and the rural Midwest during the nineteenth century, William Cronon analyzes the transition from the "first nature" of the local ecosystem to the "second nature" of regional hinterland and global economy. In a related vein, Olivier Zunz describes the successful corporate penetration of agrarian markets and, by implication, of agrarian ways of life, as the minions of International Harvester and their ilk married their own agendas to the farmers' pursuits of profit and progress. Scholars also detail the rise of the Country Life Movement, a series of reforms to restructure rural institutions along modern, bureaucratic lines, or the emergence of large-scale farmers' organizations such as the Farm Bureau, which critics regard as a betrayal of an older agrarian ethos. Finally, consumer and popular culture arrived in rural America during these years as well, first through the mail in the form of a catalogue, and then by car or radio, which transported country folk to the nearest movie theaters and the worlds beyond.[8]

The truth lies somewhere between. Like other histories, the history of the
rural experience between 1870 and 1930 is a story of change *and* continuity,
and of accommodation as well as resistance, which took place under conditions and with consequences that were not always chosen or anticipated. This
book is an attempt to explore and explain those vagaries and contradictions
and to understand the dynamics and meanings of the second great transformation in the northern countryside.

The importance of both change and continuity also applies to the history
of the first great transformation in the rural North, and this provides a useful starting point for any consideration of the second. Much of this discussion has centered on the social meanings of the rise of a market economy.
This is a primary concern of the "new rural history," and it has taken the
form of a heated debate between historians who argue that preindustrial
farmers stood in opposition to the values of an emerging industrial society
and limited their participation in the market, and historians who claim that
northern farmers were motivated by the same capitalist spirit of liberal individualism and acquisitiveness as the rest of society—the so-called social and
market perspectives.[9]
According to the former view, the expansion of the market economy en-
gendered significant changes as northern farmers began specializing in cash
crops and new forms of nonagricultural production instead of practicing
mixed agriculture to meet the needs of their households and communities.
That strategy not only made them more vulnerable to fluctuations in price
and other forces beyond their communities and beyond their control, it also
changed relationships within their communities and households. Market
pressures altered traditional interactions between farmers and their neighbors and between country people and those in the villages and towns. They
also led to a redefinition of the roles of farm women as well as new relationships between farmers and their hired hands, who increasingly came from a
distinct class of outside laborers.
Although this depiction of dramatic transformation has been tempered
and refined as newer studies have uncovered more of the nuances and details
of those relationships, the larger paradigm still overlooks important characteristics of rural life that continued to distinguish it from the mainstream of

American society long after the transition to commercial agriculture.[10] In particular, the central importance of the family farm and the primacy of the local community continued to shape the rural experience and allowed more traditional Jeffersonian beliefs of independence and local autonomy to continue to influence the lives of northern country people. This, in turn, provided country people with their own framework for negotiating and, at times, opposing, newer forces of change.

The family farm in the nineteenth-century rural North was, in the words of two economic historians, "simultaneously a complex, successful economic activity as well as an engine of family and social organization with strong noneconomic motivations." This dual nature meant that northern farmers constantly straddled the fence between agriculture as a way of life and as a way of making a living, but the relative autonomy of farm life led them to aspire to both goals and often gave them the wherewithal to succeed. In spite of the pressures and vicissitudes of the market economy, commercial family farms provided more freedom than industrial work or even small businesses, and they continued to foster a culture of independence that was of a piece with older agrarian values. Moreover, the rural North remained a society of family farms well into the twentieth century in which the family enterprise was the dominant form of economic organization as well as the main component of the rural community.[11]

That rural community also remained a primary frame of reference in spite of integration into the market economy. Indeed, as several scholars have argued, the local community became even more important during the late nineteenth century as many rural areas matured after the initial settlement period and communities there became increasingly homogeneous and interconnected because of the relative lack of new in-migration and the cumulative effects of generations of selective out-migration. This localism also resonated with more traditional Jeffersonian beliefs that emphasized local authority and the decentralized control of public life, and it continued to shape agrarian sensibilities.[12]

In ways that built on but transcended the immediate social realities of family farm and community, northern farmers also continued to see themselves as essential to the nation's commonwealth, a conviction known as agrarianism or agricultural fundamentalism. They stressed their importance not as a separate interest group, but as the basis of the larger society's well-being. This perspective shared elements with the producers' ethic, which celebrated those who actually made or grew things and was common among urban workers during this period, but it also emphasized the superiority of country life over city life. Moreover, such beliefs were not confined to agrarian society, but continued to foster a deep-seated uncertainty about urban life that was common in American culture. Here, too, Jefferson cast a long shadow.[13]

Thus, life in the rural North continued to be informed by values of independence, localism, and agricultural fundamentalism well after the first great transformation and extensive involvement in the market economy. Yet, these were the same values that were most directly threatened by the newer forces of the second great transformation. Those challenges and their resolutions took place in three discrete but interrelated arenas, and these form the organizing framework for this book.

First, rural northerners were challenged in their roles as citizens as new combinations of reformers and professionals sought to centralize authority in the state at the expense of local government and local control. Chapter 1, "And the Crooked Shall Be Made Straight," analyzes the battles that were fought over the seemingly mundane issue of road administration, a process that led to a redefinition of localism in a political sense just as the roads themselves reconfigured its meaning in a geographical one. Chapter 2, "Teach No More His Neighbor," discusses the issues of school reform and school consolidation, which also provide a prism for examining the conflicts between more traditional rural attitudes and the imperatives of a centralized, bureaucratic society.

Northern farmers were also forced to define themselves in new ways as producers and as small businessmen as they formed new organizations in order to counter the increasing powers of large-scale corporations in the marketplace. Chapters 3 and 4 offer two case studies of the social and ideological bases of farmers' organizations in the post-Populist period. "Bringing Forth Strife" tells the story of the Dairymen's League of upstate New York, a leading cooperative of milk producers, and "To Reap the Whirlwind" considers the farmers' grain elevator movement in the Midwest, which was the most common but is the least studied form of agricultural organization in that region. In both cases, agricultural producers struggled not only against their economic competitors but between their own desires for individual autonomy and local control and countervailing pressures for greater economic power and efficiency.

Finally, country people became consumers during this period and were increasingly drawn into an urban-based consumer culture, which also posed challenges to their sense of local autonomy as well as their beliefs in the superiority of country life. Chapter 5, "With All the Fragrant Powders of the Merchant," looks at rural experiences with mail-order buying and the campaigns against the mail-order houses that were waged by local merchants, ostensibly defending the local community against outsiders. The 1920s saw the proliferation of consumer culture in American society, and Chapter 6, "Not the Bread of Idleness," analyzes rural encounters with some of its chief components: the automobile, home electricity, the radio, and brand-name advertising. In this sphere, like the political and economic, country people approached new conditions in ways that were consistent with their beliefs and sensibilities, even if the consequences of their actions led them in other directions.

None of these attempts to come to terms with the second great transformation in the northern countryside is simple and clear-cut, however, either for the historical actors involved or for the historian trying to make sense of them. The rural North and the communities it contained was not a monolith with a singular perspective, but was cross-hatched by competing visions deriving from a variety of sources including class, ethnicity, gender, and age. At times, for example, the agents of larger forces of change were not outsiders, but members of the family or nearby townspeople. Thus, the process of negotiating the second great transformation involved relationships within rural households and communities as well as between those communities and the larger society.

Likewise, heartfelt efforts to negotiate between time-honored principles and new structural realities were, of necessity, marked by ambiguities and contradictions. The end result, then, is also not a simple one, either as a story of the steadfast maintenance of tradition in the face of change or the complete capitulation to a new order. Rather, it is best understood as a hybrid of the two, to use an analogy drawn from another agricultural development, which reconfigured more traditional notions of localism, independence, and agrarianism into new forms. And, this, too, represents change as well as continuity.

In a political sense, this change allowed rural northerners to continue their criticism and opposition to the dominant direction of American society, but to do so as organized interest groups that participated successfully in the new order. Farmers continued to rely on traditions of independence and the rhetoric of agricultural fundamentalism as they formed new organizations as producers and small businessmen, but in this case, those values ultimately limited their abilities to achieve centralized control and greater economic power like the corporations they opposed. With respect to consumer culture, country people used new technologies, such as the automobile and the radio, to fashion a new rural culture that transcended and undermined the smaller communities in their lives even as it paradoxically celebrated and continued old-fashioned virtues of localism and neighborliness. This offered both an alternative to and a critique of the dominant urban society, and it informed rural folk who moved to the cities as well as those who stayed in the countryside, contributing to the enduring ambivalence about urban life in American culture.

Thus, rural northerners negotiated the larger forces of the second great transformation in ways that were marked by resistance as well as accommodation and by change as well as continuity. As a result, agrarian society during the twentieth century continued to provide a counterpoint to the dominant trends in American society, and country people remained both a part of the American mainstream and apart from it. For them and for the nation as a whole, it was a mixed harvest.

Part I

CITIZENS

Prepare ye the way of the Lord,
  make straight in the desert a highway for our God.
Every valley shall be raised,
  and every mountain and hill shall be made low:
and the crooked shall be made straight,
  and the rough places a plain.

  —ISAIAH 40:3–4

AND THE CROOKED
SHALL BE MADE STRAIGHT

Rural Road Reform and the
Politics of Localism

One of the defining characteristics of the second great transformation in the
United States was the attempt of new combinations of reformers and professionals, members of the so-called new middle class, to restructure American
society and its institutions in order to make them more efficient. These efforts began in the late nineteenth century and contributed significantly to the
increased centralization of American life by creating new arenas for professional expertise, new mechanisms of control, and an expanded role for the
state, all of which undermined more local sources of authority and power.

In the northern countryside, this impulse manifested itself most directly
in a series of reforms designed to modernize rural life that achieved its
apotheosis in the Country Life Movement during the first decades of the
twentieth century. Typically advocated by outside experts, this grab bag of
governmental and nongovernmental initiatives included agricultural extension work, the formation of farmers' organizations and cooperatives, rural
church reform, and social welfare measures for the countryside, in addition
to road reform and school consolidation. Most of our understanding of this
movement, however, is based on studies of the reformers' ideas and values

rather than their intended beneficiaries, and while historians understand (and often empathize with) the cosmopolitan perspective of those who advocated the restructuring of country life, rural attitudes and experiences remain less accessible.[1]

Indeed, many rural northerners initially opposed the kind of society envisioned by the reformers. Informed by antiurban sentiments and other agrarian sensibilities that stressed the primacy of self-government, they at first resisted the self-professed expertise of these outsiders as well as related efforts to centralize the control of local institutions in the hands of the state. By the 1930s, however, country people had become more integrated into and, in certain ways, more comfortable with a translocal society. But what were the dynamics of this change, and on what terms did rural northerners come to participate in the new order?

The history of public road administration in the rural North between 1870 and 1930 illustrates some of the tensions and accommodations that shaped the political dimensions of the second great transformation in the countryside. In their efforts to make the crooked straight, advocates of road reform engaged rural inhabitants in a protracted struggle for change. At first, farmers adhered to republican principles and strove to maintain local control over their roads in the face of increasing pressures from townspeople and boosters within their communities and from engineers, bicyclists, and other urban interests on the outside. In order to overcome this rural intransigence, however, the state became progressively more involved, and by 1930, road administration had become centralized and a critical component of local government had disappeared. Thus, the battles over roads between local priorities and cosmopolitan goals helped to shape the modern state.

In the course of these events, though, rural attitudes also changed between 1870 and 1930. In one sense, the roads themselves, along with automobiles and other improvements in communications and transportation, facilitated wider contact with a broader spectrum of American society, altering the definition of the local community (changes that will be discussed later). In another sense, however, the issue of roads provided an impetus for farmers' own emergence as an organized faction in the new political order and for their embrace of a new perspective that cast them as an interest group rather than as the foundation of American society. While this new translocal rural outlook represented a significant departure from an older, more localistic political culture, paradoxically it still formed a basis for opposition to urban and industrial interests.

––––––––––

Roads in nineteenth-century rural America were predominantly local institutions, which both reflected and shaped the nature of the rural community and were bound up with the commonplace rhythms of agrarian life. Country roads were often winding and poorly located, a condition that, according to landscape historian John Stilgoe, "derived from specific, local needs not from concern with the long-distance traveler condemned to meander from farmstead to woodlot to pasture to farmstead, forever detouring around or through swamps, bogs, and hills."[2] Consequently, road administration was handled almost exclusively by local government until the end of the nineteenth century.[3] Typically, each township was subdivided into smaller road districts and placed under the authority of an elected official, known variously as a road surveyor, overseer, or pathmaster. In a system of corvée or statute labor that dated back to the Middle Ages, road construction and maintenance was carried out by every able-bodied male inhabitant in the township, who worked out a road tax based on property values as well as a poll tax.

This system of road districts, pathmasters, and statute labor was the bane of later road reformers, but it was well attuned to the realities and sensibilities of nineteenth-century rural life. A farmer worked mainly on the roads that he used the most, and he could pay his road tax with his own labor or that of his sons and hired men, as well as through the use of his draught teams, wagons, and tools, which made it less of a burden than a cash levy. Moreover, he performed this work during slack times on the farm, when his crops (and the roads, in the reformers' estimation) were not in need of attention. According to one local historian, the highway district system was preeminently a social system, for "it gave the people of the neighborhood a chance to get together and discuss the questions of the neighborhood, town and nation"; or, in the words of a late-nineteenth-century critic from Wisconsin, "The day set for work is a sort of annual picnic where farmers meet to swap stories and trade horses."[4]

Even more important, however, the system of local road districts embodied the principles of home rule and self-reliant independence that epitomized rural republican ideology. In Europe, roads were both the symbol and the agent of centralized government: the King's Highway, *camino real*, *Reichstrasse*, or *route royale*. In the American colonies, however, attempts to establish and maintain "post roads" or "royal roads" failed repeatedly. The towns of colonial Connecticut, for example, felt no obligation to provide intertown highways or public roads that would link up with the King's Highway. According to the leading authority on the subject, "self-contained and independent, they resented any supervision by a higher authority."[5] Similarly, during the turnpike-building boom of the early nineteenth century, Americans curtailed the road-building powers of the federal government and limited state governments' role to a financial one. In John Stilgoe's words: "The same fear of tyranny that forbade the keeping of a standing army retarded the building of 'Federal highways'; even the success of the National Road scarcely lessened citizen fears that a government powerful enough to build roads everywhere might use its power to erode local rights."[6]

The virtues of local government remained fixtures of the rural perspective throughout the nineteenth century, and they found explicit expression after the Civil War in response to mounting pressures to change the administration of roads. David W. Lewis, a pathmaster in Delaware County, New York, voiced widely held sentiments in his reaction to an 1892 article in *Harper's Weekly* that touted a system of national, state, and county roads: "The tendency of the times toward centralized politics, and the present utter neglect of the earlier and homelier ideas of self-development and local self-government, are here well illustrated. . . . The liberty of localities to perform their own functions in road-building and road-working is in danger, and if people do not exercise this liberty, it will be wrested from them."[7] Nor were such feelings any less pronounced in the newer midwestern states. In 1884, a group of farmers from Warren County, Iowa, linked the issue of roads to the core of republican ideology when they beseeched the state legislature: "give heed to the call of human rights and equal justice and the great principle of free Government which will leave the road laws and management as they now are in the hands of the People and not under the control of a centralized one man power and moneyed despotism."[8]

Whatever its ideological virtues, this decentralized system of road management was also the subject of sharp attack, and not just from irate and inconvenienced travelers. In Williamstown, Massachusetts, for example, complaints about the poor quality of roads began to appear in town records in 1803 and continued every year until after World War II. Nineteenth-century Vermonters commonly quipped: "This road ain't passable, it ain't even jackass-able."[9] Burgeoning cities chafed under the homegrown style of road administration and abandoned it for less anachronistic forms of government, while the needs of growing numbers of suburbanites and nearby commercial farmers in the Northeast focused concern on the poor roads leading from the hinterlands into urban areas. In general, roads for long-distance travel got less use and attention after the development of the railroads, but as the northeastern rail network matured and expansion slowed after the Civil War, poor road conditions became increasingly troublesome.

Massachusetts began to address these problems in 1869 when state legislators funded an essay competition on road making and supervision, which was followed by an extensive survey and report on current practices in the Commonwealth.[10] Although the essay competition and subsequent report were conducted under the auspices of the State Board of Agriculture, they exhibit a perspective that is decidedly cosmopolitan and professional—and out of step with the realities of rural life. The top essayists, as well as many of the less successful competitors, were all civil engineers, steeped in a professional culture that emphasized their roles as planners and architects. Their suggestions for road reform reflected that professional mentality and sought to create new positions for other civil engineers.[11]

To these reformers, the solutions to road problems were clear-cut: First and foremost, abolish the labor system and substitute a cash tax. Second, distinguish between first-, second-, and third-class roads, leaving only the last category in the hands of the townships. Finally, eliminate road districts and overseers and centralize administration at the township, county, and state levels under expert supervisors, preferably engineers, who can purchase equipment and hire skilled workers, following the best (and often the most expensive) road-making techniques. None of the reformers, however, addressed the problem of how to pay for expensive new roads, nor did they seem aware of the deep-seated commitment to local government that held sway in the countryside. At the 1870 meeting of the Massachusetts Board of Agriculture, only Dr. Loring, the president of the New England Agricultural Society, expressed any reservations and admonished the board to avoid centralized organizations, "which might interfere with local wants and interest."[12]

In contrast, the 1870 survey of Massachusetts road administration illustrates the extent of older practices in rural areas. Of the 332 towns and cities (out of a total of 337) reporting on road taxes, all of the 50 towns and cities over 5,000 relied exclusively on cash, while nearly three-fourths of the 73 towns under 1,000 continued using labor in whole or in part. The labor system was most common in the predominantly rural counties of western Massachusetts, even in the larger towns, and in Franklin County, 87 percent of the 23 towns up to 2,500 adhered to some form of statute labor. The newer forms of supervision advocated by Massachusetts road reformers were less prevalent than cash taxes, and these were also concentrated in the larger, urban areas. Even a cash tax did not necessarily lead to greater centralization, however, and well over half of the townships on the cash system still had large numbers of road officials and decentralized road districts; only three employed a full-time superintendent. As the 1870 survey indicates, then, although rural inhabitants were not completely averse to changes in road administration, they had other priorities in contrast to the proposals of the early road reformers.[13]

These "local wants and interests" become clearer in the numerous discussions of road issues that were sponsored by state boards of agriculture, farmers' clubs, and farmers' institutes throughout the North during the 1870s and 1880s.[14] Rural inhabitants persisted in placing neighborhood needs ahead of more widespread benefits, and they wanted their local governments to be responsive to those concerns. According to one of the speakers at the 1870 meeting of the Maine Board of Agriculture, many roads in the state were built by the original settlers, and relocating them was problematic: "It is very difficult to get any alteration made in those roads. Almost every selectman has some friend whose personal rights must be taken care of. . . . Here are the farms on the old roads, and the buildings, and the orchards, and here is an old gray-headed man, who has worked hard all his life, and his labors have gone for the benefit of the public, and, now he is to be deprived of his rights and privileges by taking away his road."[15] Similar considerations also determined the selection of road surveyors in New Hampshire, in the words of the chairman of the State Board of Agriculture in 1872: "Sometimes an interested party wants some particular work done near his premises, and he finds some other persons who want something done in their districts, and they put their heads together and nominate their friends and they are elected."[16]

Rural inhabitants were also worried about the increased costs inherent in proposed road reforms. "The farmers' fear of increased taxation stands seriously in the way of thorough road improvement," noted one Pennsylvanian.[17] In general, northern rural townships during the 1870s were very sensitive about tax issues; many had just retired their Civil War debts and were reluctant to take on new financial obligations. To the poorer farmers and residents who often formed the majority of local voters, a cash road tax was an economic burden. More prosperous farmers were better able to afford cash taxes, and sometimes preferred to pay cash rather than take time away from their farms to work on the roads. But they were still loathe to add to their taxes, in whatever form, because they regarded the taxes as a threat to their property values and their independence. Cash taxes also posed a particular hardship in the newer townships of the Midwest, where opposition was especially pronounced. Road reformers in Michigan, for example, pushed for a money tax, but even their proposals had to exempt new and sparsely settled areas.[18]

Apprehensions about excessive and expensive government also shaped rural concerns about proposed road reforms. Farmers from Pennsylvania and New York, for example, were leery of new government officials and warned against the creation of hordes of "engineers, superintendents, contractors, &c," or "long lists of salaried office holders, in whose hands vast sums of the people's money would melt away."[19] Elsewhere, the town meeting in Pelham, Hampshire County, Massachusetts (population 673 in 1870), passed a sarcastic motion in 1868 in response to suggested road changes: "Voted that the selectmen be instructed to hire a certain number of men to repair the highways and bridges in this town the ensuing year. Not to work themselves personally but to superintend the whole. And that Superintendence shall not exceed in cost the expense of work on said highways."[20] Needless to say, Pelham remained under the labor system and had 19 road surveyors for 48 miles of roads in 1870.

Ironically, numerous rural communities adopted cash taxes as well as more centralized township control during the 1880s in order to buy road machines.[21] Patent road scrapers came on the market in 1879 and, at a cost of less than $200, were much more affordable than the large steamrollers used in

The Champion road grader, 1886. (Courtesy of the Public Works Historical Society, Kansas City, Missouri)

cities and suburban towns.[22] One agriculturalist in Connecticut considered the road machine to be a "perfect godsend," while N. F. Underwood of Wayne County, Pennsylvania, proclaimed: "the use of the road machine in our county is saving us at least one-half of our taxes. . . . There has been more done in the last two years than before in ten years." [23] And rural communities were quick to take advantage of the new technology. According to an 1886 survey of Connecticut roads, 116 of the 129 towns reporting (out of a total of 167) had at least one patent scraper or road machine, including 26 of the 29 towns still on the district system.[24] In at least one town in Massachusetts, however, the road machine had a bumpier ride. After a long history of torturous debates and numerous reversals over the administration of local roads, the selectmen in Ashfield, Franklin County, finally set out to purchase the town's first road machine in 1883 using newly authorized cash taxes. In the end, though, sarcasm reigned, and when the town wit witnessed the trial of the new contraption, he commented: "Oh, they'll buy it quick enough if

they can ride and do the work, only they'll want a big umbrella to keep the
sun off, and a place to carry a jug of cider."[25]

Thus, the new road machines improved roads without necessitating centralized administration or higher taxes. Given the small number of Connecticut townships that adopted the machines and remained with the district system, they probably also provided a strong impetus for the consolidation of
township control. Still, the experiences of Ashfield notwithstanding, road
machines permitted a range of compromises between better roads, cost, and
decentralized control that suited rural needs and sensibilities. Left to their
own devices, rural communities during the 1880s could and did arrive at their
own balance of these considerations. They got better roads without sacrificing too much local control.

────────

But rural communities were not left to their own devices. Instead, new
pressures for "permanent improvements"—expensive macadam stone
roads—shifted the focus of road reform and heightened rural concerns
about increased costs and centralization; and as good roads advocates began
to push for macadamized roads, town and rural interests squared off against
each other.[26] In Jefferson County, Ohio, for example, an 1878 measure to
macadamize three trunk roads leading from the city of Steubenville carried
3,185 to 2,935; it passed overwhelmingly in the city itself, but was defeated
decisively in the surrounding area with some townships opposing the new
roads without dissent. In the end, the will of the majority was thwarted as attempts to build the roads were blocked by court injunctions until country
people could elect a county commissioner who was against the new roads.[27]

Farmers resisted macadamizing roads, or any expensive road improvements, because of the cost. Except for the relatively small poll tax, road taxes
were based mainly on the assessment of real property, and property owners
along or near the improved road had to pay a special added tax of up to
one-third of the cost of the improvements. Thus, in the Steubenville example, city residents owned just one-third of the assessed property, ensuring
that local farmers would pay disproportionately for new roads that primarily
benefited townspeople. If rural counties and townships were loathe to raise
taxes, the question of floating bonds and assuming debt in order to finance

road improvements was even more vexing and divided fiscally conservative farmers from their booster neighbors. In addition to the burdens of Civil War indebtedness, many rural communities in the North had a history of public and private investment in local railroads that either failed or never materialized, and their experiences made them wary of taking similar steps for better roads.[28]

By the 1880s and 1890s, however, a new force led the drive for macadam roads and transformed it into a national campaign that transcended strictly local animosities. The League of American Wheelmen (LAW) was an organization of well-heeled, urban bicycling enthusiasts—the late-nineteenth-century equivalent of present-day yuppies—who enjoyed touring the countryside on their two-wheelers, especially if they could ride on a smooth, permanent surface.[29] Although the arguments and programs advanced by the LAW were elaborations of those put forth by earlier road reformers, the LAW operated on a larger scale and in a wider arena. With substantial funding from bicycle manufacturers and dealers, the LAW published *Good Roads* magazine and distributed over 5 million pamphlets on the subject between 1889 and 1900, the most famous being *The Gospel of Good Roads, A Letter to the American Farmer* (1891). In addition, the LAW sponsored numerous meetings and conventions on road issues, and LAW officials often spoke at local farmers' institutes and other agricultural and business gatherings. Finally, the LAW agitated for both state and federal road legislation and formed a full-fledged lobbying organization, the National League for Good Roads.[30]

As bona fide members of the "new middle class," as the creators of a well-financed lobbying organization, and as conspicuous consumers in a new leisure culture, then, the LAW epitomized the new order of the second great transformation, and farmers were extremely skeptical of their motivations in addition to their long-standing concerns about costs and centralized administration. Thus, by the 1890s, urban-based road reformers and rural interests had reached an impasse over the funding of improved roads. The gradual shift to township control and cash taxes and the adoption of patent road machines enhanced the maintenance of existing roads in many northeastern communities, but these changes were not sufficient to finance the expensive macadam roads increasingly in demand. Midwestern farmers, in the throes of an agricultural depression, were even less receptive to costly road reforms, as

"How cam'st thou in this pickle?"—*Shakespeare.*

THE GOSPEL

OF

GOOD ROADS.

A Letter to the American Farmer.

BY

Isaac B. Potter

NEW YORK:
1891.

Title page from The Gospel of Good Roads, *1891.*

Stuck in the mud near New Albany, Indiana, 1898. Photograph entered in a
"muddy road" contest sponsored by the League of American Wheelmen.
(Courtesy of the State Historical Society of Wisconsin)

illustrated by a resolution passed at an 1893 Iowa farmers' convention: "We
don't want any eastern bicycle fellers or one-hoss lawyers with patent leather
boots, to tell us how to fix the roads that we use."[31] All too often, that contempt was reciprocated by the urban-based wheelmen, who saw the farmers
as the chief roadblock, if you will, to the realization of their goals.

   One possible resolution to the conflict was to provide direct state aid to localities to help defray the costs of expensive road improvements, a strategy
first proposed in 1869 by the essayists in Massachusetts and advocated by
wheelmen throughout the 1880s. That solution, however, raised other problems, which were discussed extensively in a survey of Pennsylvania's "leading
farmers and thinking men" in 1890. These spokesmen generally favored state
aid for permanent roads and recognized it as the only way to fund such expensive improvements, but they were uneasy about excessive state control at

the expense of local initiative. In the words of A. Sharpless from Chester County:

> To make the state the initial power of control over all roads within her borders . . . would soon throw into the hands of irresponsible leaders a vast political power that would prove dangerous to the integrity of our commonwealth, and in time possibly wreck our boasted independence. . . . With a revenue of seven or eight millions annually of road tax in their hands, any party could maintain itself against all comers. Its ramifications and power for evil would be felt in every township in the state with constant danger to the people.[32]

Because of these and similar objections from rural constituents, northern legislatures first experimented with more limited reforms that made it easier for localities to improve their roads but fell shy of direct state involvement.[33] During the 1890s, however, the ineffectiveness of these measures and persistent lobbying by good roads organizations led to the institution of state aid, and by 1905, some form of state assistance was available in thirteen states, including all of the Northeast and Ohio.

But rural desires to maintain local control continued to limit the role of the state in spite of the establishment of state assistance. Consequently, the first state aid programs were not sufficient, and rural areas continued to balk at expensive improvements and built few macadam or stone roads.[34] As already noted, farmers in rural Hunterdon County, New Jersey, resisted attempts to obtain state funding for stone roads and cheered when heavy traffic broke up the newly macadamized main street in Flemington, the county seat.[35] Massachusetts in 1904 had the highest percentage of improved roads of any state in the country—45.9 percent of a total of 17,092 miles—but 84 percent of these improved roads (6,579 miles) were gravel roads financed by the towns, and state aid accounted for only 523.7 miles of stone roads. However they were funded, by 1909 there were only 14,107 miles of macadam roads in urban and rural areas in the Northeast—less than 6 percent of all public roads.[36]

In New York, in a development that presaged changes elsewhere, this rural reticence led to greater state involvement and eventually resulted in the largest program of state aid in the country. Good roads advocates began lobbying for state aid and cash taxes in the mid-1890s after it became clear that county option plans were having little effect. The taxes were resisted by upstate farmers and their legislators, who claimed that farmers were usually "short" on cash and "long" on time and preferred to work off their road taxes. The Albany County farmers who appeared before the Joint Committee on Roads and Bridges in 1898 voiced all of the usual complaints and then some. In addition to pleading poverty, they worried about being subjected to the control of a state engineer, and they pointed to the current state-funded improvements on the Erie Canal as an ominous example of drastic cost overruns and political corruption that would be repeated with the new roads. One farmer pointed out that many rural towns owned road scrapers, which made dirt roads that were very good, and that the roads to be built under the provisions of the bill would be between large cities, not the rural crossroads that needed the most improvement. These attitudes had already defeated good roads measures in 1896 and 1897, causing the *New York Times* editors to decry the "whole soggy mass of rural conservatism."[37]

Later in 1898, however, the state legislature finally passed two of the laws that had previously been rejected: the Higbee-Armstrong Act (which passed the Assembly 90 to 39 after a "very spirited debate"), establishing 50 percent state support for macadam highways; and the Fuller–Plank Road Law (which had been defeated by two votes earlier in the Assembly's session), giving townships twenty-five cents for every dollar raised for road taxes if they adopted the cash system. Still, rural sensibilities were a palpable political force, according to the *New York Times*: "The 'home rule' idea is uppermost in the proposed law. Under it the whole road building machinery is set in motion by the local sentiment of the counties."[38] In spite of the financial incentives provided by the new legislation, New York townships were slow to switch to a money tax or build macadam roads: only 456 miles of the new highways were completed by 1904 and 66 percent of the 1904 road tax was still paid in labor.[39] Macadam roads remained too expensive, according to a speaker at the Hanover Farmers' Club in Chautauqua County: "The new road law is more in the interest of the wheelmen than the farmer. . . . I am interested in good roads . . . but if we should have the roads paved, so that all the people would have the benefit, the real estate would not pay the expense."[40]

In order to get better roads, then, the state was forced to buy off rural concerns and pay for the new roads entirely out of state funds—a resolution of the dilemma that was repeated later throughout the Northeast and Midwest. This seemed equitable to the residents of the New York countryside: it was redress for their tax contributions to the expensive modifications of the Erie Canal, and it meant that farmers would finally get a direct share of state monies. According to a committee of Cortland County farmers who had attended a good roads convention in Albany:

> When we think of the miserable condition of our country roads and of the small expenditure that is being made for their improvement, and then think of the millions of dollars that has been expended . . . for the opening and enlarging a ditch across the State . . . your Committee believe that the millions that use the country roads have a right, yea, are in duty bound to clamor for State aid in road improvement, and that in such a way as not to overburden the small tax-payer in the country districts.[41]

Rural opposition thus appeased, the necessary constitutional amendment passed by a wide margin in 1905 (383,188 to 117,181); and by 1908, New York enacted a $50 million bond issue and created a State Department of Highways to build thirty-seven designated state highways entirely at state expense. The new program of state roads stimulated construction, but it also generated fresh complaints reflecting older fears and concerns about state power. Farmers criticized the inefficiency and political corruption of the state highway department, the misplaced emphasis on macadam instead of earth roads, and the poor quality and durability of the new roads themselves, especially because state engineers were not familiar with local conditions and because localities were responsible for maintenance at their own expense. True to form, the highway program was less than half completed when funds ran out, so another $50 million bond issue was authorized by a constitutional amendment in 1912. This bond passed by an even wider margin than the one in 1905, in part because it apportioned even more money to rural counties. Thus, New York had an extensive network of nearly 8,000 miles of macadam and bituminous-macadam highways on the eve of World War I. The farmers, although still wary of the state, were less insistent on completely local control because of the sizable influx of state funds.[42]

In contrast to the comparatively wealthy and urbanized states of the Northeast, rural opposition to macadamized roads and other road reforms

and the rural commitment to local control were even more pronounced in
the Midwest, causing state aid and state control to come later and on a
smaller scale. In Wisconsin, the most reform-minded midwestern state, state
aid and a state highway commission were not established until 1911, after improved economic conditions and new state taxes on nonfarm sources lessened the farmers' tax bite for road reforms.[43] When it finally did pass over the
objections of two-fifths of the legislators, Wisconsin's 1911 law did not establish a system of state highways, but provided cost-sharing only for county
roads after a petition by the township. Consequently, Wisconsin funded
roads that suited rural needs and pocketbooks; two-thirds of the roads improved during the first three years of the program were dirt, gravel, or shale
country roads.

The continuing importance of localism also limited more rational planning. In Green County, for example, each supervisor on the board wanted
county road money spent in his township rather than on primary county
roads, resulting in sufficient funding for each "to build a piece of good road
as long as a dining table."[44] This combination of local control and state funding had absurd consequences in nearby Ogle County, Illinois. Several townships advanced competing proposals for the first road to be built with state
aid under the 1913 Tice Act, so the county supervisors chose a compromise
location and built a two-mile, one-lane brick road on a concrete base that did
not touch any population center and was not on a route connecting any major towns in the county. As a result, few people used the road, and it remained
in good condition into the 1970s.[45]

Iowa was the site of the first good roads convention in the United States in
1882 after a bad winter and thaw rendered the roads particularly impassable,
but Iowans resisted centralization and state control more than other mid-
westerners, so much so that even good roads advocates divided on the issue.
For example, the relatively mild Anderson Law made township consolidation
and cash road taxes mandatory in 1902 (although the $5 poll tax could still be
worked off), but only over the strenuous objections of many farmers and
farm journals who defended the virtues of local control and saw the act
mainly as a prelude to more comprehensive and more expensive changes.
Thus, the highway commission that was set up two years later was only an
educational and advisory body housed at Iowa State College; direct state aid

was not introduced until after it was required by the Federal Aid Road Act of 1916; and actual state control was not consolidated until 1929.[46]

For a time, however, a fairly humble technological innovation appeared to offer rural Iowans (as well as others) a way to have better roads for less money without abdicating local authority. Developed by D. Ward King, a Missouri farmer, the King road drag was an easily constructed device that shaped a dirt road into a slight mound rounded toward the center. After a rain, the road dried smooth and hardened, so that subsequent rainwater ran off more quickly and the road remained usable. Henry Wallace, the editor of *Wallace's Farmer*, featured the drag in numerous articles and a 1905 pamphlet, and its virtues spread quickly to states from New England to the Midwest. Even local songwriters got into the act. At drag day in Owasa, Iowa, seven young girls sang a song composed by their father with the following chorus: "Dragging the roads, dragging the roads, / Dragging the roads with the King road drag; / Hard as a bone, smooth as a hone, / The roads that lead into Owasa"; Missourians sang: "If your road is soft or rough, / Drag, brother, drag. / Once or twice will be enough, / Drag, brother, drag."[47] Because it was cheap and simple to operate, the drag became, in the words of one scholar, "the perfect weapon in the farmers' fight against good-roads advocates who desired to build expensive surfaced highways." Equally important, the drag offered the possibility of continued self-government by preempting the need for complicated organization, bonded debt, burdensome taxes, and high-salaried civil engineers.[48]

The road drag, however, failed to foment a rural-based revolution in the administration of roads or to forestall the urban-based revolution already under way. For all of its virtues, dragging foundered, in part, on the very localism it attempted to preserve. In most places, dragging was done on a volunteer basis with only sporadic and limited success, and more formal attempts to finance and administer road dragging by townships also proved disappointing. The drag itself was abandoned for more modern gasoline-powered road machinery during the 1920s, even though it was still recognized as the best method for maintaining dirt roads.[49]

In a symbolic sense, the fate of the road drag marked the more general eclipse of older ideals of local self-government, which had been so compelling in earlier road battles. As the drag's heyday waned, the expanding role

How To Make Good Dirt Roads

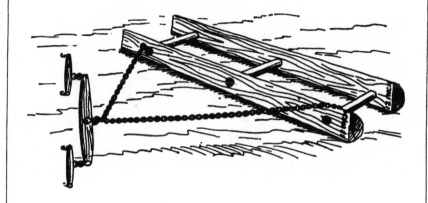

The Split Log Drag

Easy to make—easy to run—and which, rightly used, convinces the unconvinced, converts the unconverted, makes rough roads smooth, and soft roads hard. A simple implement made on the farm, which will transform the roads of the corn and grass belt.

The split log (King) road drag from a 1905 pamphlet, How to Make Good Dirt Roads, *published by Henry Wallace.*

of the federal government and the rapid adoption of the automobile generated more pressures and more revenues for road reform and the creation of
state highway systems. Appeased by these new monies, midwestern farmers
eventually followed the example of earlier New York farmers and began to
support any kind of roads for their benefit, however centralized, as long as
they didn't have to pay for them. But in order to get their share of the pie,
they first formed new organizations to represent and lobby for their interests.

The final consolidation of centralized control and the decline of local authority over rural roads came about because of the combined impact of the
federal government and the widespread adoption of the automobile after
World War I. Just as the shortcomings of township control first created pressures for greater state involvement in road matters, the subsequent limitations of county and state administration during the first two decades of the
twentieth century led road reformers to appeal to the federal government.
Initially, the idea of federal aid did not have widespread support and was even
opposed by some of the good roads advocates who testified at congressional
hearings creating the Office of Road Inquiry in 1893. After the government
instituted rural free delivery in 1896, however, Congress considered a series
of bills to fund public roads to facilitate mail delivery, and the different factions lobbied for their interests. According to the master of the National
Grange in 1908, for example, "if congress wishes to dispose wisely of the
present large surplus in the treasury it can not do better than to devote at
least $50,000,000 to the work of road improvement."[50]

This was the thinking of Representative Dorsey W. Shackleford of Missouri in 1912 when he introduced the bill that eventually became the Federal
Aid Road Act of 1916, and its somewhat rocky road to adoption reflects the
continuing conflicts between urban and rural interests and between local and
cosmopolitan priorities at a higher level of government. At first, Shackleford
proposed a scheme that would fund lesser rural farm-to-market roads while
leaving them under state control, but this died in the Senate after passing in
the House because of opposition from the American Automobile Association (AAA), which did not want money wasted on roads that "began
nowhere and ended nowhere."[51] Consequently, the act that did pass in 1916

allowed the government to fund major highways forming an interstate network, as well as rural routes. Rather than creating a national system of highways, however, the act allowed the states to select the routes and the type of road and to build and maintain them. But in order to receive federal money, they had to establish their own highway departments and get approval from the Federal Bureau of Public Roads, and these stipulations generally escalated conflicts within the states over highway spending.[52]

In addition, the growing prevalence of the automobile lent new urgency to the questions of what kind of roads to build and where to build them. Cars wreaked havoc with the expensive macadam roads advocated by good roads reformers, the inadequacies of which became all too apparent during a large cross-country convoy of trucks mobilized for World War I.[53] If trucks and automobiles created problems for the older permanent roads, however, they also embodied something of a solution for the cost of building new ones. States financed their highway departments and their cost sharing for federal monies with the proceeds of automobile, truck, and motorcycle registration fees, and as the number of motor vehicles increased, so did the available funds. In Wisconsin in 1912, for example, one-fourth of the automobile registration fees, or $28,000, went toward state roads, but in 1921, those registrations accounted for over $3.5 million. Similarly, during the 1920s, the introduction of gasoline taxes added more money for highway construction and continued to shift the burden of highway finance from the property owners to the road users. Often, however, these funds were still not enough, and bond issues were necessary, but after World War I and the mass purchase of Liberty Bonds, many states were more willing to pass them. Congress was also inspired by the experiences of the war, especially the truck convoy in 1917, and increased the total federal road appropriation to $200 million in 1919. Ironically, as part of this act, 25,000 of the war surplus trucks that had caused so many problems in 1917 were given to state highway departments for use in highway construction.[54]

But the growing number of automobiles and increased revenues did not create a consensus on road questions. Instead, new interest groups organized and argued about the disposition of road funds. On the one side, automobile clubs, especially the AAA, pushed for a federally financed system of concrete, interstate, transcontinental highways that linked urban areas and followed scenic routes across the countryside.[55] Similarly, engineers actively promoted interstate concrete highways in their professional organizations, through their domination of the Federal Bureau of Public Roads, and through their authority as state highway engineers.[56] This conflation of urban priorities and professional expertise continued to irritate rural inhabitants, however. According to a county commissioner from Reno County, Kansas, in 1920: "The hard road law gives the state engineer autocratic power over localities, and I shall resist the enforcement of the law, just as my father resisted the enforcement of the Dred Scott decision though he got into jail for it."[57]

In contrast to the automobile clubs and the highway engineers, farmers stressed the construction of less expensive roads, or even hard-surfaced ones, on so-called farm-to-market routes.[58] At first, railroads sponsored the campaign for farm-to-market roads because they were leery of competition from shipping over interstate highways. This continued a long-standing tradition of railroad support for good roads that would allow farmers to lower shipping costs and take pressure off the railroads to reduce rates. By 1916, however, the trend within the good roads movement toward interstate highways seemed inexorable, so railroads withdrew all support. Instead, during the late 1910s and the 1920s, farmers and farmers' organizations waged the battle for farm-to-market roads.[59]

The 1921 Federal Highway Act tried to accommodate both interstate and farm-to-market constituencies, and, according to a history of the Federal Highway Administration, it "ended, or at least submerged, the feud. . . . and it permanently laid to rest the idea of a national highway system under Federal control."[60] The resolution of conflict at the federal level, however, did not mean peace within the states. In fact, with increasing revenues from registrations, bond issues, and gasoline taxes, the relative importance of federal aid declined, and battles raged instead over the distribution of state highway monies. This was especially true in the Midwest, where states were building networks of expensive, hard-surfaced roads for the first time just as the farm depression of the 1920s ended agriculture's so-called golden age and newly formed farmers' organizations lobbied for rural interests.

In Illinois, for example, voters passed two large bond issues for a concrete state highway system in 1918 and 1923, and their history illustrates Illinois farmers' growing organization and legislative clout. Progressive farmers and farm journals supported the first bond issue (which passed by the large margin of 602,519 to 149,407), but they changed their tune after they saw how the funds were being distributed. In a letter to the *Prairie Farmer*, H. J. Kennedy of Kendall County voiced a common theme and railed against the urban interests who would decide where the new roads would go:

> They are war-made millionaires who stand between the farmer and the consumer of farm produce. They are the ones in whose interests the hard roads will be laid. . . . When the farmer is working in his field the big twin sixes sail by, tearing up the roads, the occupants going to some summer resort, golf links, joy rides or trips in the interest of some social affair. I know of a large town near by that in the summer time draws the farmers from 25 miles away. One road leading into this town has so much travel over it that it is absolutely impossible to keep it in shape. It has holes in it almost large enough to bury an elephant. . . . Are they going to pave this road? No, they are going to follow this road and this trail and go this way and that way, just connecting all the country clubs and summer resorts they can reach.[61]

Others appealed to agrarian virtue rather than lambaste urban frivolity when they objected to high and curvy routes selected for their scenic value rather than more direct and level routes through farming areas:

> The real scenery of Illinois is the rich farming land and the fields of corn for which the state is noted. Those are the things we want tourists to see as they travel through the state—not the clay bluffs and muddy bottoms of the Illinois River. We cannot compete with many other sections of the country in scenery of that kind, but our expanse of rich farming land is without rival anywhere in the world.[62]

State highways, then, became a major issue for the emerging Illinois Agricultural Association (Illinois's Farm Bureau) that was on its way to becoming the largest farmers' organization in the state as well as the most extensive state Farm Bureau in the country. At its annual meeting in 1919, the organization made roads a top priority and pledged that the first roads built under the $60 million bond issue would be "those most important as farm market roads." That pledge, however, was not easy to keep, according to Z. M. Holmes, chairman of the IAA road committee: "There is a growing suspicion in Illinois that the state highway department is developing into a bureaucracy that has at heart the interests of politicians and tourists rather than those of farmers" and that "the department is autocratic and will not take suggestions from anyone." Consequently, the IAA waged a concerted campaign for redress in subsequent legislation; as a result, provisions for a secondary network of farm-to-market roads dominated the $100 million bond issue in 1923. Similarly, the IAA lobbied successfully for a gasoline tax that exempted gasoline for agricultural purposes, and was used instead of property taxes to fund county roads that would not be administered by the state highway department. This tax passed in 1927 with near unanimous support from rural legislators regardless of party, and near-unanimous opposition from those representing Chicago and Cook County.[63]

The passage of this tax is significant, for by the 1930s, when it came to roads, many rural northerners had stopped bemoaning the diminution of self-government and local autonomy or worrying about costs. Rather than opposing the incursions of the second great transformation, they themselves had become organized and accommodated to it. The IAA and other farmers' organizations now willingly embraced the new order and, as established interest groups, went after their share in competition with other factions in the political process. The larger contours of this transformation are familiar to historians from studies of the emerging farm bloc and the creation of federal agricultural policies during the New Deal, but the focus on road administration gives it new dimensions. For rural northerners, much of the organizational revolution came about well before the 1930s, and the state, in addition to the federal government, provided a critical arena.

Thus, the path toward centralized road administration in the rural North was crooked, not straight. Throughout the late nineteenth and early twentieth centuries, northern farmers opposed some road reforms and advocated others because of an ideological commitment to home rule and because of concerns about costs, both of which they tried to serve by maintaining as much local control over the roads as possible. This rural attachment to local control, however, forced compromises that limited the government's powers and created the need for still further state involvement in order to overcome those limitations, propelling the issue of road administration to progressively higher levels. As townships and counties proved unable to plan larger highway systems or fund macadam roads, state aid emerged as a solution; but the states were often unable or unwilling to ignore their rural constituents, prompting increased pressures for a greater federal role. In this sense, then, the battle between rural localism and cosmopolitan priorities helped to create the modern state.

This process took place within the context of technological changes, which also had contradictory effects. Thus, while the automobile presented the most inexorable pressures for expensive highways and centralized administration, it also embodied the means to fund them, and rural worries were eventually appeased by new monies from bond issues, automobile registrations, and gasoline taxes. Along with other changes in communication and transportation, the automobile transformed the spatial significance and cultural meaning of the local community, and this also lessened the relative importance of local government.

Instead, and in contrast to the local isolation in the countryside fifty years earlier, the rural and urban North became linked by new systems of concrete roads and began to compete for new state and federal resources. Rather than defend an older vision of government and society rooted in republican traditions of home rule and agrarian fundamentalism, farmers became an interest group and campaigned for their interests in new, translocal organizations. Although this new rural perspective was a significant departure from the older, more localistic worldview that informed earlier generations of country people, it continued to form a basis for opposition to the dominant forces in society. Thus, while the new roads took rural northerners further on the torturous path of the second great transformation, it remained an uncompleted journey.

And they shall teach no more every man his neighbor,

and every man his brother,

saying, Know the Lord: for they shall all know me,

from the least of them unto the greatest of them.

— JEREMIAH 31:34

TEACH NO MORE HIS NEIGHBOR

Localism and Rural Opposition to Educational Reform

After the village of Hubbard, Trumbull County, Ohio, incorporated separately from rural Hubbard Township in 1880, the two school districts battled for control of the local high school, which had been built in the village in 1870. Although each school board nominated a different principal, the township gained the upper hand and installed its candidate, resulting in such bitterness that it was necessary to maintain an armed guard over the building. Fortunately, the parties turned to the courts to resolve their dispute, but the vacillations of the legal system only exacerbated the hard feelings. The court of common pleas initially found for the township, but the village won an appeal to the circuit court in 1882, a decision that the Ohio Supreme Court reversed in 1885, when it awarded control back to the township. Bitterness continued through another round of court battles, which also favored the township, and reached a nadir of sorts when a wall was built to divide the portion of the building used for the high school under township control from the portion used by the village for its elementary school. This Solomonic strategy failed to resolve the issue permanently, however, because the village ultimately wanted to build a better building but had neither the power nor the money to do so without the cooperation of the township. Finally, the village school board, aided by new state laws, renewed the battle in 1916 and circulated petitions for the consolidation of the township and village school districts. This effort garnered a local majority, withstood another series of court challenges, and resulted in a single school district and, eventually, a new high school.[1]

Although somewhat extreme and colorful in its details, Hubbard's educational history is of a piece with similar stories throughout the rural North between 1870 and 1930. Simply put, country schools were contested terrain during the late nineteenth and early twentieth centuries and often served as flash points for a wide range of rural concerns about changes in the nature of their communities and their place in American life. At the most local level, school battles reflected and reinforced the myriad factions, both petty and profound, that frequently characterized social relations in agricultural townships. In particular, rural northerners reacted to the changing role of the village, which mediated between an urban society that was on the rise and the surrounding countryside that was not. Thus, school issues, which were often precipitated by shrinking numbers of school-aged children, also embodied more general worries about the decline of population in agrarian communities, a little-understood but much lamented phenomenon that signaled a basic shift in American society. So, too, did they reveal country peoples' anxieties about their children's abilities to succeed in that changing world, whether schools were criticized for educating their children away from the farm, or for not preparing them well enough to make it in urban society.

Mostly, however, school issues highlighted the conflict between two competing visions of society. Even more than the efforts to improve country roads, school reform during the nineteenth and twentieth centuries represented one of the most concerted and long-lived attempts to restructure rural institutions to bring the countryside into congruence with an emerging organizational society. As such, it pitted those who were oriented toward the city and the larger society and deferred to outside expertise and authority against those who continued to stress the primacy of the local community, the sanctity of home rule, and the virtues of self-reliance.

In the end, precisely because their schools were invested with so much meaning, rural northerners were even more jealous of them than they were of their roads and were even less willing to give up control in spite of intervention by the state and other outside forces. Thus, the one-room schoolhouse remained a fixture in the northern countryside until well into the twentieth century. By 1928, there were still over 80,000 such schools in the rural North, and only 6,320 with more than one room. The vast majority of rural school consolidations did not occur until after World War II.

That same depth and multiplicity of meanings, however, also make resistance to school reform an important window on the attitudes and experiences of rural inhabitants as they faced the second great transformation in the countryside. That examination begins in Massachusetts, which was the birthplace of educational reform, and it extends first to other New England states and then to the Old Northwest, New York, and the midwestern prairies and plains.

During the nineteenth century, rural schools, like rural roads, were administered by tiny neighborhood districts, which were subdivisions of the township. In Massachusetts in 1850, for example, 316 of the state's 333 townships and cities relied on 2,818 autonomous districts to administer their schools, for an average of 9 per township, with some towns having as many as 30, 40, or even 50 separate districts. Although the details of administration varied from state to state, the country school district typically had the power to determine how long the school term would be and how to spend the local property tax that was assessed to support the school. The annual district meeting also elected a committee or an individual with the power to hire (and fire) the teacher, set the curriculum, and equip and maintain the schoolhouse. State governments established nominal authority in matters such as establishing minimum standards for the length of the school term or the qualifications of teachers, which they enforced by withholding small appropriations. But, in reality, the school districts maintained de facto and ultimate control.

This decentralized system of control was the nemesis of those concerned with educational reform. Beginning with Horace Mann, who became Massachusetts's first secretary of education in 1837, school officials throughout the North regularly and repeatedly criticized what they perceived to be the evils of the district system. Even those who initially supported it changed their minds. According to George S. Boutwell, who was secretary of the

Massachusetts board in 1859: "I entered upon the duties of the office I now hold with some faith in the district system; my observation and experience have destroyed that faith entirely. It is a system admirably calculated to secure poor schools, incompetent teachers, [and] consequent waste of public money."[2]

The schools that Boutwell complained about were poor buildings on poorer sites. These "shrines to Minerva," as one critic sarcastically referred to them, typically occupied undesirable land: "a barren ledge by the roadside, a gravelly knoll, the steeply sloping side of a bosky ravine, the apex of the angle of intersecting roads."[3] The schoolhouses themselves were often small, crowded, dimly lit, poorly ventilated, inadequately heated, and in need of repair. Moreover, the quality of the schools varied substantially between towns and between districts within the same town, and these disparities became even more pronounced as village centers grew in size and more remote rural districts lost population and property value over the course of the nineteenth century.

Reformers also complained about poor teachers. In general, there was little continuity from year to year because each new school committee hired a new teacher and often got started too late or did not pay enough to procure capable ones. Or they used their authority to hire relatives and friends regardless of qualifications and abilities. As Boutwell put it: "The quality of the school depends upon the character of the teacher; and the character of the teacher depends upon accident, or the caprice, prejudices, or convenience of the committee-man."[4]

Mostly, however, reformers detested the pettiness and lack of educational vision that they felt characterized district administration. According to Boston school supervisor George H. Martin in 1894, each school district became a center of political activity, where

> Questions involving the fate of nations have been decided with less expenditure of time, less stirring of passions, less vociferation of declamation and denunciation, than the location of a fifteen-by-twenty district schoolhouse. I have known such a question to call for ten district meetings, scattered over two years, bringing down from mountain farms three miles away men who had no children to be schooled, and who had not taken the trouble to vote in a presidential election during the period.[5]

Local disputes over the location of the schoolhouse, the hiring and firing of teachers, and the selection of school committeemen had a long afterlife, in Martin's words:

A rankling sense of injustice remained; smoldering embers ready to kindle into flame; an old score waiting to be paid off, maybe in the town meeting, perhaps in the election to the General Court, possibly in a church quarrel. Within a half-dozen years I have discovered more than one such "ancient grudge" not yet fed fat enough.[6]

And indignations that finally did ignite raged with "the bitterness of a Kentucky vendetta and the protraction of an English suit in chancery." Thus, while district administration may have been "the high-water mark of modern democracy," in Martin's view it was also "the low-water mark of the Massachusetts school system."[7]

By way of solution, reformers urged several types of changes. Following the lead of Horace Mann, educators in Massachusetts and throughout the North sought measures that would lengthen the school year and compel attendance. They also advocated the professional training and certification of teachers as well as minimum standards for school buildings and curricular materials, all to be determined and administered by the state's department of education. Similarly, they promoted the creation of graded schools and high schools. To accomplish these and other reforms, they wanted to place district schools under the more centralized control of the township, which would better enforce standards and help equalize the disparities between the different districts. Mann pinned his hopes on moral suasion by the enlightened few in each community, typically the half-dozen men and women who comprised the township's school committee, which usually advocated reform but was powerless to implement it. As he wrote of them, "Let the intelligent visit the ignorant day by day, as the oculist visits the blind man and detaches the scales from his eyes, until the living sense leaps to the living light."[8]

Many of those who lived in the rural school districts and patronized the schools, however, did not consider themselves blind. Rather, their point of view was informed by the economic, social, and ideological realities of agrarian life. In Boxford, Massachusetts, a rural town of about one thousand, for example, farmers located schoolyards in the swamps or rocky fields because they were reluctant to give up any land that could be used for agricultural purposes. Similarly, farmers set winter and summer school terms that complemented the cycle of agricultural production, particularly strawberry picking and sheep shearing, in order to ensure that their children would be able to help them on the farm. If they needed their children's labor while school was in session, they often kept them at home, a practice that was accepted by rural school officials in spite of state truancy laws.[9]

Economy was also an important consideration for the district schools, and Boxford farmers regularly rejected entreaties by the town's school committee to make costly improvements or adopt new materials. District 7, for example, spent three meetings in 1843 debating whether to build an outhouse before giving limited and grudging approval to "only such a building as the [committee in charge] thinks absolutely necessary." By the same token, Boxford schools continued the traditional custom of allowing students to furnish their own textbooks, which were handed down from older cousins and siblings, rather than adopt the newer, standardized texts advocated by educational reformers. This practice saved money, but it also reaffirmed the old and familiar, appealing to both the fiscal and ideological conservatism of the local inhabitants.

At a more fundamental level, farmers in Boxford were motivated by an ideology that stressed the independence and equality of the local inhabitants, and this made them reluctant to accede control to outsiders, whether from Boston or the other side of town, or to institute distinctions among themselves. They resisted efforts to professionalize and certify teachers, which they saw as an attempt to diminish their authority to hire and fire as they saw fit. Questions of location were also important because district schools were key neighborhood institutions that were regularly used for singing schools, debating societies, public lectures, and religious meetings when classes were not in session. Thus, while the repeated and contentious meetings devoted to locating new schoolhouses may have reflected community factions and jealousies, they were also informed by rural concerns that all citizens be treated equally and that no neighborhood or family enjoy too much of an advantage in public matters at the expense of others.

In 1864, the Boxford School Committee, which supported township rather than district control of the schools, complained about local attitudes and despaired of their chances of success: "so firmly are the larger part of our citizens attached to this system, so fully are they persuaded that centralized power is dangerous . . . that we do not with much hope look for better things. Yet this has been a costly mistake, which has done more to retard the progress of an enlightened and enlarged system of instruction, than any and all other causes combined." [10] As George H. Martin described this rural opposition more generally, the school district was "the palladium of popular liberty, to be defended to the last," and the town system was "an entering wedge to centralization and despotism," against which "backwoods orators in town meetings eloquently appealed to the memory of Patrick Henry and the heroes of Lexington and Bunker Hill." [11]

Thus, the initial efforts to restructure rural schools and put them under township control reflected a polarization of views. Educational reformers strove to improve the often sorry state of country schools, and they found willing allies in what they considered to be the more enlightened residents of the village centers. This coalition was opposed by large numbers of rural inhabitants, who, during the second half of the nineteenth century, were still committed to the principles of home rule and self-government and who were leery of the expenses entailed by the proposed changes.

Because of the pervasiveness of rural fears of "centralization and despotism," efforts to do away with the district system in Massachusetts and elsewhere in New England had a torturous history. An 1853 state law allowed town school committees to discontinue districts unless the town voted triennially to continue them, but this law was repealed in 1857. The spring session of the legislature summarily abolished the school districts in 1859, but a special session was called the next fall in order to reverse that legislation. Similarly, an 1869 act abolishing the school districts passed unanimously in the Senate and with only nine negative votes in the House, but it, too, was nullified the next year by another law that allowed any town to return to the district system with a two-thirds vote. [12]

After this act, a number of Massachusetts communities chose not to return to the district system. In Boxford, for example, townspeople defeated local initiatives for the abolition of district powers in 1866 and 1869, but after state law ended the district system later in 1869, they did not vote subsequently to reinstate it. Other townships followed the same pattern or moved away from the district system voluntarily under other statutes that allowed them to do so. Indeed, by the time the state legislature abolished the district system totally and permanently in 1882, only forty-five townships were affected by the legislation.[13]

The district system, however, remained popular among small, relatively isolated rural townships, especially in the western counties, and more than sixty mustered the two-thirds necessary to reinstate it during the early 1870s. The complaints of their town school committees give a good indication of the depths of feelings involved.[14] The Raynham school committee, for example, felt compelled to apologize to the state board for its town's decision, which it regarded as a futile attempt "to block the wheels of civilization." "A more unjust and mischievous Act, we believe, never passed into a law," wrote the Agawam school committee after its town reverted to the district system. The Charlemont, Franklin County, school committee was even more revulsed by the recent turn of events: "One word in regard to the district system. It is well known that the town voted to go back to the district system, yet we hardly know where we are and words cannot better express our condition than to use scripture: 'The dog has returned to its vomit again, and the sow that was washed to its wallowing in the mire.'"[15]

Similar conflicts occurred throughout rural New England as Vermont, Maine, and New Hampshire also established the township system between 1880 and 1894. Significantly, this period witnessed the extension of school election voting rights to women. Women voters, however, had no distinctive politics with respect to education and did not spearhead these changes. Rather, their votes spanned the spectrum of school issues to the same degree that male votes did, and, once in office, female school officials behaved comparably to their male counterparts. Although women voters tended to vote for women candidates to a greater degree, this was primarily an extension of local suffrage and temperance efforts and not a reflection of specific gender-based positions on educational reform.[16]

In Vermont, the legislature initially required towns to vote on the district versus the town system in 1885, but only sixteen towns adopted the new system, and another five tried it for a few years before switching back. The town of Chelsea, for example, either voted against the township system repeatedly and by a large margin throughout 1880s, or they voted to pass over the agenda item at town meetings and did not consider it at all. The pattern was the same in neighboring Thetford, where the vote against the township system was even more lopsided, reflecting the lesser importance of the village center in that town. In the words of one study of Vermont, "The suggestion for the end of local district control and the beginning of town-wide school consolidation evoked tremendous controversy and awakened strong feelings as local boards, parents, and politicians argued with professional educators. Community control became a major issue."[17]

Nor did the 1892 abolition of the district system in Vermont end debate. As one reader wrote to the Corinth local paper: "The real true down-to-bottom objection to the town school system is that it deprives so many of a chance to hold a little office; many a man who couldn't get elected hog constable at town meeting could be on the skule kermitty." This provoked an equally blunt response: "As I am one of the hornets spoken of, I wish to say it is a poor rule that will not work both ways. The real, right-down-and-get-there of the town school system is to give office to a few smart men that cannot get elected selectmen or hog constable either (the honor is about the same), but can be elected one of the board of school directors. We have got plenty of crazy laws now and want no more of them. It would be better for the state if the legislature would let the school laws alone."[18]

The adoption of township control, whether voluntarily or in response to the state, did not necessarily signify acceptance of the perspectives of educational reformers or the agendas of their village allies. Country people typically embraced township control and closed district schools as a pragmatic cost-saving response to the diminishing numbers of school-age children. This demographic change came about because of the combination of population decline and an aging local population, and it occurred in increasing numbers of New England communities during the second half of the nineteenth century. Thus, the numbers of rural schools with fewer than twenty pupils—many with ten, five, or even two—increased dramatically in New England after the Civil War. When district administration was abandoned in New Hampshire at the end of the century, for example, nearly one-third of the state's 2,684 schools had twelve or fewer pupils, and about 40 percent of those had six or fewer.[19]

Some aspects of rural educational reform, then, were ironically propelled by traditional rural concerns about cost rather than more "modern" values.

Thus, when Peru, Massachusetts, voted against returning to the district system in 1871, the town school committee, which advocated closing some of the smaller schools, justified the change primarily in terms of economics rather than education: "A teacher can as easily manage and instruct a school of twenty-five as twelve. And the expense of educating a pupil in the smaller schools is double the sum expended for a pupil in the larger. As long as we maintain so many small schools, we cannot do justice to the young, without greatly increasing our school appropriations." In response to the criticism that the children would have to walk too far to school, the committee also betrayed the secondary importance of educational content when it observed that the walk would be good for them and would counteract the "pernicious effects" of being confined for hours in a close or heated room. For many declining towns, then, the move away from district control was consistent with traditional rural concerns for economy and frugality even as it superseded other agrarian commitments to home rule and self-government.[20]

Those same rural concerns for frugality, however, led country people to resist other educational reforms that cost more money and were justified primarily in terms of professional educators' conceptions of educational quality. Borrowing from changes that they had implemented in urban school districts, reformers tried to establish more formal supervision by professional educators. An 1870 Massachusetts law designed for rural areas, for example, permitted two or more towns to unite for the purposes of hiring a school superintendent, but only seventeen towns took advantage of it.

Similarly, educational reformers also wanted to extend their urban accomplishments by establishing high schools and graded elementary schools in rural villages. Farmers, however, were especially reluctant to embrace such expensive changes that reflected the interests of those who lived in the village centers rather than the countryside. George Martin, writing in 1894, attributed this resistance to the "new measures" to the selectivity of out-migration, which left behind an older, more conservative agricultural population whose families had already been educated. "In towns containing a village center, growing populous under the new order of things," he noted, the movement for a town high school led to a struggle between the village and the outskirts that was "an occasion for an annual tug of war," which lasted for years.[21]

The town of Boxford, Massachusetts, for example, refused to satisfy East Boxford's ambitions for a public high school during the 1890s, which would have put it on a par with West Boxford, a village with fewer people but with a private sectarian academy. Instead, the town decided that it was cheaper and less divisive to pay tuition and transportation costs for its aspiring students to go to public high schools in neighboring towns.[22]

Walpole, New Hampshire (population 2,163 in 1890), was the site of even more dramatic struggles between farm and village interests that were fueled by frugality. Already the veterans of numerous battles over abolishing school districts and establishing a township system, the town's factions went at it again in 1892 when two hundred residents of North Walpole, which was a growing industrial village across the river from Bellows Falls, Vermont, chartered a special train to attend the annual school meeting in Walpole Village in order to push for a new $10,000 school building. The more numerous farmers, who lived near Walpole Village in the southern part of the township and who owned most of the town's property, voted their resolution down. When the election of the farmers' candidate for school board was overturned because of a technicality (his middle initial was left off the ballot), though, North Walpole gained a majority on the board and called a special meeting two weeks later in North Walpole to reconsider the issue. Five hundred and thirteen attended that meeting, but after the chartered train transporting the farmers left at 6 P.M., those who remained brought the issue of a new school to a vote and passed it, 176 to 0. The courts eventually declared the initial election valid, which nullified that evening meeting. But after several more meetings, which included a failed motion that school meetings be held every two weeks for the entertainment of summer visitors, North Walpole eventually got a new school, albeit one that cost much less than $10,000.[23]

At the end of the century, the growing movement to close small schools and transport students at public expense, a process known as consolidation, reflected both rural concerns with saving money and the more expensive ambitions of villagers and educational reformers.[24] According to an 1891 survey, Massachusetts towns closed district schools and transported pupils to other schools for "two distinct purposes—one financial and the other educational." As the author of the survey reported: "In many of the towns of the State, the depopulation of the districts outside the villages has made it cheaper to transport to other schools the few pupils living in the districts than to teach them *in situ*. In other towns, the desire to make strong central schools, and the purpose to give all the children of the town the benefit of better teachers, better appliances, and better supervision, have been the dominant motives to determine consolidation."[25]

More detailed accounts of school consolidations in western Massachusetts between 1890 and 1895 also indicate the split motives behind the movement. In general, the two types of towns that were most active in consolidating schools and transporting students were those that were growing and those that were declining. Towns that experienced an expansion in their nonagricultural population often shut down outlying rural schools and transported students to the center, especially after they had built a new, more modern school building. Palmer in Hampden County, which grew from 6,520 in 1890 to 7,801 in 1900, for example, shut down three schools between 1890 and 1895 and transported eight grammar school students as well as forty-three high schoolers, most probably to a newly constructed $10,500 building. By contrast, nearby Blandford, which declined from 871 to 836 during the same period, did not build any new buildings when it closed two schools, but transported the ten displaced students to other one-room district schools that remained open. Rural townships that were more stable, like Agawam or Wales, were less likely either to consolidate schools or to transport students.[26]

Whether it was brought on by the expansion and ascendance of village interests or the decline of old, established country neighborhoods, the actual process of closing and consolidating rural schools was long, painful, and vexing. Concord was regarded as a pioneer of this movement, and it began in 1880 by consolidating the five schools in Concord Village into a new eight-room graded school, the Emerson School.[27] The town school committee then turned its attention to the five district schools in the open countryside, whose students could also be served by the new village school or another one in West Concord. But that process took ten years and was marked by a series of petitions and counterpetitions and periods when the school committee held off in the face of especially strenuous opposition. Only the persistence of the successive school boards, which, according to the superintendent's account, "never lost sight of the end in view, nor relaxed their efforts," allowed all of Concord's students to go to a primary school located in one of the town's two village centers.[28]

Boxford also had a rocky experience. Districts 1 and 2 and then 5 and 6 were consolidated in 1897 and 1898, and the town provided transportation.

After parents protested that farm values would drop and that their children were at risk, the town reopened schools in Districts 5 and 1 in 1899. Two years later, Boxford went along with a movement to form a union district with Reading, Middleton, and Topsfield in order to hire a new superintendent, who turned out to be very progressive and advocated new school buildings, playgrounds, and other costly improvements. Although Boxford and Middleton pushed for a different superintendent who would be more conservative and spend less money, Reading and Topsfield, which were larger towns, did not agree, so Boxford and Middleton withdrew from the union in 1903.[29]

Because of local resistance and concerns about cost, then, school consolidation progressed slowly in rural New England, especially when it involved closing all outlying schools and creating a new graded school in the village center. By 1905 Massachusetts had consolidated more schools and spent more to transport students to them (over $200,000) than any other state, but it still had over five hundred schools with twenty-five or fewer students, mainly in the rural western townships, and as late as 1918, one-room school houses comprised over one-third of the schools in towns of less than five thousand.[30] In New Hampshire, Vermont, and Maine, rural towns typically consolidated by closing and transporting students from smaller one-room schools to nearby larger one-room schools, a process that reduced the total number of schools in New Hampshire only by about 25 percent between 1885 and 1911. But few towns built the multiroom schools advocated by educational reformers.[31]

Thus, the progress of school reform in rural New England was shaped by different and even contradictory sets of concerns during the decades between the Civil War and the turn of the century. On the one hand, rural inhabitants resisted proposed changes because of their expense and their diminution of local prerogatives and because they reflected and reinforced the values and pretensions of those who lived in the villages. When farmers did support the efforts to close and consolidate rural schools under township control, they did so primarily because of their desires to economize and better allocate scarce resources. On the other hand, educational reformers and their village allies pushed for improvements in educational quality, such as new graded elementary schools and high schools, which cost more money rather than less. As rural depopulation spread to other regions, and as educators became increasingly organized and professionalized and integrated into broader reform movements concerned with the problems of rural life, these contradictions became even more pronounced, and the conflicts between them became more widespread and took on new dimensions.

What began in New England spread to the rest of the country, as is the case in much of American history, and by the beginning of the twentieth century, the effort to consolidate rural schools had become a national movement. As professional educators and their organizations defined and took control of the movement, however, the economizing impulses that had undergirded much rural school reform in New England were eclipsed by an emphasis on more expensive changes that reflected new theories about modern education and the role of the school in the community, which also promoted an agenda of professional expansion.

Progressive educational reformers strove to consolidate small rural schools and create new, larger ones in order to replicate key aspects of urban education in the countryside and to better prepare rural youth for full participation in an organizational society. In addition to administration by professional educators and the differentiation of students by grade and subject, the size of the new consolidated schools allowed expanded facilities such as auditoriums and gymnasiums, which supported a range of curricular and extracurricular activities that went beyond traditional emphases on the three Rs. This reflected progressive educators' assumptions that the school was an important agent of socialization, which prepared its students for community life in the broadest sense as opposed to a narrower emphasis on learning. Those amenities also enabled the consolidated school to serve as a rural community center, which became a priority of the Country Life Movement. And, also in conjunction with the Country Life Movement, educational reformers advocated agricultural education and home economics as part of the new curriculum in order to lessen the "inefficiencies" of rural life.[32]

Rural northerners were also concerned about educational quality and their children's future, but they continued to oppose many of the proposed reforms. Moreover, the tenor of that opposition changed in reaction to the reformers' increased scope and ambition as well as their arrogance and condescension. In addition to traditional concerns about self-government, costs, and the expanding power of village interests, country people began to see school issues in ways that transcended the local community and reflected a new panoply of anxieties about the basic direction of American society. Increasingly, they framed their opposition to rural school consolidation during the twentieth century in terms of the bureaucratization and professionalization of American society as a whole as well as the large scale and impersonality of modern urban life. Thus, in ways both real and symbolic, battles over school issues became a referendum on some of the defining characteristics of the second great transformation in the countryside.

The earliest and most celebrated instance of rural school consolidation outside of Massachusetts illustrates the emergence of these differing perspectives. Kingsville in Ashtabula County in northeastern Ohio consolidated its schools in 1893. Like many other rural communities in the Old Northwest during this period, the township experienced population decline and went from 1,712 to 1,412 between 1890 and 1900. Thus, when one weak school district needed a new building, a group of community leaders decided that it would be cheaper and wiser to transport rural children to an existing school in the village rather than build any new buildings in the countryside. The Ohio legislature passed a special law for the township in 1894 that enabled it to allocate public funds for such transportation, and the next general assembly passed similar special legislation for other communities in Stark, Ashtabula, and Portage Counties, privileges that later bills in 1898 and 1904 extended throughout the state.[33]

The Kingsville plan, as it came to be known, was appropriated by educational reformers who touted it, publicized it, and ironically transformed it from a local effort to save money into a paragon of educational improvement and a model for educational reformers throughout the nation. Edward Erf's 1899 article on Kingsville schools in the *Arena*, for example, was quickly reprinted in the annual report of the U.S. Bureau of Education. Two years later that same report published a more extensive description, "A Visit to the Centralized Schools of Ohio," by O. J. Kern, the superintendent of schools of Winnebago County, Illinois. In both cases, the authors gave glowing accounts and highlighted the superior education provided by the new system. According to the Erf article, which Kern quoted as well, pupils from the most remote part of the township now had access to an excellent graded school education, and "The mingling of the pupils from the subdistricts and the village has had a deepening and broadening influence on the former without any disadvantage to the latter."[34]

Erf's condescending assumption that only rural youth benefited from contact with village students, who at best escaped such interactions unscathed and unsullied, must have grated against rural Ohioans' sensibilities. Their attitudes about educational reform emerge more clearly in the ongoing debate about school consolidation and centralization that was carried on in the pages of the *Ohio Farmer* in the wake of the Kingsville experiment. Initially, rural advocates of school reform based their arguments on issues of cost as well as educational quality. J. F. Greene of Erie County, who gave an address on the subject to a state farmers' institute, urged centralization as the solution for poor and expensive schools brought on by population loss. As he wrote in 1898, "We are now reaching the conditions in our population existing in the New England states thirty years ago, that of decimated numbers of pupils in the rural schools."[35]

In light of the greater expenses entailed by the new schools, however, reformers quickly played down appeals to economy and stressed the quality of the education offered by the new system, which, they argued, was necessary to prepare rural youth to compete in the larger society. Willis E. Morehouse of Huntsburg admitted that taxes were higher after centralization, but pointed with pride to the fact that their high school graduates were accepted into all of the leading colleges and universities in the state without prior examination.[36] To C. G. Williams of Trumbull County, such assurances were worth the extra expense. His community spent considerably more for the new system, but he felt that they were getting much better schools: "No truly patriotic citizen will complain of taxes for school purposes if the community gets value received for money expended."[37]

The majority of correspondents to the *Ohio Farmer* had different ideas as to what constituted good value for their tax dollars, and they objected not only to the expense of the new system, but to its orientation toward and emulation of urban society. For many, college admission for their children was neither a goal nor an option. Others felt that values of independence were a better guarantor of their children's success, whether on the farm or off, than the subjects and activities embodied in the newer curricula, and that these were best instilled by country schools rather than by more "modern" institutions. G.S.F. of Sandusky County, for example, defended the country school as a vital community institution and the site of numerous meetings and activities, but he also thought it superior on pedagogical grounds. The best people in the country got their start in district schools, he argued, and much of that success can be attributed to the independence that was fostered by the one-room school.[38] In the same vein, J.S.M. of Clinton County thought that getting rid of teachers and hiring more hacks so that all pupils could be taught under one roof was "monumental stupidity." As he wrote, "Instead of education we get jobbery and the minds of the children are fed upon false ideals and error. . . . Let us have done with this question of centralization."[39]

These rural Ohioans also rejected the notion that the city was superior to the country and that consolidated schools were therefore a step forward. Daniel E. White of Litchfield, Medina County, initially favored centralization but changed his mind because of worries about corruption, an ironic inversion of reformers' complaints about improprieties under the district system. "Cities are full of corruption," he wrote, "and centralization is on the same road." Such fears were realized in Kinsman, Ohio, according to another letter, when taxes skyrocketed after the school board built a high school in a poor location that one of the board members had an interest in, and also awarded themselves transportation contracts for more money than they were worth.[40]

Criticisms of the long wagon rides that centralization entailed were also common, and rural parents fretted about their children's exposure to the elements and to the low morals of the hack driver and the village centers. One commentator worried that country schoolchildren would pass by open saloons on their way to school in the village, something that would never happen in their own neighborhoods. "Somebody says the dear children are acquiring grace and culture by contact in the central school," he wrote, perhaps anticipating Erf's arguments. "Maybe so, but I have always supposed there was a good deal of flexibility in a merry skip along the country road, a butterfly chase, or the gathering of a cluster of early sparkling, dew-decked violets for the teacher's desk. Such grace is free and easy to the body, happifying to the mind, invigorating to both mind and body, and quite exempt from affectation or artificiality." Significantly, this author was not inalterably opposed to consolidation. Rather, he thought that it should be considered only when it saved money and after weighing the disadvantages of getting rid of country schools.[41]

These attitudes were not confined to Ohio, and other sources reveal a similar array of opinions elsewhere in the Midwest. According to a 1900 Indiana survey of county school superintendents, most expressed support for school consolidation and claimed that their trustees felt likewise, but their enthusiasm for change was often tempered by the poor condition of local roads and the significant opposition of local school patrons.[42] The Carroll County superintendent, for example, described his trustees' support for closing small schools and for other reforms, which was couched primarily in economic terms: "They also think that much better school work could be done at less expense by consolidating all the schools in the township. I think they are in favor of it only where a graded school is already established near the center of the township and where the roads are good." Carroll County school patrons, however, felt differently, and at one school meeting where a proposed consolidation was discussed, the superintendent reported: "Patrons came prejudiced, thinking we were going to rob them of their school and build up the school at Camden. They were almost unanimously against us. We set forth the plan, but they raised all forms of objections and never would submit."[43]

Although reformers routinely claimed that country people who initially opposed the new system changed their minds after experiencing it, the 1900 survey provides numerous examples to the contrary. In Harrison Township, Henry County, local inhabitants wanted a new schoolhouse built but the trustee did not think there were enough students to warrant it, so he had them transported instead. According to the superintendent's statement, "The pupils and patrons decided to oppose it, and have done so. They call the hack the 'ice wagon,' although it is well inclosed [sic]. Other districts, fearing a trustee might do them likewise, made it a trustee election issue and won."[44]

Posey County residents were also generally "in favor of holding to the small schools," even though the idea of consolidation had been much discussed at the county teachers' association and also at farmers' institutes. Objections were even stronger in Warrick County, where, in contrast to Posey

Portrait of the one-room Halcyon School near Black River Falls, Wisconsin,
ca. 1890–1910. (Courtesy of the State Historical Society of Wisconsin)

County, trustees would not even talk about the idea much less try it, leading
the county superintendent to throw up his hands and lament that "it will not
be tried for a number of years, or until the law compels it. People are wanting
schoolhouses on every 100 acres of land."[45]

In general, then, even though some rural Indiana townships closed some
of their smaller schools, the majority of the state's 92 counties had little experience with rural school consolidation in 1900, particularly if it involved
transporting students, and those that did adopted the practice in only one or
two townships. In 1900, 679 small schools had been abandoned, but the state
still had over 4,000 schools with fewer than 20 students, and almost 600 with
fewer than 10. In 1901, the legislature passed a law that gave school trustees
the authority (but, again, did not compel them) to close schools in which the
average attendance was less than 12. Between 1901 and 1906, this law reduced the number of schools with 5 or fewer students from 108 to 40, and
the number of schools with 10 or fewer from 487 to 400, but it had little

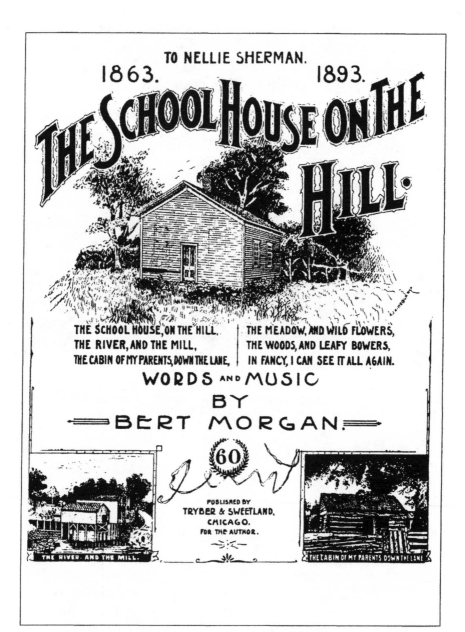

Sheet music celebrating the country school, 1893.

effect on the numbers of rural schools with more than 10 pupils. Significantly, Warrick County, which had been so opposed to school consolidation in 1900, did not close any of its schools in response to the new law, and had the largest number of small schools of any county in the state.[46]

A similar survey of Iowa county school superintendents in 1901 found even less experience with consolidation than in Indiana and, if anything, even more opposition on the part of rural patrons. Consolidation had been adopted by only 63 districts in 28 of the state's nearly 99 counties. Where it did occur, rural Iowans closed small schools not so much to achieve educational reform as to save money, and then only if the proximity of other schools or the good quality of local roads did not make transportation a problem. In Grundy County, even the county superintendent opposed the new system and summed up his objections in a way that encapsulates rural worries about participating fully in an organizational society. He believed that country schools provided better training in the common branches of learning than the much-vaunted graded schools. As he put it, "In the grades it is too much of a machine grind."[47]

In order to overcome such rural resistance, professional educators and their agencies, particularly the education faculties of state normal schools and universities, the U.S. Bureau of Education, and the different state departments of public instruction, mounted an all-out campaign to promote rural school consolidation during the first decades of the twentieth century. These efforts received additional boosts from the Country Life Movement, which also saw rural education as a key area in need of reform, as well as from the U.S. Department of Agriculture and its different extension efforts. Consequently, the amount of writing and attention devoted to the "rural school problem" increased exponentially, and educators lobbied state legislatures to pass laws promoting their agenda.[48]

Rather than limiting their efforts to closing or improving smaller rural schools, educational reformers redoubled their advocacy of complete consolidation and centralization and the construction of new graded elementary schools and well-equipped high schools. Regardless of their source, their reports and bulletins reflected a certain sameness and painted an overly happy picture of the benefits of consolidation as well as its progress. These publications typically summarized the history of the movement and offered digests of current laws affecting rural school reform and compilations of statistics showing its spread. They also featured case histories of successful consolidation efforts in different rural communities replete with numerous photographs depicting stolid but modern brick consolidated school buildings, well-ordered classes using up-to-date facilities, and all manner of organized extracurricular activities, including school orchestras, athletic teams, and pageants and dramatic productions.

Reformers paid particular attention to the physical improvements that consolidation enabled, exhibiting at times the sort of "edifice complex" that has often characterized educational administration. In contrast to wood-frame district schoolhouses, which continued the same vernacular styles that characterized farmhouses and country churches, the new consolidated school buildings were often the largest structures in the community and utilized different materials and aesthetics to make more grandiose and formal architectural statements. In his 1910 bulletin for the U.S. Department of Agriculture, for example, George W. Knorr noted that the buildings themselves were an important part of the consolidation movement. "When new buildings are erected they usually represent the best efforts of the community, and are the objects of local pride," he wrote. Local pride did not come cheap, however, and costs ranged from $8,000 to $12,000 for a "serviceable, substantial, and modern four or five room building"; school buildings in wealthy agricultural areas could cost $20,000 or more. Moreover, Knorr pointed out, there were a number of architectural firms specializing in the "peculiar requirements of these schools," and he recommended that such specialists be engaged.[49]

As might be expected, rural school patrons continued to balk at such expensive propositions. In several instances, however, private philanthropy bridged the gap between educators' dreams and rural fiscal realities. William Henry Miner provided what was, perhaps, the most generous and ostentatious of these gifts to his hometown of Chazy, Clinton County, New York, in 1915. After the township accepted his proposal and voted to centralize its small schools and spend $17,000 for a new building, Miner paid for the rest of the costs, furnished buses to transport the students, and established an endowment fund for the new school's continued operation. The new school

A typical consolidated school in Indiana with the old one-room school used as the janitor's cottage. From A. C. Monahan, Consolidation of Rural Schools and Transportation of Pupils at Public Expense, *U.S. Bureau of Education, Bulletin 604, No. 30, Washington, D.C., 1914.*

was an elegant five-story California Mission–style building with an Otis elevator and entrance hall walls of Italian marble, a carillon 71 feet higher than the roof with 40 tons of brass bells, an auditorium for 1,100, two gymnasiums with swimming pools for boys and girls, and 44 rooms, including a special mahogany-paneled Shakespeare room and a white Cicero room complete with classical statues.[50]

In addition to such private bequests, different states also provided a modicum of financial support for the new schools. Minnesota, which adopted the most generous policy of any state with the 1911 Holmberg Act, gave annual support of $750, $1,000, and $1,500, for schools of two, three, and four or more rooms respectively, as well as up to $1,500 for initial building costs. In order to ensure the proper use of public funds, the same act also fixed standards for the area of the consolidated school district, buildings, equipment, teachers' qualifications, industrial courses, and transportation. By the same token, Wisconsin passed a law in 1913 that gave aid for the construction of new consolidated schools ranging from $500 for a one-room school that combined two or more school districts to $5,000 for a graded elementary and high school that united all of the districts in the township, as well as annual support for transportation costs. A similar law in Iowa provided up to $500 for equipment and $750 in annual support for school buildings with four or more rooms.[51]

State legislatures also tried to promote rural school consolidation during the early 1900s by making it easier for the issue to be brought to a vote and adopted. Typically this legislation lowered the percentage or number of school patrons required to petition to have the issue considered, and it allowed consolidation by a majority of votes in all the affected districts taken as a whole rather than requiring a majority in each separate school district, which had effectively given each district a veto. In addition, county or township education officials in some states also had the power to close small schools and transport students regardless of the wishes of the affected patrons.

In spite of publicity, state aid and other legislation, and the best efforts of educational reformers, rural school consolidation ultimately depended on the willingness of local inhabitants, and it proceeded very slowly. In some states, such as Illinois, rural opposition prevented any enabling legislation from being passed. Elsewhere, the easier laws or the money provided by the state were not sufficient to stimulate widespread consolidation. Even in states where education officials had the power to close small schools, they were often unwilling to suffer the political consequences of that decision.

If anything, the intensified campaign by professional educators only heightened rural suspicions of school consolidation and added new dimensions to their opposition. This was particularly true in New York, where the state finally abolished the district system in favor of township control in 1917, after more than forty years of failed legislative attempts. Although state superintendents of education began complaining about the district system in New York as early as 1844, and a bill to abolish it was first introduced in 1877, staunch opposition typically prevented consideration much less passage of any enabling legislation. The bill that ultimately did pass was introduced and promoted by the New York State Education Department in the wake of its 1915 report, which stressed the need to improve New York's rural schools. According to that report, 8,430 of the state's 11,642 elementary schools were one-room schools, and 3,580 of these had an average attendance of ten or fewer including 13 schools with only one pupil, 74 with two, and 172 with three, as well as a handful of districts that allegedly hired a teacher in order to claim the state's appropriation for schools that had no students at all. As a result of the education department's efforts, in May 1917 the bill creating the Township Unit System passed the Assembly by a vote of 77 to 54 and was approved by the Senate by 40 to 7.[52]

The outcry from the countryside, however, was immediate and intense. Rural voters overwhelmingly demanded repeal of the township system and filled local newspapers and grange halls throughout the state with often emotional letters and resolutions expressing their opinions. Indeed, they turned up the political heat so much that Governor Whitman, who had originally advocated the new law but was up for renomination, changed his mind and urged repeal in his annual message to the legislature on January 2, 1918. State legislators had also gotten the same message from their constituents, and they repealed the township law three months later by a vote of 107 to 36 in the House and 34 to 9 in the Senate.

Rural New Yorkers opposed the township system for a variety of reasons. Mostly, they resented the higher taxes that township control represented. Although supporters of the law claimed that it equalized the tax burden throughout the township and primarily benefited the more remote and poorer school districts that had the highest tax rates, others remained skeptical and saw the law as serving village, not rural, interests. According to one report of farmers' opinions, the township decreased village taxes but increased the farmer's taxes by 200 to 300 percent, "giving him in return the privilege of sending his children to the village school, which however he can not exercise on account of climatic and topographical conditions."[53] In his letter to the *Ogdensburg News*, James D. Moore of Lisbon, New York, sneered at the cosmopolitan pretenses of local village residents and sarcastically urged his fellow farmers to embrace the new system cheerfully:

Come up ye jolly farmer men and pay your Machold-township-school-system taxes. Don't be ugly if they happen to be a few hundred percent higher than the old fashioned sort. Remember that, as everywhere else, so in educational matters, you can't be strictly highbrow and up-to-date unless you are willing to pay the price. Moreover, what is your loss is perhaps other people's gain. . . . This is the intent of the Machold law, that a uniform tax rate by compelling you to help pay for the more expensive buildings, teachers and equipment of the village school and thus making the expense the same to you whether you send your children there or to their own district school will in time pry you loose from that "little red schoolhouse" and make you willing to be consolidated and centralized.[54]

As well as stirring long-standing rural resentments of village ambitions, the fact that taxes were raised substantially without any direct vote led to other time-honored rhetoric, which reflected older republican sensibilities. J. Grant Morse of Madison County objected to paying for the bonded indebtedness of surrounding union districts as well as the incorporated village, which had built a $20,000 school. "It seems to us," he wrote to the *Rural New Yorker*, "to be just about such a situation as faced the early colonists and instigated a famous tea party—taxation without representation." Another farmer worried about the expansion of Heuvelton High School, which local country folk would be taxed to pay for: "If we had half the courage of our colonial forefathers we'd be up and doing something to break the chain that has been thrown around us. Instead we endure this unjust taxation also the satisfied smiles of the villagers, whose tax is much reduced and although we say a great deal we do nothing. . . . Are we going to submit?"[55]

Other protestors put the same attitudes in a more contemporary context and labeled the township law an extension of kaiserism, the ideological as well as the genealogical descendant of King George. According to a letter signed "Ruralite" in Mechanicville to the *Troy Record*, the law violated all the principles of home rule, and, "instead of being known as a township school it should be entitled an act to establish kaiser rule over the rural district, the kaiser being personified by the State Education Department."[56] Emmet B. Kirbe was a member of the Taylor, New York, board of education, and was sworn to try to make the new law work. "But I don't like it," he wrote, because it was wrong in principle: "It places control of schools too far from the people; in short reverting towards the Kaiserist form of government. They tell us we are fighting Germany to destroy autocracy. . . . Shall we, then, admit that we are incapable of local government? No, and forever no! Shall we say England was right when in 1784, she told us that republican form of government would be a failure? I hope not!"[57] A grange member from Wayville was even more succinct and vowed, in the name of democracy, to fight "the Hohenzollerns to a finish whether they hail from Albany or Berlin."[58]

Many of the New York farmers' protestations against the township school law, then, reflected common and familiar themes in rural political culture and agrarian ideology. The insistence on home rule and decentralized control, for example, also informed rural opposition to road reform and to the different efforts to centralize farmers' own organizations, such as the Dairymen's League, which will be discussed later.[59] Even the invocation of the kaiser had a precedent in mid-nineteenth-century objections to Horace Mann's desire to emulate the centralized Prussian school system in Massachusetts. By the same token, rural distrust of and animosity toward village interests had also shaped myriad issues in the countryside for many years.

Rural opposition to the New York township system law in 1917 and 1918 reflected these familiar sensibilities, but it also revealed new sources of complaint and anxiety. In particular, much of the new rhetoric criticized the state's embrace of professional expertise and authority as well as the more general organizational culture that this represented. In this respect, rural New Yorkers objected not so much to the tax increases per se, but to the fact that the additional revenues were used to pay for what were, in their minds, unnecessary frills or educational fads that were sanctioned and advocated by professional educators.

In particular, irksome and expensive requirements for sanitary chemical toilets and physical education instruction in all rural schools symbolized the excesses and inappropriateness of the professional educators' agenda. Although neither of these mandates were part of the 1917 township school law, but were enacted a year earlier, country people used the campaign against the township system as an opportunity to rail against them. Actually, the new toilets were not required by any legislation but were decreed by the State Education Department. Given the fact that most farmers before the 1920s did not choose to buy such facilities for their own homes, being forced by the state to do so for the schools stirred resentment. According to one letter to State Senator Morris Halliday from a group of taxpayers and residents of school district 7, Reading, Schuyler County, New York:

We have just finished paying a large tax because of being compelled to practically rebuild and refurnish our schoolhouse, with toilets, etc. Now we hear the new "sanitary closet" has arrived at a cost of only about $150, or more. Probably some one particular closet picked out as being the best one (for some pockets at Albany) which spells graft. There has not been an epidemic in our section in the memory of our oldest resident, and why the taxpayers in rural districts should be burdened with oppressive taxation for such utterly needless innovations is a matter we propose to look into.[60]

New toilets, however, were relatively inexpensive compared to the physical education instructors required by the Welsh-Slater Physical Training Law of 1916. Orleans County rural schools, for example, were required to employ three physical trainers at an annual salary of $1,200 each plus expenses. In the minds of many rural inhabitants, this was an unadulterated waste of money because farm boys and girls were very active and had no need for specially designated physical education. According to one nativist landowner: "In the great city of New York, with its enormous population of underbred and underfed aliens, there may be need for such fads as 'physical training.' But our farmer boys and girls are not housed in tenements, and do get plenty of exercise in their walks to and from school, and in helping their parents in farm work and doing chores."[61]

This was not good enough for the law's defenders, however. "I am one of those articles classified by your contributors as Impositions, Abominations, Nuisances, etc.,—a Physical Director," wrote Vesta McKee to the *Rural New Yorker*; she went on to argue for physical education as well as a range of progressive school reforms. Another correspondent observed that even though the working strength and longevity of the farmer were proverbial, the "clean cut, glossy, rubber muscled, high school athletic" was preferable to the "bowed, muscle bound, gnarled farm boy." Such matters were best left to the professionals, for "the psychology of play, or games, of erect carriage, proper breathing, the development of co-ordination of mind and muscle, of eye and movement, are things that have been deeply studied." And the experts in Albany, who knew more about these things than the average farmer, considered these studies carefully before installing the physical culture system in the rural schools. "Some of them came from the farm themselves," noted the writer, condescendingly. "They are smart men, too. That is why they came."[62]

Rural school patrons had a different assessment of such arcane professional knowledge. According to Charles R. Traver of Dutchess County: "It certainly seems the height of folly to have a high-priced teacher come around once a week to teach the pupils of the rural schools to hop on one foot, throw bean bags, or a big rubber ball etc., or to practice them in different motion exercises. . . . This part of the program has brought the Education Department into more contempt and disfavor than anything they have put over on us in many a year."[63]

Another writer from Ulster County complained, "Were parents more familiar with the required stunts and supervised games, the whole scheme would be ridiculed to oblivion." Even one observer who favored the idea of physical education thought that it would be better taught by the regular teachers after some training rather than by high-priced specialists: "Mathematically it figured out that we are paying $5 per hour to get our youngsters' feet educated and 50 cents per hour to have their heads attended to and wits sharpened." Clearly, this writer's wits were plenty sharp enough in spite of, or, perhaps, because of, his education in a rural district school.[64]

To its defenders, then, the rural school provided a focus of opposition to the authority of professional expertise and the organizational society that it served. According to the plea of "A Rural Mother," which another reader regarded as one of the best articles on the subject that he had read, centralization was "paternalism with a vengeance": "Individuality will be lost, the pride taken in 'our' school and 'our' teacher gone and in a few years the country schools will be run by one or two man power. . . . Haven't the parents who bear the children anything to say? Must they yield those children up to be educated as some man or men with certain ideas in their heads, deem best?"[65]

By contrast, the "little red schoolhouse" was a bulwark of personalism in an increasingly faceless society. "A Rural Mother" complained about carting the children off in the early morning "to a place appointed by outsiders." As she put it, "Now every one knows that all children are not alike in temperament, etc., but no matter, bundle them all in, as a farmer ships his calves to a distant pasture, and even he distinguishes between the weak and the strong." Or, as one boy in her community said: "When we get to high schools we are just one of the units to make the whole, we don't count as individuals as we did in our school."[66]

Significantly, then, the "little red schoolhouse" became as much an icon for rural northerners in their opposition to the new order as the big brick consolidated school building was for the educators in their advocacy of it.

Anti–school reform postcard, Broadhead, Wisconsin, 1890.
(Courtesy of the State Historical Society of Wisconsin)

For both sides, the buildings simultaneously symbolized their values and embodied their agendas. Increasingly, for country people, their schools provided a sanctuary for the individualism and small scale of local life that were being threatened by the new, organizational society. And, under the often leaky roof of their one-room schools, they marshaled a host of agrarian traditions as they sought to preserve their scarce capital and their time-honored rights of self-government and independence in the face of challenges from nearby villagers and faraway professional educators.

———————

Thus, the one-room schoolhouse remained a fixture in the northern countryside throughout the first part of the twentieth century even after decades of educators' active campaigning for consolidated schools. As of 1920, the overwhelming majority of rural schools in the North were still one-room schoolhouses. In New England, the percentage of small country schools out of the total number of schools (including city schools) ranged from a low of 25 or 27 percent in relatively urbanized Rhode Island and Massachusetts to 68, 70, and 76 percent, respectively, in New Hampshire, Vermont, and Maine. Between two-thirds and three-fourths of the schools in Pennsylvania and New York were also one-room country schools, and comparable statistics were even higher in the Midwest. Indiana and Ohio had the largest number of consolidated schools of any states in the country, but well over 60 percent of their schools were still one-room buildings. Minnesota had a few dozen consolidations after the 1911 Holmberg Act, but as of 1920, 7,668 of the state's 9,077 schools (85 percent) remained typical country schoolhouses, a percentage that also characterized Wisconsin, Kansas, and Nebraska. Finally, Iowa had both the largest number and the highest percentage of one-room rural schools, accounting for just under 90 percent of the state's 12,716 schoolhouses.[67]

During the 1920s, the ready availability of gasoline-powered school buses and the more widespread improvement of country roads helped remove some of the most obvious obstacles that professional educators had blamed for their lack of success. Such triumphs over time and distance failed to spur significant additional rural school consolidation, however. By 1928, the rural North had over 80,000 schools, but only 6,320 of them had more than one room, and many of these were not part of consolidated districts. Likewise, the percentage of students who attended consolidated schools was also low, ranging from a high of only 18 percent in Minnesota to 2.8 percent in Illinois and 1.5 percent in New Hampshire.[68]

Moreover, the movement for consolidation appeared to have stalled. In Iowa in 1926, for example, only 385 of the state's approximately 10,000 rural schools were consolidated; 18 of those consolidations occurred after 1920 and 4 after 1921. According to Viggo Justesen, who visited rural schools throughout the state in 1930 and reported on them in *Wallace's Farmer*, "That the one-room school is doomed seems largely a dream of the professional educators, who still have the consolidated school bug in their systems, long after many farmers who have had to pay the added tax burden have been cured of it."[69]

That lack of momentum led to new measures. In the wake of the defeat of its township system law, the New York State Education Department convinced Governor Al Smith and the legislature to enact a new law in 1925 that encouraged small rural schools to combine into central rural districts. The new law required only a majority vote in all of the affected districts rather than a majority in each, and, in order to promote consolidation, the state paid for 50 percent of the costs of transportation and 25 percent of the cost of the construction of the new central schools. For New York farm families, however, this was déjà vu all over again, and the pages of the *Rural New Yorker* filled with angry diatribes against the law and news of meetings of the Rural School Improvement Society, which was formed to oppose it. In one instance, the paper snidely published a circular boasting about the new centralized district in Madrid, St. Lawrence County, which described its three modern buses, "equipped with heaters, hydraulic shock absorbers and many other conveniences," together with a picture of one of those buses disabled by the side of a snowy and icy road. "They Crowed Too Soon," read the headline. The combination of such small moral victories and rural political agitation failed to overturn the 1925 law, as it had a decade earlier, but rural opposition continued to limit the number of school consolidations in spite of the financial incentives provided by the state. As of 1938, only 250 central rural districts had been established, and New York still had almost 8,000 old-fashioned country school districts.[70]

Frustration with the slow pace of rural school consolidation in Indiana, a state that earlier education reformers had been more optimistic about, led

them to push for the establishment of even larger county districts during the
1920s. With funding from John D. Rockefeller, the General Education Board
(GEB) sent Frank P. Bachman, an E.D. from Teachers' College, to survey Indiana's rural schools in 1923. Bachman published his findings in a 304-page
report and drafted legislation for the establishment of a county unit system to
replace township control, but the state legislature rejected his proposals in
the face of opposition from township school officials. After this defeat, the
GEB mounted a demonstration project of the new system in Johnson and
LaGrange Counties, but public opinion against county control remained so
strong that, ultimately, both the project and subsequent bills for a county unit
system failed.[71]

The failed attempt to institute a county system in Indiana, however, provided a harbinger of future trends. After the depression, which effectively
curtailed rural school consolidation except where New Deal funds paid for
the new buildings, educational reformers tried to sidestep rural opposition
by creating larger administrative districts without requiring consolidation.
Reorganization, as this process was known, allowed professional educators
to establish firmer control over the school system, making eventual consolidation easier at some point in the future.

That strategy simply led to the repeat of earlier battles. In Kansas, for example, the 1945 school reorganization law was challenged by different county
associations and the statewide Kansas Rural School Association before being
declared unconstitutional by the Kansas Supreme Court and replaced by a
new act in 1947 that neither the opponents or the supporters of the earlier
law regarded with much enthusiasm. A similar reorganization law in Illinois
led to at least one protracted battle that spanned the entire postwar era when
residents of Killmer attempted to secede from their new larger district in
order to continue their own schools. School reorganization was also contentious in Adams County, Nebraska, during the same period. Back in Indiana, rural opposition kept the Indiana School Reorganization Act from being
passed until 1959.[72]

By the second half of the twentieth century, however, the process of reorganization and consolidation was facilitated by both the commitment of
more public funds and the further acculturation of rural Americans into a society dominated by large-scale organizations and professional expertise,
changes that had not yet taken place by 1930. Yet, even though most rural

schools today are consolidated and the one-room schoolhouse is a museum piece or a curiosity from another era, advocates of educational reorganization and reform won few easy victories. In what is, perhaps, the ultimate irony, some education professors in recent years have reassessed the conventional wisdom that bigger is better and are advocating the revitalization of the smaller country school. Whether rural people have also come full circle and are now opposing them remains to be seen.[73]

Between the end of the Civil War and 1930, rural northerners resisted school reform for a variety of reasons. Still informed by the precepts of rural republicanism, northern farm people during the middle decades of the nineteenth century insisted on local control of their schools by small neighborhood districts. As the progressive depopulation of older agricultural communities made that system an increasingly costly one, rural inhabitants centralized the administration of their schools at the township level and closed some of the smaller ones, sacrificing a measure of self-government in order to save money.

In spite of such changes, residents of the countryside continued to be leery of costly changes that were proposed by educational reformers, particularly graded elementary schools and high schools housed in new, more modern school buildings. At first, this opposition was directed primarily against nearby villagers, who benefited disproportionately from such improvements even though the farmers bore the bulk of their expense. As professional educators became increasingly organized and zealous in their efforts to control and restructure country schools during the first decades of the twentieth century, rural resentments shifted to them. Once again, country people voiced familiar objections to outside concentrations of power and the decline of local control, and school reform became a target for a host of complaints about the large scale and impersonality of modern society. For all of these reasons, then, rural northerners continued to resist attempts to reshape their schools and effectively stymied the fulfillment of one of the major impulses of progressive reform in the countryside well into the twentieth century.

This history of rural school reform differs significantly from the changes in road administration, and it is instructive to compare them. As Charles Sumner once observed, "the road and the schoolmaster are the two most important agents in advancing civilization," but farmers initially resisted efforts to reform both out of concerns for the ideological centrality of local self-government, frugality, and animosity toward the pretensions of nearby villagers and the arrogance of outside experts.[74] By 1930, however, rural northerners had made their peace with changes in road administration in ways they were not yet prepared to do with respect to the schools.

At its most basic, the definition of a good road was a question of science and engineering, and rural interests eventually argued not so much about what constituted good roads as about who was going to pay for them. Infusions of funds from state and federal governments as well as substantial revenues from automobile registrations and gasoline taxes shifted that financial burden away from the farmers and largely settled the issue. By contrast, the definition of a good school or a good education was less a matter of science, regardless of the pretensions of professional educators. It remained more in the realm of metaphysics than physics or, at least, of culture and ideology. In contrast to the impact of the automobile on road administration, then, there were no technological fixes that provided easy resolutions to the conflicts inherent in school reform, and, because it was a gray zone, the state was less willing or able to commit enough of its resources to be a decisive force. Instead, rural schools remained contested terrain for much of the twentieth century, and rural opposition to educational reform became a measure of the countryside's distance from the second great transformation of American society. The new roads may have brought country people closer in a physical and even a political sense, but they remained aloof in other ways, as the history of rural school reform makes clear.

Part II
PRODUCERS

Surely the churning of milk bringeth forth butter,

and the wringing of the nose bringeth forth blood:

so the forcing of wrath bringeth forth strife.

— PROVERBS 30:33

3

BRINGING FORTH STRIFE

The Ironies of Dairy Organization
in the New York Milkshed

Economic changes during the late nineteenth and early twentieth centuries also threatened the importance of the local community and the independence of small producers in the rural North. Increasingly, the American economy became dominated by large-scale corporations and organizations that reflected the specific and separate interests of business and labor. For farmers, however, these developments posed particular challenges. Informed by the precepts of Jeffersonian republicanism, country people at first eschewed large concentrations of power as well as separate class interests, which, in their minds, threatened to corrupt the commonwealth. Their earliest responses to corporate power, the Grange and Populist movements, had definitely pursued goals particular to farmers, but did so from a perspective of agricultural fundamentalism: the belief that the welfare of the nation as a whole depended upon the welfare of its farmers, who, in the words of the old Grange song, is the man who feeds them all. In the face of these new, large, outside forces, farmers in these movements strove to preserve their own independence and the autonomy of their local communities and, at times, even a vision of America as a cooperative commonwealth that was based on those values.

After the failure of Populism and in the wake of the growing power of big business, such a perspective became increasingly problematic, and agricultural spokesmen began to call for new types of organizations that stressed the separate interests of agriculture. Turn-of-the-century farmers accepted the need for new interest-based organizations reluctantly, however, and then primarily as a response to the prior organization of capital and labor. According to Alva Agee, a farmer from Gallia County, Ohio, in 1892, farmers' groups "should promote class feeling only sufficiently to counteract the influence of others . . . and this feature should be dropped when the cause for its existence passes away."[1] In contrast, the permanence of distinct interests was much more apparent by 1903, as was the need for new strategies. In the words of a speaker at the Scott County, Iowa, Farmers' Institute: "And both organized capital and labor have come to stay. . . . The farmer has looked upon this industrial upheaval complacently, believing it was only a question of time when everything would be back to its old channels again . . . but that thing has been exploded and in order to meet these new conditions we have but one course to follow, and that is the course the capitalist and the laboring man has pursued—power by organization."[2]

The goals, methods, and ideology of these new farmers' organizations, however, were very much open to debate, and between 1900 and 1930, agriculturalists experimented with a variety of arrangements and tactics in order to redress their relative lack of power in the marketplace. Farmers built on their own histories of cooperation and organization and continued to act upon their traditional antipathy toward middlemen and their belief in a producers' ethic. But they also had to balance ancestral desires for independence and local autonomy and long-standing fears of monopoly power and consolidated control against the need for effective organization in an increasingly centralized marketplace. Yet, because of farmers' identities as producers and small businessmen, neither big businesses nor labor unions provided wholly satisfactory models, and they were forced to forge their own path. As a result, attempts to organize agricultural producers during the early twentieth century were marked by conflict, contradiction, and, at times, profound ambivalence, in which leaders who were more comfortable with the new corporate order often opposed members who were not.

These efforts at organization, most notably the development of agricultural cooperatives and the rise of the Farm Bureau, have not been well understood. Grant McConnell laments the abandonment of the Granger and Populist commitments to democracy in its broadest sense in favor of the narrower and more circumscribed agenda of a special interest group that was well integrated into a corporate political economy. This portrayal of discontinuity, however, is informed by a romanticization of the earlier period and a critique of the American Farm Bureau Federation's behavior at the national level after 1937, but not by a close study of the local dynamics and the ideological and social bases of the new farmers' organizations during their formative years. Theodore Saloutos and John Hicks too readily assume that these twentieth-century farmers' organizations were direct continuations of older sensibilities. But, they argue, both the earlier movements and the later groups pursued only limited goals and interests that were of a piece with the dominant framework of American society, rather than in opposition to it.[3]

To understand the place of northern farmers as producers in an emerging organizational society during the first decades of the twentieth century, then, it is necessary to reconstruct the complexities of agricultural organization and agrarian ideology at the local level. This chapter analyzes the dramatic history of dairy organization in New York State between 1880 and 1930, particularly the Dairymen's League, which was a leading agricultural cooperative. The early development of the Dairymen's League was animated by a strong grassroots activism throughout the milkshed, which climaxed in the dramatic milk strike of 1916. The subsequent transformation of the league after the strike, which many regarded as a betrayal of that struggle, was, in large part, the product of the separation of the leadership from the membership as they pursued their own corporate agenda. Thus, what began as a movement of producers against middlemen in order to protect the independence of the small businessman-farmer against the imperatives of monopolistic corporations went awry as the organization the farmers created itself became a big business and acted accordingly. Both in their embrace of the new organization and subsequent disaffection, then, one can find measures of the farmers' responses to the second great transformation in the northern countryside.

Beginning after the Civil War, the growth of urban markets for country milk led to new forms of collective action among New York dairy farmers.[4] As New York City consumers became increasingly dissatisfied with the poor nutritional quality of local milk, most of which was produced by unsanitary dairies that fed its cows swill or distillery slop, railroads began transporting purer country milk into the city within a radius of about one hundred miles.[5] This expansion of the milk trade, however, created new problems. Farmers regularly complained that urban milk dealers paid too little for their milk and accused them of watering it or adulterating it with chalk and flour in order to increase profits — charges that dealers just as frequently turned back on the farmers. Farmers also griped against both the dealers and the railroads for damaging or losing their milk cans and for not providing the facilities necessary for the milk trade.

As a result, dairymen began to organize along their railroad lines and formed route protective associations.[6] The Harlem Milk Producers' Protective Association was established in 1880 by dairymen east of the Hudson River along the Harlem Railroad; farmers west of the Hudson along the Erie, the Midland, and the Sussex railroads organized in 1881 and 1882. The largest of these groups, the Erie Mutual Milk Producers' Association, included almost seven hundred of the eight hundred or so producers shipping on the Erie line, and won significant concessions from the railroad.[7] At the same time, however, the leading milk dealers and creamery operators also organized and formed the New York Milk Exchange, Limited, in 1882, in order to set prices. When the producers' associations west of the Hudson requested an increase in prices in 1883, the exchange refused to meet their demands, and the dairymen called for a milk strike, probably the first organized withholding from an urban market in the United States.[8]

Feelings ran strong at the March 12 strike meeting in the Goshen Courthouse in Orange County, home of the Erie Mutual Milk Producers' Association. According to the reporter from the *New York Times*, hundreds of dairy farmers crowded the courthouse, and "venerable milk producers shook their whitened beards vigorously as they declared their purpose to 'let the cows kick over the pails' until the City dealers came to terms." Striking farmers were more circumspect when it came to their neighbors, however, and they rejected a plan to publicly list and scorn all those who refused to hold back their milk. In several cases, those farmers supported the strike but felt bound to honor their contracts with the milk dealers, and the strikers did not want to shame them. Their neighbors' milk, though, was fair game. At the March 15 meeting, D. E. Chase, whom the *Times* also described as a white-bearded farmer, felt morally and legally obligated by his written contract to continue shipping milk to a New York dealer, even though his sympathies were with the strikers. "Three or four other farmers made similar statements," the paper reported, "and County Treasurer William E. Mapes provoked laughter and applause by remarking: 'It seems to me that here are some good cases for spilling.'"[9]

Numerous unofficial "spilling committees"—groups of irate dairymen and their employees—overturned milk cans at local railroad depots, and after the first week of the strike, milk shipments to the city were down more than 50 percent. At least one of these groups consisted of African Americans, probably hired by the striking farmers. On March 20, according to the *Times*, a party of "colored men" dumped twenty-two cans belonging to the Orange County Milk Association, an established company of farmers and dealers that was opposed to the strike, and a spilling committee of "about 12 or 13 negroes," maybe the same group, went into action at nearby Bennett's Station.[10]

However dramatic, these altercations were not very violent and posed little threat to the social order. In spite of the fact that both strikers and nonstrikers were sometimes armed, only one shooting was reported, and it inflicted a "painful but not dangerous wound" to a young man's lower leg. Initially, county sheriffs and other law enforcement officials refused to go after the spillers or to protect the shipments of nonstriking producers, nor did the courts inflict severe sanctions against them, regardless of their race. When a black man, John Richardson, was arrested and arraigned at the same Goshen Courthouse for assaulting a nonstriking dairy farmer and spilling his milk, he was defended by the Erie Milk Producers' Association's attorney and was fined $5 and compelled to give a $250 bond to keep the peace. In the words of the *Times*, "the Court room was crowded and the farmers' sympathy was undeniably with the prisoner. . . . Both the amount of the fine and the bond were promptly forthcoming from the farmers in the Court room."[11]

On the ninth day of the strike, the Milk Exchange met with a committee of producers and offered to raise prices for the next few months, but did not agree to any increase after June. With their strike fund well subscribed, the farmers were reluctant to compromise. Their leaders, however, argued otherwise. "It is a nice thing to talk about holding the fort," declared Howard Shaw before a meeting of one thousand at the Goshen Courthouse, "but it is a deuced sight harder thing to hold the fort." The Midland Railroad, which had withheld milk at first, was now shipping almost a normal supply. Similarly, law enforcement officials could no longer ignore pressures to go after spillers and protect dairymen who wanted to ship. The president of the producers' association, W. P. Richardson, was also in favor of a compromise and a speedy resolution to benefit the Erie Railroad, which was losing $1,000 per day in freights, because he regarded the line as a good friend of the farmers. At the strike's end, the smaller independent dealers and creamery operators were willing to accept the farmers' prices for twelve months, but the exchange persisted in offering its own price, which was typically 15 to 20 percent less.[12]

The strike, which was over and lost in two weeks, was a clear expression of the dairymen's animosities toward the middlemen and a reflection of their commitment to a producers' ethic. In the words of the author of a letter to the *Country Gentleman*: "I always rejoice when I see reports of successful combinations among farmers to defend themselves against those who grow rich by handling their products. Farming is not such easy work that it can be indulged in merely that others may get rich, though with proper reward, it is about as pleasant a business as I know of. Nor can any honest man, it seems to me, deny that the man who in measure creates wealth ought to receive the largest share of the profit from it."[13] The strikers enjoyed widespread support in their communities and in the big city newspapers for many of the same reasons.

Popular support and a high level of dissatisfaction notwithstanding, the strike gained only a short-term increase in prices and did little to change the long-term problems of milk marketing. Several structural factors contributed to the farmers' failure. The strike was poorly timed, coming at the beginning of the peak milk-producing season when supplies were large, and it could only last a short time because the producers' organizations made no provisions for disposing of the milk that was not shipped or sold. The strikers also failed to organize the entire milkshed, especially the dairy areas east of the Hudson River, and many local creameries west of the river shipped their milk to the New York dealers instead of processing it.

The strike was also shaped by the farmers' sensibilities as small businessmen and respectable members of the community. These dairymen were hardly marginal producers on the fringes of a market economy. As the *Times* reported, one indignant milk producer put the whole issue in very businesslike terms and thought it most unfair that milk farmers with farms and stock worth $20,000 were scarcely making a living, while the owner of a New York milk route grew rich off an investment of a few hundred dollars in a horse and wagon. "I think it would be safe to say that the average milk producer in Orange and the neighboring milk counties does not make at present more than 2½ per cent on his invested capital."[14]

Ultimately, it was these attitudes, in spite of traditional animosities toward middlemen, that limited farmers' willingness to pursue more drastic strategies in order to achieve their goals. Resentments against the combinations of New York dealers were simply not enough to transcend the divergent interests within the milkshed as well as the strikers' own reluctance and inability to alienate their neighbors or "friendly" railroads and dealers.

———————

After 1883, the structure of the dairy industry changed and became even more centralized and monopolistic, and in place of the older association of dealers, huge and highly capitalized corporations began to dominate the purchase of milk in the New York milkshed. As a result, dairy farmers experienced a loss of independence and control akin to that endured by skilled workers during the same period, and, as small businessmen, they chafed even more against the monopolistic powers of the new corporations. These newer sensibilities led to renewed organization in the milkshed.

The Borden's Condensed Milk Company was the largest of these new corporations. Typical of the big businesses of the period, Borden's emerged during the 1890s out of the consolidation and reorganization of the New York Condensed Milk Company, which distributed fluid milk as well as manufacturing the condensed product using the expensive vacuum condenser that had been invented by Gail Borden in 1856. According to the *American Agriculturalist* in 1895 and the *Milk Reporter* in 1896, Borden's manufactured 225,000 quarts per day. It had numerous country milk collection stations, condenseries at Elgin and Algonquin, Illinois, and at Wassaic, Brewster, Purdys, Walkill, and Deposit, New York, and bottling plants at three New York towns. When Borden's incorporated in New Jersey in 1899, it was capitalized at $20 million. The Anglo-Swiss Milk Company was almost as old as Borden's and had factories in the United States and Europe, and Borden's acquired its American operations in 1902 for $4 million. Sheffield Farms–Slawson-Decker Company, later known as Sealtest, was the other big dairy concern dominating the New York market.[15]

Dealing with such huge businesses greatly undermined the dairy farmer's independence, and Borden's in particular exercised substantial control over its producers. To ensure the taste of the milk, only certain mill feeds could be fed, and ensilage (which permitted a longer milking season), malt grains, linseed meal, turnips, and barley sprouts were expressly forbidden. Herds were subject to inspection by a company veterinarian whose decree was final; no Holsteins were permitted, and cows had to be brushed regularly. Similarly, company barn inspectors passed judgment on stables, which had to be white-washed and cleared of manure. The milk's temperature was strictly regulated, the milk had to be strained, and the cans were covered with a costly canvas that the company sold to the farmers for a profit; milk that grew too warm or failed to meet these conditions was refused by milk station managers, often arbitrarily. All in all, Borden's standard contract exceeded eighteen hundred words. Such measures guaranteed quality control, and, according to the *Rural New Yorker*, as long as Borden's paid higher prices for their milk, farmers usually felt rewarded for their extra efforts. Similarly, when the company faced strong local competition in buying the milk, it eased up on the enforcement of its requirements. But these conditions were rare, and while Borden's cows may have been contented, Borden's dairy farmers became increasingly less so.[16]

Whatever the monetary rewards, the lack of control and power inherent in dealing with a large corporation was bothersome. When farmers east of the Hudson, in Brewster, New York, organized and asked for better prices after a price cut in 1899, Borden's threatened to close down its factory. At first, all but a few refused to sign up on the September contract day, but after the threat many eventually accepted the company's terms.[17] In Otsego County, Borden's raised its prices 10 to 15 percent in 1903 in order to defuse an organizing effort among the farmers.[18]

"Contract day" was particularly onerous: "I want to remind you of the contract days when you would line up at the plant early in the morning. It required no whips or chains to enslave you thus. You used to scramble madly and even fight to be among the first to sign away your economic liberty. . . .

Standing there in line like a bunch of volunteer convicts, anxious to sign up for the next six months hard labor!"[19] Or, as an official of the successful organization that grew out of such discontent recalled in 1919, three years after their big victory: "More than once I have stood in that line and have seen men with flashing eyes, as if indignant at the humiliation of it all; and more than once I have stated to my associates, 'Men, some day this system will be smashed, and I pray that I may be one of the men who will help smash it.'"[20]

In addition to the growing power of private corporations, New York dairy farmers also had to contend with the New York City Board and Department of Health as it began to regulate the dairy industry in order to control the spread of tuberculosis from contaminated cow's milk. Beginning in 1902, all country dairy farms and plants supplying milk to New York City had to have permits from the Health Department, which required regular physical examination of the cows and used official score cards to check compliance with detailed regulations. In 1907, the Health Department demanded that farmers clip the tails of their cows in order to minimize the spread of bacteria, prompting one rural Odd Fellows chapter to parade a freshly washed cow under a banner labeled "What New York City Demands!" followed by a group of farmers wielding what purported to be a large toothbrush and manicure set for the animal. In addition, farmers leveled countercharges against the dealers about the filthy, germ-infested milk cans they returned to them and which their wives had to clean.[21]

The big change came in 1911–12. Milk was graded and all milk sold in New York City had to be pasteurized except for special Grade A raw and certified milk, which was from tuberculin-tested cows and produced under exceptionally sanitary conditions. Although dairy farmers benefited to a degree from the elimination of competition from unwholesome milk, the main effect of state regulation was to reinforce the growing power of the large corporations. Small dealers and individual farmers could not afford the expensive equipment required to pasteurize milk and had to get out of the business of selling milk directly to the New York City market. This led to further consolidation of the milk market, which limited the options farmers had for selling their milk and strengthened the ability of the bigger operations to dictate conditions and prices.[22]

Given these conditions at the turn of twentieth century, the eventual triumph of organized dairy farmers was by no means apparent. If anything, the

expansion of the milkshed and the overbearing influence of the big dairy corporations made farmers' cooperation and organization that much more
difficult, especially for the Five States Milk Producers' Association (FSMPA),
which attempted to mobilize all producers shipping to New York during the
period. By 1903, milk was being shipped into New York from over three hundred miles away, and the center of the New York milkshed was in Chenango
County, two hundred miles northwest of the city. After the Interstate Commerce Commission established differential rail rates in 1897, dairy farmers
who lived closer to the city enjoyed a 6-cent-per-can advantage and were reluctant to join with those further out. Similarly, farmers who lived near a factory that produced condensed milk and had a ready market for their milk
without shipping it were less inclined to combine with those who did not and
refused to take any actions that would aggravate their buyers. Some dairy
farmers set up cooperative creameries in an effort to have alternative outlets
for their milk and gain greater independence from the dealers, but creameries
that were too successful or offered too much competition were bought out
by the big companies.[23] Even the cooperative creameries that persisted, however, were reluctant to limit their local prerogatives in order to band together
and market their produce collectively.[24]

It took a new organization, the Dairymen's League, to transcend these divisions and mount an effective challenge against the "milk trust." Significantly, the league had its start in the Grange and union halls of upstate New
York.[25] O. W. Mapes, a participant in the 1883 strike, first got the idea for a
new dairy organization in 1904 and discussed the matter with John Schindler,
a trade union leader in Middletown, New York, who loaned him copies of local union by-laws to study. Mapes continued this interest as the lecturer of
the Walkill River Grange in Orange County, where he arranged programs on
the subject. The Pomona Grange of Orange County agreed to sponsor the
new organization until it got five hundred signatures, and on August 24,
1907, seven hundred dairy farmers from Orange, Sullivan, and Ulster Counties in New York, and Sussex County, New Jersey, met in Middletown and
formed a separate organization.[26]

In his article in the *Rural New Yorker* announcing the formation of the
league, Mapes revealed the influence of his contact with labor leaders and his
study of the union movement:

Farmers have been watching the success of labor unions in bringing
about conditions that are advantageous to themselves and families and
are at least convinced that our only hope lies in co-operation and organization. These 700 men have signed an iron-clad agreement, whereby they expect to stand or fall together, and emancipate themselves from the shack-
les which milk dealers and health department officials seem determined
they shall wear. . . . Farmers as units are helpless when they come up
against great corporations and firms of dealers with their millions of capital, or against health departments of great cities with their almost unlim-
ited power to adopt drastic rules. Bound together into a great partnership or organization they will have a power which will be recognized and
respected.[27]

Other agriculturalists, however, were more cautious about emulating organized labor. In an earlier article entitled, "Co-Operation among Farmers,"
Edgar L. Vincent of Broome County, New York, strongly advocated organization among farmers but worried that farmers' unions might take away their
freedom of action: "Without stopping to inquire as to the actual good laboring men are receiving from unions to which they belong, it may well be questioned whether farmers would be greatly benefitted from entering organizations based on the same principles as those governing labor unions."[28]

The league pledged to organize wherever there was a creamery, con-
densery, or shipping station sending milk to the New York market, and it was
open to any producer living within a reasonable wagon haul, "provided he is
not interested as a dealer in milk." The initial excitement was great, according
to Bartow W. Bull of Orange County, who remembered one of the league's
early organizing drives: "I had a wonderful mare here. I think it was over four
days and four nights we didn't take her out of the saddle."[29]

Fiery rhetoric and frenetic organizing notwithstanding, however, the
league leadership actually pursued a somewhat conservative strategy, in part
to avoid repeating the mistakes of previous organizations. The league was set
up as a conventional joint-stock corporation with officers, a board of directors, and an executive committee; farmers who signed on as members became stockholders and were assessed at the rate of 25 cents per cow to cover
the costs of organizing and administration. At an early meeting, it was decided over Mapes's opposition that the league would operate as a bargaining

agent only; rather than negotiate for a five-year period as the FSMPA had attempted without success, the league sought to fix prices for six months at a time. Even that bargaining would not take place until the league established a "controlling factor" in the New York market, which was set at 50,000 cows in 1907 and achieved in 1910.[30] Organizing proceeded steadily, and by the end of 1913, the league represented over 8,000 farmers and 130,000 cows in almost 300 locals, still less than 25 percent of the New York milkshed. In spite of the expansion of the organization, however, league leaders continued to hold back on confronting the dealers. Instead, they began to promote a long-term plan to develop cooperative creameries in order to give the league the ability to process surplus milk not demanded by the dealers, therefore gaining more control over the market.

The caution and conservatism of the league leaders caused growing consternation among the local membership, and, ultimately, it was their wrath that forced the league to take action. Feelings ran hot, especially in the newer areas of the milkshed. When the local at Sherburne in Chenango County was organized in 1912, the speaker grew so distraught over the pitiable condition of the dairymen that he wept. Although the league eventually let him go as an organizer, his display of emotion worked wonders at Sherburne and the majority joined up. Once organized, Chenango County immediately started to push for direct confrontation with the dealers and sent their delegates to league meetings demanding a fair price for milk. Over and over again, the executive committee met, decided that the time was not ripe, and sent the delegates home. In the words of Kenneth Scott, later the manager of the county Farm Bureau, "The train load of dairymen going back to Utica from all over this part of the State were wild with indignation at the futility of the leadership which the league possessed. They practically decided that the league was dead and its leaders a bunch of cowards and traitors."[31]

The situation came to a head after a successful strike by Chicago-area milk producers in the spring of 1916. Immediately, H. J. Kershaw, a league director from Chenango County, called on the league to do the same thing, but Vice President F. H. Thompson wrote to Kershaw arguing that the Chicago producers had more resources and were better organized than the New York dairymen. Speaking for the executive committee (which was smaller and more conservative than the board of directors), he noted: "It is also our belief that the necessity of resorting to the forcible and strenuous, if not illegal methods, used in the western strike would tend ultimately to impair if not de-feat the purposes for which the League was organized."[32] Kershaw's dissatis-faction was echoed by farmers in the older dairy regions as well, especially Mapes, who also wrote to Thompson and accused him of being one of the "chief reactionaries . . . and opposed to the employment of any labor union or Strike methods." In particular, Mapes objected to the emphasis on build-ing new cooperative creameries and processing plants instead of direct ac-tion: "Producers of the older shipping territory first organized and . . . de-cided that what is called the labor union plan was the simplest and quickest way to accomplish our object. . . . Why is it that you now refuse to stand by your bargain and seek to turn the League to a new plan which is sure to hold up the whole movement indefinitely?"[33]

On June 1, 1916, Chenango County dairymen voted unanimously to se-cede from the league if no action was taken, and that same day the league di-rectors finally decided to demand higher prices in the fall. Later that summer, however, John Y. Gerow, the league president, made a disastrous speaking tour of the region, in which he demonstrated that he was "constitutionally in-capable of acting aggressively." Gerow continued to advocate the new plan to develop cooperative creameries instead of direct action, "something en-tirely foreign to anything the Dairymen's League was formed for as we the dairymen of Chenango Co. understand it," according to N. M. Condon, who attended one of the speeches.[34] Local dairy farmers swore out affidavits against Gerow and passed resolutions demanding his resignation, prompting Kershaw and E. P. Smith, the county Farm Bureau agent, to take to the road in the Farm Bureau flivver to visit all the league directors and argue for their position. This came to be known as the Paul Revere Ride of the Dairymen's League (although in a historically mixed metaphor, Kershaw was also called the Moses of the organization), and as a result of the campaign, the directors forced Gerow's ouster and began planning for a strike.[35]

Support for the strike grew. Throughout the summer there were meetings to promote cooperation and organize new chapters up and down the New York milkshed. At the same time, broader public support for the dairy farm-ers developed as the Wicks Committee of the New York State Legislature in-vestigated farmers' complaints and conducted hearings during the summer of 1916 that demonstrated the dairymen's need to get a better price for their milk in order to make a modest living.[36]

In August, the league invited W. J. Kittle of the Chicago Milk Producers' Association to address its membership in Orange County, New York, and then in Sussex County, New Jersey, in what was, in the estimation of the dealers' periodical, the *Milk Reporter*, the largest producers' meeting ever held there.[37] According to the *American Agriculturalist*, a conservative farm paper that supported the league, "The interest is widespread and producers are not going to be side-tracked by suave promises. The favorable effect of the Chicago milk strike is not a ghost, but a real live success that has awakened dairymen all over the country."[38] Earlier that summer, the president of the Chicago association had defended his organization's use of "labor union tactics" in the pages of the *Rural New Yorker*:

> Looking back over the situation, and asking myself whether we could have won without the picketing and turning back producers who had started to town with their milk, I am forced to say that I believe we would have lost. Many farmers who could not be reached by reason were quickened in their thought when determined men stepped in front of their horses and asked them if they did not think they were doing themselves and their neighbors a wrong that would take years to correct. . . . Where necessary some of the most conservative, sensible and thrifty farmers we have, got into the wagons and handed the milk to others who set it beside the road.[39]

In the wake of Kittle's visit, it appeared, league members and their leaders were prepared to do the same.

In contrast to the 1883 strike, the Dairymen's League's action in 1916 achieved a quick victory. On September 9, 1916, the league's Executive Committee demanded a 25 percent increase over the previous year's price of milk.[40] Although both Borden's and Sheffield Farms–Slawson-Decker immediately raised their prices by 11 percent, the league admonished its members not to deliver milk after October 1 without notice from them. Once the withholding began, independent dealers representing about one-third of the market agreed to the league's price within a week; while the so-called big three— Borden's, Sheffield Farms–Slawson-Decker, and Mutual-McDermott—accepted the same terms and settled one week later on October 14.[41]

Just as grassroots enthusiasm was responsible for the strike, the spirit and dedication of local league members ensured its success, making it a dramatic and often singular event in their lives. At its height, 18,000 dairy farmers had joined the league and almost 75 percent of the milk supply to New York City was cut off. All told, one observer estimated, more than 100,000 producers were active in or sympathetic to the strike.[42]

Unlike the 1883 episode, dairymen were no longer compromised by ambivalent feelings. When the local at Worcester in Otsego County was organized in 1916 at the first strike meeting, for example, farmers were reluctant to sign because the popular Borden's manager was present. According to a witness, the chairman declared that he was a good friend of this manager yesterday and today and would be tomorrow—"signing up would make no difference," he said. As a result, every man present signed. In the words of the observer, "This was typical of many other places. Men who had never made speeches before and who have never made speeches since, had such full hearts that they made speeches then."[43]

In several communities, striking farmers set up cooperative creameries or cheese factories to process the milk that was being held off the market, and this contributed to local pride and the élan of the league. Initially, a few county agents took an active role in coordinating these and other strike activities even though this was against policy (as well as the conventional historical wisdom concerning the conservatism and pro-business orientation of the Farm Bureau). Farm Bureaus typically received support from the dealers and local distributors, but this was often rescinded after the strike. Borden's, for example, had contributed $250 to the Orange County Farm Bureau and objected when county agent Tom Milliman worked for the strike. Other county agents, however, followed his example, and, as John Dillon put it, "Soon the Farm Bureaus in most of the dairy counties were in the work in shirt sleeves and did helpful work, and it popularized the 'boys' in their counties." In the words of one former agent in Oneida County, "if you didn't believe in the Dairymen's League, if you didn't work for it and fight for it, you might say you couldn't be a county agent."[44]

Striking and dealing with the surplus milk became a family affair as well, and farm women played an important role. According to a dairyman from Catatonk, Tioga County: "Churns put away long before were brought out,

OFFICIAL BU~~LLETIN~~

---OF---

THE DAIRYMEN'S LEAGUE

Friday	Sept. 22, 1916.	No. 3

You can't catch seven o'clock after the whistle blows. The whistle will blow October 1st. **Be Prepared.**

We are going to fight it out on our prices if it takes all winter.

A stitch in time saves nine. **Look for the weak places in your Branch.**

Orange County reports but a few scattering farmers outside the League.

Some dealers in Orange County have told those outside the League that they will not take their milk unless they join the League.

Orange County has doubled the number of League cows since this campaign started.

Fifteen Borden plants in Orange County. All patrons standing solid as a rock.

Ulster County is well organized.

Unless the dealers meet our price October 1st, the actual fighting is on. Get your machine guns on the firing line for business October first.

Orange County is planning a League parade.

St. Lawrence County is standing by the League.

The dealers are trying to tie up all the cans. **You tie up all the milk.**

Levy Dairy Company is trying to buy milk from the co-operative plants.

180 distributors in New York city are in position to deliver milk at one cent a quart less than is charged by the big dealers and are prepared to pay the farmer one cent increase for which the League is fighting.

Executive Committee Dairymen's League.

Dairymen's League strike bulletin, 1916. (Courtesy of the Division of Rare and Manuscript Collections, Cornell University Library) cleaned and scalded for another period of use"; with veal and pork prices high, farmers were happy to have the skim milk to feed their animals. Elsewhere, dairy wives put the excess milk to more festive uses, and one woman remembers eating lots of ice cream, whipped cream on everything, and rice puddings and custards—a veritable "feast of milk."[45]

As preparations for the strike progressed, support for the league became almost universal, transcending divisions within the community. Initially, league members tended to be the younger farmers, "but the older ones came along once it got active." Irish Catholic dairymen also joined the largely Protestant organization. "They had a priest somewhere, I guess in Jersey or thereabouts," recalled Bartow W. Bull. "If they didn't join the League he put the sticks right on them. He was a great fellow. But he believed in the Dairymen's League and he believed in having his parishioners join the League."[46] Mabel G. Feint wrote in the *American Agriculturalist* that few farmers refused to cooperate in Cortland County, "and these were attended to individually without violence, but with very strong moral persuasion from members of the League and its loyal friends."[47] In Tioga County, according to a different reporter one month after the strike: "One of the most surprising things about the strike was the almost complete unanimity of the dairymen in supporting it. It was a very small number who insisted upon their right to ship their milk in defiance of their neighbors, and life for these promptly became very uncomfortable. . . . It wasn't a happy existence that they led for a few days, and most of them capitulated and joined the League before the strike was many days old."[48]

The farmers who continued to ship their milk in spite of the strike got their milk dumped even though this was not officially sanctioned by the league. Typically, however, league representatives compensated nonstriking farmers for their losses on the spot. In one instance, dumping became a lighthearted battle of wits. Bartow W. Bull remembers dumping milk with his brother at a neighbor's farm: "He was a smart old fellow. We knew him well. Ebenezer and I pulled his milk out of the vat—three or four cans—and when we dumped it, it was full of water. Heh, they didn't have any milk in them. Oh he was a good one."[49]

In another case, however, dumping left deeper scars. According to Bull's daughter, a cousin of theirs, someone who had always been very close to them and took care of their children whenever anyone was sick, was the daughter of a milk dealer, and she and her husband continued to send their milk to New York in spite of the strike. When a group of farmers spilled their milk, they blamed Bull. "But he would never think of dumping their milk because they had been close to us for so many years," Helen Bull recalled. They were mad at him for dumping their milk and he was mad at them for thinking that he did it. "This was a rift that has never healed," she lamented. In general, she was much less sanguine about the spilling that occurred, even though she considered the noncooperators scabs: "This was really war and everybody felt badly—you know—they didn't like to look at each other after this had happened. They were ashamed of it. On the other hand they felt that they had to fight for this way of life."[50]

Clearly, the strike was a peak experience in many people's lives; for many, it sanctified a fervent commitment to the Dairymen's League. John J. Dillon remembered the first meeting of the league after the great victory: "The dairymen were in good spirits. . . . It was not the paltry forty-five cents a cwt. extra for milk they rejoiced over. They had thrown off the yoke of tyranny. They had discovered their own power. They realized a new-born confidence in themselves. They felt the inspiration of hope and trust for the future of their dairy business. They felt full of good humor."[51] Others celebrated the strike as an emancipation from economic bondage, which restored human dignity in place of servitude and humiliation.[52]

Several reminiscences describe involvement in the league in religious terms. In the words of a Cornell graduate who was a county agent in Oneida County at the time, "I mean there was a religious furor about coops back in those days that has not prevailed in recent years. This was true both in the case of the G.L.F. [Grange-League-Federation cooperative stores and feed dealers] and the Dairymen's League." For Helen Bull, the league was the family faith, complete with sacraments and codes of behavior. "We wouldn't think of drinking a glass of Sheffield milk or anything like that," she noted. Later, as the home demonstration agent in Lewis County, she lived with the sister of the president of the Sheffield Milk Producers' Association, whose brother regarded her warily because her name was Helen Bull. In the same vein, her parents wondered how she could associate with someone from "the other side."[53]

The excitement of the strike and the depth of feeling it generated, however, temporarily masked more profound differences among league members and between the membership and the leadership of the organization. The successful use of "labor union" tactics, for example, did not signify a common ideology, much less a radical one, and in the wake of the 1916 victory, competing visions of the league's role began to crystallize. According to Fred Sexauer, president of the league during the 1930s: "When, in 1916, the circumstances were just right for a successful movement, this created the psychological situation where people, in effect, fought together, won together; where reasons and causes didn't mean so much. They had acted together without thinking very deeply. . . . Divisions came later as you got deeper into the analysis of marketing problems and the necessity for people to reason things rather than be emotional. At that point they began to divide."[54]

After the strike, the league's leaders began to confront these long-term problems of milk marketing, however, and fundamental disagreements emerged, particularly over the mechanisms to guarantee an outlet for all milk and process the surplus that was not bought for use as fluid milk. This was important to have more leverage with the dealers and more control over the market, but it eventually resulted in an organization that was increasingly capital-intensive, centralized, and removed from the same grassroots involvement and control that had animated the league in the first place.

Initially, the Dairymen's League did not own any milk collection stations or processing plants, but encouraged and facilitated the cooperative ownership of local facilities by groups of farmers. These efforts did not solve the larger problems, however, because there were not enough locally controlled plants to take care of all of the milk, and, acting independently, local cooperatives often struck their own deals instead of abiding by league prices and policies. Limited as they were, however, such arrangements reflected dairy farmers' deep-seated commitment to independence and local autonomy and their reluctance to submit to more centralized management, even by their own organization.

As a next step, the league's leadership formed a federation of these farmer-owned plants, the Cooperative Milk Producers' Marketing Association, and purchased the Modern Dairy Company, which it reincorporated as the Country Milk Company, to provide a marketing outlet for the new association.

There were still not enough local cooperatives to handle all the milk, though. Instead, after the league waged a second dairy strike in 1919 that was less successful than the earlier one, a group of its directors spearheaded its reorganization into the Dairymen's League Cooperative Association (DLCA), which took over completely in 1922.

In contrast to the older league, the DLCA had the power to buy and control country milk stations, processing plants, and other facilities related to the milk business. It also required its members to sign "ironclad" contracts agreeing to commit their milk to the DLCA for one year and to pool it with the other members of the association and receive the same price whether that milk was sold as fluid milk or manufactured into cheese, butter, ice cream, or condensed milk. As a result, although the pooled price was lower than the Class I price for fluid milk, the DLCA took all the milk produced, which the dealers did not. This became particularly urgent after one-fourth of the league members lost their markets in October 1920, when many major milk manufacturing plants in the New York milkshed shut down due to excessive inventories of canned milk and other products.[55]

This reorganization proved extremely controversial and divisive. According to Fred Sexauer, the many meetings that discussed the new plans were "wild meetings":

> There was always opposition. . . . The fact that someone lost his market because the manufacturer closed up his plants wasn't very realistic to the fellow whose milk was going every day. . . . This whole new philosophy that you had to share with somebody else in order to maintain a market was asking people to believe a whole lot in a relatively short period of time. . . . People who believed in this new idea, and saw the necessity for this, had no patience with those who didn't see it. Bitter words were said that drove people apart. These things were argued and discussed on church steps and at family gatherings. This split churches, communities and families.[56]

In general, dairymen in more distant areas, especially those who lost their markets due to plant closings, were more likely to sign the new contracts than farmers in more traditional fluid milk counties; but, as Sexauer's statement implies, the DLCA plan was hotly contested within dairy communities throughout the milkshed.

Although it may have made good "business" sense, the new plan grew out of the corporate and professional cultures that epitomized the second great transformation of American society and did not reflect the more traditional sensibilities of New York dairy farmers as producers or small businessmen. In contrast to the farmer-activists who had spearheaded the 1916 strike, the league directors who pushed for reorganization were "hard-headed business types" and "lawyers and accountants with peripheral farming interests," who were paid high salaries.[57] They had strong allies among other so-called progressive agriculturalists and extensive ties to the Cornell University Agricultural College. Cornell-trained county agents typically threw the weight of the Farm Bureau behind the new plan, and faculty at the college were instrumental in helping to organize and manage the GLF, a league-sponsored cooperative supply company that also evolved into a big business.[58] In the agricultural press, the *American Agriculturalist* supported the DLCA as part of its larger vision of a more modern and businesslike agriculture, and the editor of the *Dairymen's League News*, former county agent E. R. Eastman, became editor of that publication in the 1920s.[59]

To its opponents, the new organization did not epitomize cooperation so much as it resembled the coercive corporations they had struggled to overcome. This criticism of the DLCA was spearheaded by John J. Dillon of the *Rural New Yorker*, who was particularly galled by what he saw as the undemocratic structure of the new organization and its perversion of the cooperative ideal. Many dairymen agreed with Dillon. According to one letter he received from a dairy farmer:

> The producers who signed the pooling contract have been led to believe that they are members of the co-operative association. This is not true. . . . The relation of dairymen is simply that of individuals entering a contract with a corporation. The association consists of only a handful of men, most of whom are appointed officers, who have the right under contract to make the price of milk, to collect for it and take out whatever amount they please. They own and control millions of dollars worth of plants and equipment purchased by the producers' money. The dairymen are required to sign away their right to an accounting.[60]

Dillon and others were also bothered by the close relationship between the DLCA and Borden's, the dairymen's old nemesis. In what Dillon argued was a quid pro quo, the DLCA and Borden's colluded to split the milk industry into country and city operations. Many of the country milk stations that the DLCA owned were purchased from Borden's when that corporation threatened to close them down in 1920 because of the league's high prices. The DLCA agreed not to compete with Borden's by marketing milk and ice cream directly in New York City, while Borden's agreed to buy milk from the DLCA. Similarly, the DLCA bought out large independent dealers, such as the Empire State Dairy Company, Clover Farms, Inc., and Evans Dairy Co., that had plants in the country and competed with Borden's in the city, and then sold the city-end operations to Borden's. In some locations, there had been two or three plants owned by different dealers; but as the league gained control, it dismantled the extra facilities and reduced the number of choices available to local farmers, forcing them to join the DLCA pool or go out of business. At times, the league continued to operate its new acquisitions as subsidiaries in their own names. "In this way," writes Dillon, "the organization became a holding company and a milk dealer itself, as well as an agent for the sale of farmers' milk."[61] Overall, between 1920 and 1930, the DLCA purchased more than two hundred plants and condenseries in the New York milkshed.

Part of Dillon's vitriol against the league stemmed from his own difficult personality and his long-standing feuds with the more conservative league leaders, whom he regarded as selfish autocrats who aspired to be big businessmen.[62] At a deeper level, however, Dillon's animosity was based on a commitment to local autonomy and an opposition to centralized control that stemmed from older, republican sensibilities, which continued to resonate among dairy farmers in upstate New York even as they became increasingly anachronistic. "Jefferson was a cooperator," according to Dillon in 1923. "The form of government that he conceived is called democratic. It might just as properly be called cooperative." In his editorials and books on the subject, Dillon urged the preservation of local control and local initiative in farmers' organizations in the milkshed: "the temptation to standardize individual and community enterprise, initiative and effort through a large single organization does not afford the best promise of success." It was, for him and his followers, an article of faith: "Cooperation is a protest against intrigue, and force, and monopoly, and to use them in the name of cooperation is to clothe Satan in the livery of the church." According to Edward S.

Foster, who was the Chautauqua County agent during this period, many New York farm families regarded the *Rural New Yorker* as their bible, and at meetings there would always be someone in the crowd who would haul out a copy and start reading from it. "There was lots of controversy," he noted, "never a dull moment."[63]

Whether Dillon's vision of decentralized organization and local control was ultimately practical or not is open to question. In any event, the top-down strategy of the DLCA became the dominant perspective within the league during the 1920s, and it cost them much of the grassroots support they had gained during the strike. At its end in 1922, the Dairymen's League, Inc. was organized into 1,146 locals in six states and had over 100,000 members with more than a million cows, or between 80 and 90 percent of all producers for the New York market and the principal secondary markets in the milkshed. That same year, only 57,500 producers had agreed to pool their milk and join the DLCA, which superseded the league; by 1927, the number of active poolers was down to 33,000, or a third of the league's largest membership. In part, New York–area dairymen acted out of economic self-interest: many of the 15,000 or so producers close to New York who could regularly get higher fluid milk prices did so, and others got higher prices by joining associations of nonpooling farmers like the Sheffield Producers' Cooperative Association, a pseudo-cooperative organized by the Sheffield Company, which refused to deal with the DLCA. Still others, urged on by John J. Dillon, formed the Non-Pooling Dairymen's Cooperative Association, which consisted of former Dairymen's Leaguers and acted only as a bargaining agent for its members.[64]

Ultimately, however, these dairymen and others dropped out of the league because the DLCA failed to convince them to do otherwise. In its transformation from a bargaining agent for individual farmers and a supporter of local cooperatives into a huge, capital-intensive, centralized, and multifaceted corporation, the league lost touch with the grassroots militance that had animated its beginnings. Its large scale and a series of bad business decisions made it less efficient and less competitive in an economic sense, but its remote and sometimes coercive management style made it less compelling emotionally and ideologically. In contrast to the often heady days of its youth, by the 1930s the DLCA had become a consistent bulwark against change in the New York milkshed. During the first part of the decade, it strenuously opposed state and federal legislation to regulate milk marketing in the New York area as well as more general New Deal agricultural policies. In the late thirties, it led overt and covert actions to undermine a new organization of dairymen with close ties to organized labor, the Dairy Farmers' Union, which, in contrast to the league, pledged to remain pure by owning nothing and encouraging the growth of independent local cooperatives.[65]

The ironies of dairy organization in the New York milkshed are manifold. It is ironic, if not tragic, that the spirited militance of the 1916 strike eventually resulted in such a conservative and hidebound institution. The very ginger embrace of trade union tactics that was hedged by concerns about coercion and the abrogation of individual freedoms paradoxically evolved into a coercive organization of a different sort, in which collective behavior was imposed from on high rather than emanating from below. Finally, farmers who had originally opposed monopolies from an ideological perspective that combined the sensibilities of a producers' ethic with those of a small businessman became the, at times unwilling, instruments of a new big business that behaved monopolistically in order to control the market.

That these developments seem ironic, however, underscores the fact that the history of the Dairymen's League was not the inevitable triumph of a more "modern" and progressive—or, in the estimation of its critics, a more conservative and less democratic—form of organization. Instead, many dairy farmers held onto an alternative vision of decentralized organization that had its roots in older republican notions of local control as the guarantor of individual autonomy, and as the league's leadership moved in new directions, they did not follow. These disparities between the grass roots and the leadership and between the early spirit of the league and what it became force us to reassess the meanings of farmers' organizations during the first part of the twentieth century.

Nor were such ideological conflicts and organizational ironies limited to the Northeast or to dairy farmers. In the Midwest, it seems, the farmers' commitment to decentralized organization was even stronger, or at least more successful. When R. D. Cooper left his post as head of the Dairymen's League in 1921 and tried to organize Wisconsin dairymen along the same lines, they rejected centralized control and "ironclad" contracts in favor of a looser federation of local cooperatives. Centralized cooperatives that did establish themselves, typically under the aegis of the Farm Bureau, often chafed against the imperatives of local groups and led to a dampening of grassroots enthusiasm and a substantial falling off in Farm Bureau membership by the end of the decade.[66]

Commercial farmers during the first third of the twentieth century were poised between two worlds and two worldviews. They were independent producers and small businessmen in an age of big business and organizational revolution. Their vision of an ideal society became increasingly anachronistic as changes in technology and business structure moved American society toward larger institutions and greater centralization. To the farmers, these forces proved both troubling and irresistible. At first, they organized on the basis of their moral authority as producers and the antimonopolistic sentiments of small businessmen in order to redress their relative lack of power in the marketplace. To expand that power, however, their leaders felt compelled to refashion the organization into a giant corporation and pursued a path that contradicted that original perspective. New York dairy farmers fought the good fight in 1916, but by the 1930s, its meanings had become obscure.

For they have sown the wind,

    and they shall reap the whirlwind:

It hath no stalk: the bud shall yield no meal:

if so be it yield,

    the strangers shall swallow it up.

    —HOSEA 8:7

4

TO REAP THE WHIRLWIND

The Social and Ideological Bases of Farmers' Grain Elevators

As the economy of the United States became dominated by large-scale monopolistic and oligopolistic business interests during the late nineteenth and early twentieth centuries, American farmers formed local cooperatives in order to redress their disadvantages in the marketplace. These producers' cooperatives became by far the most common farmers' organizations in the country, and although definitive figures are difficult to reconstruct, by the mid-1920s, there were more than ten thousand of them with over two million members.[1]

Scholars, however, have given relatively short shrift to these important institutions, regarding them mainly as watered-down vestiges of earlier and ideologically richer agrarian crusades, which subscribed primarily to limited economic goals rather than a more far-reaching and alternative vision of cooperative commonwealth. Yet precisely because they were supported by so many people, it is important to take a closer look at what these farmers' cooperatives were in addition to what they were not, and to analyze their social and ideological bases as an index of changing agrarian sensibilities during the second great transformation of American society. Farmers' grain elevators were among the earliest as well as the most common and widespread farmers' organizations in the Midwest. By the middle of the 1920s, there were over

5,000 farmers' elevators with more than 500,000 members or stockholders; they represented an investment in excess of $90 million and conducted over $800 million in business annually.

In contrast to other agricultural movements, farmers' grain elevators were usually not the products of a larger organization with an overarching structure and ideology, but were homegrown institutions that embodied a broad spectrum of often contradictory values and beliefs. These cooperatives were often borne of dramatic and even heroic struggles against both the perceived tyranny of merchants within the community and the increasing power of the distant trusts and combinations that dominated the grain trade during this period. As such, they became important community institutions that reflected rural desires to maintain local control and individual autonomy in an increasingly centralized society.

Farmers' grain elevators built on and continued traditional agrarian animosities toward the middleman. As commercial ventures concerned with the bottom line, however, they were also informed by a small businessman's perspective that stressed sound economic practices as well as individual freedom and autonomy, and this limited broader collective action and more profound critiques of the prevailing system. And, reflecting worries that were shared by farmers as well as small businessmen, farmers' elevators struggled with the challenges posed by an emerging corporate order, which, during the 1920s, was embodied increasingly by other, newer agricultural organizations such as the American Farm Bureau Federation.

Thus, in addition to their more basic economic functions, farmers' elevators became important touchstones in the rural community's sense of itself and of the place of the small community in the larger society. By the 1920s, however, the centrality of the local community and the very viability of local institutions were being threatened. Farmers' elevators were a focal point for these tensions and struggles, and their history helps us uncover an important dimension of the second great transformation in the northern countryside.

———

Writing in *Harper's Monthly*, G. W. Schatzel described the scene in St. Charles, Minnesota, on September 18, 1868, as wheat buyers met the farmers who brought their wagons to town to market their crops:

Everything has two sides and two halves. The opposite side of a farmer, who sells wheat, is the wheat buyer, who purchases it from him. These wheat buyers are a class by themselves. At all the wheat outlets a few houses do all the business of buying it. These hire their buyers, who stand on the street from morning till night, bidding for the grain as fast as the wagons come in. . . . all make a dash at the farmer, who, of course, tries to take advantage of this rivalry and gets as big a price as he can.

"It is," Schatzel went on, "a very animating spectacle, this business of buying wheat."

Some are going off, having just deposited their loads at the hopper; others are arriving to replenish the ranks. Some have oxen before them, others have horses. All are white to the view, with their rows of sacks filled out plump with the grain. There is shouting and running and confusion.[2]

Increasingly, however, new and powerful interests tried to impose order on that confusion, and this lessened the farmer's advantage in playing one buyer against another. As the expansion of the rail network in the Upper Midwest shifted the grain trade away from seasonal and unreliable water routes, it created new classes of local middlemen and new patterns of inter- action with central grain markets. Although railroads initially were not di- rectly involved in purchasing and storing grain at local markets, they influ- enced the grain trade by exercising control over those who did. In some cases, railroads promoted "wheat rings," groups of shippers along its route who received special rebates and preferential treatment with respect to infor- mation, storage, and sales at the terminal markets. In other cases, railroads, perennially short of capital, contracted with individuals to build and operate local storage elevators and gave them exclusive privileges, often by refusing to allow competitors to build additional facilities on their tracks.[3]

While the railroads and their associates claimed that these practices were necessary in order to be competitive and actually resulted in higher wheat prices, farmers had a different point of view. Grain farmers were already resentful of high and discriminatory railroad rates, which were often set by pooling agreements rather than by competitive factors, and they were plagued by a disquieting sense that their financial destinies were controlled by the mysterious machinations of suspect urban institutions such as the Chicago

Board of Trade and the Milwaukee Chamber of Commerce. Thus, the new arrangements in their local markets seemed to be yet another manifestation of the excessive and growing powers of nonproducing middlemen and monopoly control from afar.

These sentiments helped fuel the rise of the Grange movement during the 1870s, which advocated legislation to curb the abuses of the railroads. In addition, some local Granges started their own cooperative grain elevators in order to provide alternative marketing arrangements. As early as 1869, the Minneapolis-based *Farmers' Union*, which regularly supported the Grange, suggested that farmers store their own grain and bargain for favorable freight rates; significantly, the first farmers' elevator to file incorporation papers in Iowa formed later that year as the Farmers' Union Elevator. By the 1870s, these operations typically had Grange-related titles such as Patron's Joint Stock Company, Grange Elevator, and Elevator and Warehouse Association of Patrons of Husbandry. Altogether, more than forty such elevators were established in Iowa between 1867 and 1877, with 1874 as the peak year. One contemporary claimed that one-third of the grain elevators and warehouses in the state were owned or controlled by the Grange; other writers have asserted that, at its peak, the Grange handled at least 50 percent of the grain in the state.[4]

That peak was short-lived, however, and, as was the case with other Grange businesses such as cooperative supply houses and the manufacture of farm implements, these farmers' grain elevators and warehouses quickly failed. Only six of the forty-two elevators founded in Iowa during this period remained in operation for more than five years; by 1883, none of them were still in business even though Iowa had been a focal point of the movement. Patrons' elevators typically suffered from a lack of capital and a dearth of business acumen. According to one study, "There was a very inadequate understanding of the grain business or appreciation of the necessity for business skill and experience. Rivalry for office was keen and 'Grange politics' altogether too much of a factor. Only too often, as a result, the position of manager went as a plum to some farmer who was a good Granger, but a very poor grain man."[5]

Not all of the blame rests with the victims. One Iowa farmer, in an 1873 book on the Grange, commented on the rebates that railroads gave to grain dealers:

I thought, when the idea of cooperative shipment was first proposed, that these favors were given solely on account of the amount of business that these men brought to the railroads. I supposed that the deductions were simply those that would be naturally made to wholesale trade, and in speeches to the farmers I told them so. But we have learned differently, for when our farmers have combined and offered freight in large quantities to the railroad companies, they have refused to give us the advantages which they give to the favorites. . . . The terms of these contracts are secret. But we know that they must be considerable, or these men would not have made so much money.[6]

During the 1880s, those arrangements became more widespread, if no less secret, with the rise of the large grain syndicates and their line elevators, the largest being Peavey with eight hundred elevators in 1898, and Armour in second place with seven hundred.[7] This was part of the more general restructuring of the American economy at the end of the nineteenth century. Big businesses typically consolidated horizontally by eliminating or swallowing up their direct competitors, and they expanded their operations vertically to include backward linkages to raw materials and forward linkages to marketing and distribution. In the case of the grain syndicates, they worked closely with the railroads. The two often held controlling stock in each others' companies and had interlocking directorates, allowing them to enjoy illegal advantages as well as legitimate economies of scale. Another technique was the control of terminal facilities. P. D. Armour, for example, combined buying and selling with the public warehousing of grain and eventually controlled the terminal storage facilities in Chicago, eliminating any truly public facility there and forcing his competitors, in the words of one contemporary, "to pay tribute to Armour if they used the houses which he was licensed to operate." Likewise, the grain syndicates tried to eliminate competition from smaller, independent elevators and grain buyers in the local markets and country shipping stations by outbidding them and taking advantage of favoritism in railroad rates and grading and handling. When those measures proved insufficient, they simply arranged to fix prices and divide up the local business with their surviving competitors.[8]

As wheat prices plummeted during the 1880s and 1890s due to this increased lack of competitive bidding in local markets and to new wheat supplies from other countries, which depressed the world market, midwestern grain farmers again turned to collective action and organized cooperative grain elevators. In Minnesota, the Farmers' Alliance and the Populist Party attempted to organize their own elevator lines with terminal facilities in Minneapolis and Duluth, but neither effort enjoyed much success. The Farmers' Alliance also inspired several Minnesota communities to organize their own elevators, but, in general, the alliance was much less involved in these efforts than the Grange had been earlier, especially in the other grain-producing states. Rather, midwestern Populists were leery of the Grange's previous business failures and concentrated on political and legislative action such as the regulation of railroads and public elevators in terminal markets. These actions, however, had little effect on conditions in the local markets that most farmers dealt with.[9]

Instead, the farmers' elevators that were started during the 1880s and 1890s developed sporadically as homegrown affairs and were typically not the products of any particular movement or ideology. As such, they reflected a wide range of goals and attitudes, from long-standing agrarian animosities toward middlemen and trusts, to the more calculating perspective of economic self-interest trying to generate local competition that would increase the prices they got for their grain. By the same token, these elevators represented varying degrees of commitment to cooperative principles. At one end of the spectrum, companies allowed only one vote per member regardless of the number of shares owned and limited the payment of cash dividends. At the other end, however, were joint-stock companies that were controlled by the largest shareholders, which could yield significant returns and often represented lucrative investments for local farmers and businessmen.

The history of the Rockwell Cooperative Society in Cerro Gordo County, Iowa, which was one of the earliest and most successful of these farmers' elevators, illustrates both the potential and the limitations of these organizations. Rockwell was a "well-balanced community, whose citizens are about equally divided in descent among the Irish, the Germans, and the 'Yankees.'" Yet that same writer was also cognizant of local conflicts: he remembered accompanying his father, an active Granger, to a nearby grain elevator where the man in charge was missing an ear, supposedly bitten off in a squabble by an enraged farmer who felt cheated. Thomas McManus, an Irish immigrant

who lived in Dougherty Township, probably also wanted to bite off someone's ear after he spent a day in 1888 hauling his load of wheat to three different communities over a distance of thirty-two miles and received bids at
the same price in each location. The suspected pooling agreement became
public after a series of disagreements broke the grain dealers' ranks, and this
caused local farmers to consider cooperative marketing.[10]

After a brief organizing period, the Rockwell Cooperative Society was formally established in early 1889. Its first board members, known as the "Lucky
Thirteen," included some of the most successful farmers in the community
as well as men who had worked away from the farm and who had previous
experience in other agrarian movements. Norman Densmore, "a man of
ability," was a native of New York and became the society's first president at
the age of sixty-one. He had worked in railroad construction, was a teacher,
and had been active in farmers' organizations in Wisconsin before moving to
Iowa in 1877. William Barragy, who was the first to promote the idea of a cooperative, was "an outspoken man" who hated subterfuge and unfairness,
and had been a bridge builder for the railroad before taking up farming.
Thomas McManus arrived from Ireland in 1862 at the age of nineteen and
settled in Cerro Gordo County in 1871. And Andrew Johnson, an immigrant
from Germany, was one of two brothers who arrived poor in 1868, worked
as agricultural laborers, and eventually owned their own farm of nine hundred acres that they worked with thirty horses.[11]

The society initially planned to build its own elevator, causing some consternation among local businessmen who worried that the town could not
support a third elevator. Instead, they bought out one of the other elevators,
but they still faced significant local opposition. The local bank, which owned
the remaining elevator, refused them credit and, to scare away investors and
patrons, circulated letters stating that the new elevator was financially un-
sound and mortgaged. The society managed to procure a loan for operating
capital from a friendly banker in nearby Mason City, however, and opened its
doors for business. Immediately, its competitor raised its price for grain four
or five cents per bushel, lowered its price for coal two dollars a ton, and sold
lumber for five dollars less per thousand feet. According to one account,
"it was not long till they were receiving grain from members of the new cooperative society."[12]

The Rockwell Cooperative Society countered this pressure by establishing a maintenance, or penalty, clause that required its members to pay a fixed charge per bushel of grain whether they sold it to the farmers' elevator or elsewhere. That charge enabled the society to withstand the competition and maintain a fair market outlet long after the other elevators no longer quoted such favorable prices, and it was a successful device that was to be repeated by many other farmers' elevators in similar situations. A number of members calculated the bottom line and behaved accordingly, approaching the society as a business proposition rather than an ideological commitment. Thus, when competitors offered prices that more than made up for the penalty charge or represented a shorter haul for them, they frequently sold grain to the opposition. As long as those members paid the penalty charge, however, their outside transactions represented no loss to the cooperative society, and they were able to maintain their membership and their ability to get members' discounts and premiums on future transactions as well as any dividends on their shares.[13]

There were other members, however, who refused to deal with the competition at any price. That loyalty and spirit was exemplified by Frank Campbell, the very successful manager of the society from 1893 through the 1920s. Campbell had made Rockwell one of the best shipping points on the Iowa Central Railroad, doing over $350,000 worth of business in its tenth year. He was subsequently invited to a gathering of grain men and railroad officials at Mason City, where they tried to woo him away from the cooperative society with offers of his own business and a much higher salary, which he repeatedly rejected. "If you will not accept our offer," said the group's spokesman, "we ourselves will finance an elevator in Rockwell, and ruin your society there." "All right," answered the high-strung and excitable Mr. Campbell, shaking his fist. "Come on. I'm ready for you."[14]

As the Rockwell Cooperative Society survived, it expanded into sidelines, which enhanced its members' benefits, but also added to the society's list of enemies. According to a 1911 article on the beginnings of the cooperative, the society fought against the railroads, the grain trust, lumber and coal trusts, the Iowa implement dealers association, and merchants in their own town. The most important of these sidelines was lumber, and when the society bought a local lumberyard in 1893, they entered into direct competition against John Paul, a multimillionaire who owned a chain of lumberyards across the Upper Midwest. Although Paul owned yards in nearby Hampton and Mason City as well as the one in Rockwell, he sold lumber and coal much cheaper there in order to undermine the cooperative. Society members refused to patronize him, however, and after ten years they were able to buy him out and build a new lumber shed on the site.[15]

Even G. B. Rockwell, the founder and namesake of the town, became sympathetic. As the battle waged between the society and John Paul, Rockwell got up and spoke at the community's first farmers' institute after hearing a paper on cooperation: "Gentlemen, when you started the co-operative society at Rockwell, I did not believe in it. But you have demonstrated its benefits. In the meantime, I have been buying lumber of John Paul out in Dakota for my farms there; and I have come to wish that he had more of the milk of human kindness." Given Mr. Rockwell's earlier opposition and the bitterness of local businessmen toward the cooperative, those remarks, in the words of one witness, "caused a ripple of mirth to pass through the audience."[16]

Farmers tried to spread such mirth in other grain-growing communities as they endeavored to emulate Rockwell's success, and the number of farmers' elevators increased slowly but steadily. Four other elevators organized in Cerro Gordo County, and together with Rockwell they formed a short-lived association among themselves. For Iowa as a whole, 52 farmers' elevators were formed between 1886 and 1903, and 30 of these were in operation in 1903. Percentages were better in Illinois, where 30 of the 34 farmers' elevators organized between 1884 and 1902 were in business at the end of the period.[17]

Like Rockwell, a number of these elevators embodied some ideological commitment to cooperation, but they were also paying business propositions. The new competition that they provided typically raised the local price of a bushel of wheat by 5 cents; for farmers marketing one thousand bushels (not a large crop), that represented an immediate additional income of $50, which quickly made up the cost of buying a membership share.

———

Increasingly, efforts to start new farmers' elevators had to overcome more than local sources of competition and opposition. Partly in response to the farmers' actions, independent elevators and line elevator companies, the so-called regular grain dealers, formed new organizations, which continued their previous patterns of collusion on a larger statewide and regional basis. Rather than squelching the farmers' movement, however, these dealers' associations paradoxically gave it one of its biggest boosts, especially after their activities became a matter of public record during hearings by the state and federal governments.

The Illinois Grain Dealers' Association, which formed in 1896, was the first of these new organizations; its counterpart in Iowa began four years later, joining similar organizations throughout the grain belt. These associations tried to regulate competition among their members by covertly setting prices and dividing up the grain business, but they also tried to eliminate competition from the so-called irregular dealers. At first they went after "scoop shovellers" who loaded grain onto railroad cars directly from the wagons and thus capitalized on high prices without bearing the fixed expenses of maintaining a year-round facility. Most of their activities, however, targeted farmers' elevators, especially those that relied on the penalty clause, which the "regular" dealers regarded as a restraint on trade and an unfair competitive advantage. In particular, the grain dealers' associations used their vast numerical superiority to enforce a boycott against commission agencies and others who did business with the "irregulars" in order to cut off their access to terminal markets.[18]

This boycott, which took place during the first decade of the twentieth century, first came to public light in 1903 during the course of hearings by the Illinois Railroad and Warehouse Commission on the complaint of D. H. Curry & Co. against the Illinois Central Railroad. Curry & Co. was a "regular" grain elevator located on the tracks of the Chicago and Alton R.R. in Mason City, Illinois, that also wanted to ship its wheat on the Illinois Central. But, they complained, the Illinois Central refused to provide them with cars even though it provided many to the Farmers' Grain & Coal Company, an "irregular" competitor that was located on the Illinois Central tracks. By way of response, the Illinois Central did not deny this disparity, but claimed that its discrimination was justified because "D. H. Curry & Co. had gone into a conspiracy with a number of other grain men or grain companies to prevent said Farmers' Grain & Coal Co. from getting cars to ship their grain and to prevent commission men and buyers at other markets from buying or handling [their] grain."[19]

There is no small irony in these complaints by a "regular" dealer against

the same discriminatory practices that had long been used, with their bless-
ings, to hinder farmers' efforts to market their grain directly. By the same
token, the way in which the Illinois Central justified its actions is also replete with contradictions, for the railroad was an unlikely champion of a
farmers' organization. Rather, the Illinois Central was probably motivated
primarily by corporate self-interest and its desire to protect the only shipper
in Mason City that was located on their line, whether they were a "regular"
dealer or not.

Regardless of its self-interest and whatever its opinions about farmers' organizations more generally, the evidence that the railroad gave at the hearing
was both revealing and damning. It presented numerous letters to the Farmers' Grain and Coal Company from Chicago commission agents, which supported its specific accusations of conspiracy, and the commission also heard
testimony that corroborated and amplified the documentary record. One of
the company's regular brokers summarily cut off its relationship even though
"our past business has been satisfactory," and recommended transferring the
account to some other house. Those efforts were futile, however, according
to a letter from another firm that rejected their business: "Inasmuch as we are
members of the Grain Dealers' Association, and have subscribed to the rules,
we do not feel that it would be honorable to solicit your business and regret
very much to inform you that we cannot do so." Moreover, a number of
these brokers testified at the hearing that A. W. Lloyd, a special agent of the
Illinois Grain Dealers' Association, advised them personally not to handle
the grain of the farmers' elevators and led them to believe that anyone who
did so would get no further business from association members.[20]

Thus, the commission found ample evidence of a conspiracy against the
farmers' elevators on the part of the Illinois Grain Dealers' Association and
D. H. Curry & Co. The law that it was designed to enforce, however, concerned the actions of the railroad and clearly prohibited it from discriminat-
ing between one shipper or another, "whether he is a buyer or a farmer desir-
ing to ship his own grain." Consequently, the commission ordered the Illinois
Central to provide cars for D. H. Curry & Co., but it took no action about the
grain dealers' boycott.[21]

Subsequently, the U.S. Interstate Commerce Commission also investigated
the grain trade and held hearings in 1906 in Chicago, Kansas City, Omaha,
Des Moines, Milwaukee, Minneapolis, and Duluth, and these hearings pro-

vided further evidence of the scope and scale of the grain dealers' boycott and their other practices. The commissioners revisited the Mason City incident, but they also heard similar stories from other locations. In Omaha, they listened to Thomas D. Worrall, who had been a grain dealer and a member of the Nebraska Grain Dealers' Association. Initially, according to Worrall, the association was beneficial and had been formed for the purpose of getting better weights and inspections and improving conditions in the trade. Quickly, however, they began pooling and fixing prices and coerced independent grain dealers into going along. After the secretary of the Kansas Grain Dealers' Association was sent to prison for similar activities, Worrall changed his mind, and when he started handling grain for a farmers' company in Elgin, Nebraska, his former colleagues boycotted him. Worrall fought back and brought suit against the Nebraska Grain Dealers' Association and forty-six different elevator operators, and he published a book, *The Grain Trust Exposed*, which recounted his experiences as both a "regular" and an "irregular" grain dealer.[22]

In Des Moines, the commission gathered much evidence about the actions of the Iowa Grain Dealers' Association and its secretary, George A. Wells. First, they heard testimony from C. G. Messerole, who had also started as an independent grain dealer but switched to the farmers' elevator movement after he refused offers to join the association and fix prices. As manager of the farmers' elevator in Gowrie, Iowa, Messerole had difficulty finding agents who would handle the farmers' grain, and was turned down repeatedly by commission firms acting on Wells's instructions.[23]

For a time, Messerole was able to conduct business only by keeping secret the names of the firms that he dealt with. To counter this, the grain combine persuaded a young man "without a habitation, and without an occupation" to purchase shares in the farmers' company in order to demand an inspection of the books that would reveal those names. When this request was denied, he sued the farmers' grain elevator, and appealed the subsequent negative decision to the Iowa Supreme Court, where he also lost. According to the written opinion in the case, the plaintiff, Richard M. Funck, was a "malicious meddler" who was part of an "organized system of 'boycott' that has been applied to the defendant for several years by the so-called 'regular' dealers. . . . It is true that the plaintiff asks nothing in this case that is of itself illegal," continued the opinion. "But must the court aid in a conspiracy to its final goal simply because it travels this part of the way over a legal highway? We think not."[24]

Just as Messerole's access to terminal markets was about to disappear completely, he was approached by two firms in Chicago that made a specialty of the farmers' elevator trade: Lowell Hoit & Co. and Eschenberg & Dalton. According to letters written by the hearing's next witness, George A. Wells, secretary of the Iowa Grain Dealers' Association, that organization actively tried to prevent these agents from doing business with "irregular" dealers. At first, Wells paradoxically urged members of the association to give some business to Lowell Hoit & Co., so that they would be better able to influence them not to do business with such firms in the future. "Do not raise the question about the farmers' elevator companies in your first letter," he wrote, "but take that up with them later, after having given them some business."[25]

With respect to Eschenberg & Dalton, Wells first sent them a warning that if they did business with "irregular" dealers, the "regular" dealers would be notified, to which they replied defiantly: "Interfere with our business at your own peril." He then sent a letter to his association's membership reporting that the firm had received shipments from the Farmers' Elevator Company of Dougherty, Iowa, which was organized on the "Rockwell plan" and used the penalty clause. "I would suggest that you correspond with Eschenberg & Dalton," he wrote, "if you feel that you do not care to do business with terminal dealers that are taking business from such farmers' elevator companies." In fact, a number of "regular" Iowa dealers did write such letters, as did some dealers from other states who were not even members of the Iowa association, and, according to one estimate, Eschenberg & Dalton lost 90 percent of their business and kept afloat only because of the increasing numbers of farmers' elevators.[26]

Actually, the Dougherty Farmers' Elevator that so concerned George Wells had just been organized by Thomas McManus, one of the original founders of the Rockwell Cooperative Society, and was located in his home township about ten miles from Rockwell. At first, the Northwestern Railroad had refused to grant an elevator site on its tracks to the new cooperative. Mc-Manus responded by placing a bill before the Iowa State Legislature that would force railroads to provide sites to all farmers' elevators that requested them. The Northwestern relented and agreed to award the site at Dougherty if McManus would withdraw the bill, which he did, and he subsequently became known as the "Patrick Henry of Dougherty Township."[27]

That title was apt, for like the eighteenth-century patriot, McManus and others active in the farmers' elevator movement were also concerned about the corruptions of large and distant concentrations of power. From their own dealings with the local agents of these organizations, and in the wake of the various trials and hearings, the arrogance and abuses of that power were self-evident and had to be resisted. Yet, as they fought the railroads, the grain combinations, and the grain dealers' associations, McManus, Worrall, Messerole, and their supporters were not advocating a fundamental restructuring of social relationships—they were not advocates of radical change. Rather, they wanted to restore conditions of fairness and freedom in the marketplace that had been destroyed by the truly revolutionary force of the time, the rise of large-scale interests.

Beginning in 1904, in fact, there were many such patriots, although not necessarily revolutionaries, throughout the grain states. If anything, the adverse publicity generated by the different hearings marked the beginning of the end of the grain dealers' boycott, and this proved to be a tremendous boon to the farmers' elevator movement. In Illinois, for example, the number of farmers' elevators increased from 30 at the end of 1902 to more than 100 in 1905 and more than 200 in 1911. There were 121 farmers' elevators in Iowa in 1906, 95 of which had been organized during the previous three years; this figure more than doubled again over the next three years. By the same token, the movement expanded in other states, as large numbers of new farmers' elevators started operations in Minnesota, Nebraska, and the Dakotas.[28]

This rapid growth was due to a combination of factors. One of the most important was the farmers' new ability to fight fire with fire, or, in this case, organization with organization. The first of these, the Farmers' Grain Dealers' Association of Illinois, was established in 1903 as a direct response to the revelations in the Mason City case, which was, in the words of its first general letter, "one of the most open and high-handed violations of the laws of trade and decency this country ever witnessed." Formed "for the purpose of combining our forces and combating any future attempts to drive us out of business," the association invited farmers to organize new elevator companies, included an application for membership in its letter, and stressed the benefits of collective action: "Combined we are powerful enough to hold our own and meet all comers."[29]

The Iowa Association started the following year at a convention held, significantly, at Rockwell, and elected Norman Densmore as its first president. Other farmers' grain dealers' associations formed during this period in Nebraska, North and South Dakota, Kansas, Oklahoma, Ohio, Indiana, Minnesota, and Missouri, and a national organization, the Farmers' National Grain Dealers' Association, started in Minneapolis in 1912. All of these associations strengthened their ranks by actively organizing new elevator companies, often in response to direct requests for assistance, and they used their growing clout to force balky railroads to provide favorable elevator sites or build sidetracks for their members' facilities. Significantly, however, they did not exercise or attempt to exercise any direct control over their member elevators, which remained under local management.[30]

These new associations endorsed a monthly periodical, the *American Cooperative Journal*, which regularly trumpeted the progress of the farmers' elevator movement while detailing the sins and transgressions of the "regular" dealers. The *Journal* was founded in 1905 by C. G. Messerole, who, in addition to managing the Gowrie, Iowa, farmers' elevator, was the first permanent secretary of the Iowa Farmers' Grain Dealers' Association. In 1911, a group of the state farmers' grain dealers' associations actually purchased the *American Cooperative Journal* and made it their official organ. Together with their annual meetings, which were covered by the *Journal* as well as mainstream press, it was the most important vehicle for publicizing the movement, and it played a leading role in promoting farmers' cooperatives generally.[31]

In addition to the efforts of these state and national farmers' associations, the two commission houses that were willing to do business with them also helped to organize new farmers' elevators. Outlawed by the "regular" dealers' associations, these firms depended on an increasing volume of cooperative shipments in order to stay in business, so they actively encouraged the formation of new ones. One agent from Lowell Hoit & Co., William M. Stickney, claimed that he traveled almost continuously for three years and spoke about the need for farmers' elevators in about 175 different places, of which only two or three failed to organize new companies. In his estimation, this campaign cost the firm between $15,000 and $20,000. E. G. Drum, who did the same for Eschenberg & Dalton, was said to be a "whirlwind" and a "flame" who organized eight elevators for every ten towns that he visited. In contrast to earlier promotion schemes for cooperative creameries by unscrupulous operators trying to sell machinery and building contracts, this was a symbiotic rather than an exploitative relationship. Farmers' elevators needed the outlet to terminal markets and the marketing expertise that the commission firms provided, and the firms, in turn, needed the business.[32]

The state also played an important role in the growth of farmers' grain elevators. It encouraged the more general development of agricultural cooperatives, which was one of the recommendations of the 1908 Country Life Commission, and provided a more favorable and supportive climate for them. The U.S. Department of Agriculture created the Office of Markets in 1913 (later the Office of Markets and Rural Organization), which assigned staff members to survey and study cooperatives and to work with them. That work dovetailed and was increasingly coordinated with the extension and research efforts of the land grant universities and with the newly formed marketing departments in the different states. Finally, beginning with Wisconsin in 1911, a number of states passed cooperative laws, which defined the characteristics of agricultural cooperatives and protected them from prosecution under antitrust statutes, a legislative trajectory that culminated at the federal level with the passage of the Capper-Volstead Act in 1922.[33]

Thus, the new state and national farmers' associations, the sympathetic commission houses, and the state all provided important encouragement and support and established a framework for the further expansion of the farmers' elevator movement. Ultimately, however, the new farmers' elevators were local institutions whose spread and success depended on the determination of thousands of farmers in scores of communities, often in the face of significant opposition. Even as the movement as a whole gained strength, the struggles that characterized Rockwell, Mason City, and Dougherty township were repeated in towns and villages throughout the Midwest.

In Grelton, Henry County, Ohio, for example, the farmers' elevator overcame rumor campaigns by its competitors, the withholding of railroad cars, and personal threats against its manager as well as attempts to hire him away. In Utica, Illinois, farmers fought a series of battles in the town's government and local courts in order to get a railroad switch to its facility and ship its grain. The committee of the cooperative that handled all of this was known as the Trouble Committee, and was reported to be "very glad to be discharged" after it was all over, and sympathized "with any one who attempts to tread on sacred soil with their shoes on." The early history of the Farmers' Mercantile & Supply Company of Elkhart Lake, Wisconsin, was a struggle between local farmers and the Laun Brothers, a local monopoly run by three brothers who had become "wealthy, opulent and oppressive and arrogant and sought to control the public and keep them in subjugation." Similarly, the founders of the Farmers' Grain and Supply Company of Ord, Nebraska, had to overcome the animus of local merchants when they acquired a vacant grain elevator in 1915 and went on to become one of the largest cooperative businesses in the state, with 650 stockholders in 1920.[34]

Some elevators developed as expressions of ethnic cooperation and solidarity, especially in the ethnically homogeneous communities of the Midwest. Hull, Iowa, for example, had a very successful farmers' grain elevator that began in 1893 and expanded to include an extensive array of sidelines as well as a cooperative creamery. The *American Cooperative Journal* attributed this success to the community's ethnicity and the example of the Dutch cooperative movement: "Probably one of the biggest reasons for the co-operative successes at Hull is that a great many of the residents there are Hollanders. There are many other communities in Iowa where the Holland people predominate, and as a rule they are excellent co-operative centers."[35] In the same vein, Clark's Grove, Minnesota, was a Danish community that started one of the earliest cooperative creameries in the state in 1890 after one of its residents visited Denmark and learned about the cooperative movement there. The organizational meeting was held in the Danish Baptist church, and the constitution and by-laws were written in Danish. The success of that creamery led, in turn, to a farmers' elevator, as well as a cooperative store and a lumberyard. Cooperation was also important in the farming communities of Trempealeau County, Wisconsin, where Norwegians were the predominant ethnic group and prior experience with cooperatives in the old country provided a ready model, even though the cooperatives themselves involved several different ethnic groups. The Finns had a long history of cooperation, often influenced by left-wing politics, and as some Finnish

workers and miners abandoned industry for agriculture in the twentieth century, they formed cooperatives, including grain elevators and other marketing
organizations, in their rural communities.[36]

Whether ethnically homogeneous or ethnically mixed, farmers' grain elevators were important local institutions and involved significant cross-
sections of the community. In addition to the annual or semiannual stockholders' meetings, and often in conjunction with them, farmers' elevators
held picnics for their members, which added a social dimension to their significance. According to a leading observer of the movement: "These picnics
are in the nature of general celebrations in which sports of various kinds are
provided as well as good musical and literary programs. Among other numbers there will usually be an address which will consider the farmers' elevator movement, some farm problems, or political questions." The Yorkville,
Illinois, Farmers' Elevator Company, for example, closed for business on a
sunny June Saturday in 1910 and held its annual meeting at Van Emon's
Grove, where its membership enjoyed ball games and other amusements as
well as each other's company, and heard addresses by the district's congress-
man and William M. Stickney, the agent from Lowell Hoit & Co.[37]

Given the powerful combination of these factors—new farmers' associations, the active support of sympathetic brokers, the role of the state, and,
above all, the importance of elevators as reflections of local determination
and as community institutions—the rapid growth of farmers' elevators,
which had begun to take off in 1904, continued on its trajectory, skyrocketed,
and did not peak until the early 1920s. Illinois increased from 103 elevators in
1905, to 203 in 1911, to 514 in 1921; Iowa went from 76 to 511 during the
same period. According to other sources, 400,000 farmers owned stock in
farmers' elevators in 1919, 520,000 in 1925, and, in 1923, there were over
5,000 farmers' elevators representing an investment of more than $90 million
and handling $625 million of grain annually. In Illinois, Iowa, Minnesota, the
Dakotas, Nebraska, and Kansas, farmers' elevators handled fully 60 percent
of the grain that was shipped. In addition, sideline businesses by farmers' elevators were also important and accounted for more than $200 million of
business annually.[38]

In the face of such dramatic growth, opposition by the "regular" grain
dealers became a thing of the past. The boycott had broken down completely

FARMERS'
ELEVATOR
MEETING

The Annual Meeting and Picnic of the stockholders of the Farmers' Elevator Company of Yorkville will be held at

VAN EMON'S GROVE, SATURDAY, JUNE 18, 1910

A business meeting will be called at 10:30 a. m., to elect two directors and transact such other business as may come before the meeting. In the afternoon, beginning at 1:30 o'clock, addresses will be given by

Congressman Adkins
and
Hon. W. M. Stickney, of Chicago

Ball games and other amusments, which will be arranged later, will take place after the speaking. Come and bring your families. Bring your dinners and make a day of it. A good time is assured everybody.

THE ELEVATOR WILL BE CLOSED ALL DAY

FARMERS' ELEVATOR CO.,
E. B. THOMAS, Secretary.

Announcement for the Annual Picnic of the Yorkville, Illinois, Farmers' Elevator Company, 1910. (Courtesy of the Regional History Center, Northern Illinois University Archives)

by 1910, and in 1911, the *American Cooperative Journal* published a list of no fewer than twenty-seven firms in Chicago alone that solicited business from farmers' elevators. The grain dealers also failed in their 1911 legal challenge of the penalty clause as being in restraint of trade, when they tried to annul the charter of a farmers' elevator that practiced it. Instead, the judge ruled that although the clause may have injured the business of competitors, those competitors were middlemen, not the public. Rather, the penalty clause was an arrangement among stockholders in a private corporation and was not contrary to public policy.[39] Thus, when the Iowa Grain Dealers' Association reorganized as the Western Grain Dealers' Association and met in Des Moines in 1910, George Wells, who was still secretary, reported that, because membership had declined from 800 to 500 elevators, their income had been materially reduced and they were running a deficit—all of which was gleefully reported by the *Journal*. In fact, many line elevators had closed or sold out in the face of competition from the farmers, and a number of independents actually became farmers' elevators, often in defiance of the weakening grain dealers' associations.[40]

In numerical, organizational, and economic terms, then, the farmers' elevator movement was a striking success. It reduced the margin added by middlemen at country marketing points, often raising the local price of grain by as much as 10 percent, and it helped eliminate much of the chicanery on weights, dockage, and grading that had been such common complaints against the line and independent elevators. These elevators were important institutions in many midwestern communities, and their individual histories, often so full of drama and struggle against the forces of opposition, became important frames of reference and cultural touchstones for farmers throughout the grain states.

The farmers' elevator movement spread because it resonated with a number of commonly held rural values and sensibilities rather than challenging them. It drew on deep-seated agrarian attitudes that opposed middlemen and monopoly, but it also reflected the mentality of small businessmen, who believed in the fundamental importance of individual freedom and recoiled from collective coercion. Both perspectives stressed the primacy of the lo-

A typical farmers' grain elevator, Amiret, Minnesota, 1916.
(Courtesy of the Minnesota Historical Society)

cal community and local control and resisted centralized concentrations of power.

After the grain elevators became established, however, the contradictions and limitations inherent in these perspectives became more apparent, and the larger ideological and political significance of the movement became more ambiguous. Increasingly, farmers' elevators confronted their own reluctance to embrace more far-reaching change as well as their inability as local institutions to influence larger developments. They also found themselves at odds with the efforts of newer agricultural organizations to bring a more large-scale, corporate order to the rural North to rectify those shortcomings.

In one sense, the farmers' grain elevator movement continued the anti-middleman and antimonopoly ethos of earlier agrarian crusades. Cover illustrations and cartoons from the *American Cooperative Journal* during the rapid expansion of the movement regularly depicted the line elevators as fat robber barons and monopolists in top hats and morning coats, or they invoked parallels between the farmers' cooperative movement and the American Revolution and other motifs representing freedom from tyranny. The thousands of participants in the local struggles to create farmers' elevators, like the ones in Grelton, Ohio, and Elkhart Lake, Wisconsin, shared and were animated by similar sentiments.

But the rhetoric of the farmers' elevator movement contained little of the agricultural fundamentalism that had characterized earlier efforts informed by those same principles. "Why should the farmer not organize?" asked the *American Cooperative Journal* in 1909:

> What other business on earth has not organized? . . . This is a nation of organized interests, and, under the proper management, the country is better off because of the organization of farmers. When the farmer's products leave him, they are taken by the railroads which are organized, then they go to the manufacturers who are organized, and when they reach the farmer again as a finished product, they come from mercantile organizations. The producers of all this great wealth (and wealth producing products) represent the only link in the chain that is not strongly and concretely organized.[41]

Farmers, then, were simply one business interest among many, and the only one that was not "strongly and concretely" organized. They were integral to American society only in the sense that their products formed the basis for much of its wealth, not as the moral backbone and compass of the republic.

Nor did the farmers' elevator movement transcend its narrowly defined economic mission. In spite of its appeals to more traditional agrarian sensibilities, it was cast primarily as a business proposition that had few implications, radical or otherwise, beyond the local marketing of grain and supplies. Even those elevators that were most strongly committed to cooperative principles acted in this limited context rather than advocating a "cooperative commonwealth" for the larger society. The different farmers' grain growers' associations typically lobbied for cooperative laws and took positions in favor of other progressive legislation, but, for the most part, the movement eschewed politics.

Cover illustration from the American Cooperative Journal, *February 1914.*

MAY, 1914   TEN CENTS

GRAIN

COAL & LUMBER

AMERICAN
CO-OPERATIVE
JOURNAL

LIVE STOCK

DAIRY

CHICAGO   MINNEAPOLIS

Cover illustration from the American Cooperative Journal, *May 1914.*

Cover illustration from the American Cooperative Journal, *July 1914.*

AUGUST, 1914

TEN CENTS

AMERICAN CO-OPERATIVE JOURNAL

CHICAGO

MINNEAPOLIS

Cover illustration from the American Cooperative Journal, *August 1914.*

These ideological limits are captured by two illustrations from the *American Cooperative Journal.* In one drawing from 1918, a thermometer marks the degrees of improvement in farmers' elevator operations. The gauge ranges from 0 degrees, representing no farmers' elevators, to 80 degrees, which is the ideal, to 90 degrees and over, which is labeled: "Blood Heat, Dangerous: Entering Politics, etc." In a related vein, another cartoon nearly two years later, entitled "The Straw That Breaks the Camel's Back," reflects the movement's distance from organized labor, especially after the strike-torn period following World War I. The worker wields a big club labeled "Strike" and only wants to work six hours a day; he is blocking the farmer, who is already hampered by low prices and high costs, by demanding even lower wheat prices.[42]

Rather than offering an alternative vision of the social order, then, farmers' elevators, which had often grown out of specific struggles in their communities, remained local institutions that served a local clientele and reflected their character, but did not attempt to reach beyond them. As long as the elevator movement was growing and engaged in the good fight against its opponents, however, all of these limitations remained in the background, muted by the momentum of events. Ironically, the movement's very success brought them to the fore, and as individual cooperatives became secure and began to age, problems emerged within the different organizations.

These contradictions and limitations first surfaced in the numerous debates over reorganization that were stimulated by new state cooperative laws and the aging of the early farmers' companies. Before the 1910s, farmers' grain elevators had incorporated as joint-stock companies, primarily because there were no laws on the books that defined cooperative forms of organization. In spite of that organizational structure, however, they often adopted some combination of cooperative features. In addition to using the penalty clause to encourage membership loyalty, many farmers' elevator companies initially limited the amount of stock that an individual could purchase, restricted stock ownership to farmers in the community, allowed each member one vote regardless of the number of shares he owned, and paid only small dividends, typically to cover interest on the original investment. Others, however, followed none of these practices.

"The Straw That Breaks the Camel's Back,"
American Cooperative Journal, *1920.*

With the passage of time, the character of a number of these institutions changed as they drifted from cooperation to more typical business operations. Members retired from farming and moved away from the community, and some sold their stock to townspeople, lessening the specifically agrarian and cooperative character of the enterprise.[43] Some companies became farmers' elevators in name only, and held onto the old title primarily for advertising purposes. The Northfield Farmers' Elevator and Mercantile Company in Minnesota, for example, was started by farmers in 1896, but its stock gradually came to rest in the hands of businessmen and absentee owners in Colorado and California who were interested in high dividends rather than the betterment of the farmers' market. Thus, when a new farmers' elevator was organized as a true cooperative in nearby Dennison, local farmers drove the extra miles and patronized it instead, causing the Northfield company to go out of business. Elsewhere in Minnesota, those problems were exacerbated by a shift out of wheat and into livestock production, which reduced the importance of the elevators and led some of them to curtail the payment of patronage dividends.[44]

The cooperative spirit waned as well in the Danish settlement of Nysted, Nebraska, according to the reminiscences of the son of a Danish farm family. Continuing a movement they were familiar with in Denmark, the Nebraska settlers organized cooperative elevators, lumberyards, shipping associations, creameries, and credit associations. Their allegiance to those cooperatives weakened over time, though, and farmers who had been "cultural individualists and economic collectivists" became "cultural collectivists and economic individualists," who "went and bought their goods where they could get them a trifle cheaper and thereby ruined their own associations." Even Rockwell, the movement's "mother church," faced similar problems by the 1920s; according to one history, "some had come to feel that the society existed peculiarly as a money-making institution for those who had built it up."[45]

The Latham, Illinois, Farmers' Grain Company also illustrates the limited commitment to cooperative principles characteristic of some joint-stock companies, according to a 1920 article from the *Prairie Farmer*. Founded in 1904, the elevator was capitalized at $10,000, and no one could own more than eight shares or $400 worth of stock. Between 1917 and 1919, however, the company declared a total of 340 percent in dividends, and a lawsuit resulted when it was revealed that five of the directors had illegally bought more than their share of stock at reduced prices, either in secret or through members of their families. One director allegedly owned thirty-one shares. "It is a sorry mess," noted the author. "It has split a neighborhood. It has all but wrecked a thriving elevator company." He recommended that farmers' elevators organize under the Illinois cooperative law, which limited shares and dividends and redistributed profits according to patronage. "Anyway," he wrote, "those dividends were too large. . . . That money did not belong to the farmers who owned stock, it belonged to the farmers who raised grain. . . . The lesson to be learned is that a higher sort of cooperative spirit must be developed in farmers' business enterprises."[46]

As new state laws defined and legitimated that higher sort of cooperative spirit, and as the original charters of older elevators expired, both old and new companies were forced to evaluate their organizational philosophies and choose among the alternatives. Under the new laws, cooperatives had to limit shares and annual dividends to shareholders, and they paid patronage dividends to members and nonmembers alike based on the amount of their business, although one typically became a member of the cooperative simply by doing business with it. These provisions, however, proved to be sticking points to reorganization, especially among the older farmers' elevators, which were more reluctant to adopt them than the newer companies formed after the passage of state cooperative laws.

Reorganization as a cooperative raised problems about what to do with the surplus capital that had accrued and extended membership privileges to those who had refused to join the cause at the outset, when local battles were raging. The sentiments expressed by one Iowa farmer who wrote to the *American Cooperative Journal* were not uncommon: "If it was not for the capital of some of the farmers who feed all their grain but who came to the front when the stock was sold to start the farmers' elevator, they would still be selling to some old line man who would prorate his good will and make all the profit he could out of his give."[47]

The editor of the *Journal* responded by acknowledging the contributions and risks of the founders but admonished them not to be selfish in terms characteristic of an earlier producers' ethic:

Most of the early investors have had their money back long ago in dividends and increased prices on grain. Now if they are retired or for any reason are not able to do much business with the company, they should be satisfied with a reasonable interest on their investment. When they demand more they become capitalists or, we might say, speculators looking for big returns on money rather than co-operators who are building up a company for the protection of the community as a price maker.[48]

Because of the prevalence of older companies and their vested interests, then, a smaller percentage of the farmers' elevators in Illinois and Iowa were organized under the new cooperative laws than elsewhere in the grain belt. According to the Federal Trade Commission's 1918 survey, only 29 percent of the farmers' elevators in Illinois and 35 percent of those in Iowa paid patronage dividends, as opposed to an average of 68 percent overall. By 1928, though, 58 percent of Illinois farmers' elevators were organized on the cooperative plan, and 57 percent of the farmers' elevators in Iowa in 1931 were incorporated under one of that state's two cooperative laws. This increase was due primarily to the organization of new elevators as cooperatives, however, for only 44 of the older companies in Illinois had actually changed their form of organization to conform to the new law. Significantly, according to the 1931 Iowa survey, farmers' elevators that organized or reorganized as cooperatives proved to be the stronger institutions over the long run.[49]

Even successful reorganization, however, could not transcend the ideological limitations of the farmers' elevators or rekindle the fiery emotions that had fueled their founding. Again, the experiences of the Rockwell Cooperative Society are instructive. The society managed its transition to the new form of cooperative organization and the more democratic selection of officers in 1924, after it allowed proxies for absentee stockholders to get a local majority of voters. (The vote was 288 to 20.) Still, in the absence of new struggles and any overarching ideological agenda, much of the old élan had disappeared even though the history and "high points" of the society's accomplishments were recounted regularly at co-op meetings. But, according to one observer, "oft repeated, these facts were losing their potency." Rather, "the spirit of loyalty in the younger generation seemed incomparable to that of an earlier generation," and some of them even questioned the necessity of a cooperative society. It was certainly no match for the burgeoning consumer culture of the 1920s as the community's youth got in their cars and drove to nearby Mason City, Iowa, to patronize the stylish new chain store, forcing the society to abandon one of its sidelines and shut down its clothing store in 1929.[50]

In addition to sorting out new internal organizational arrangements, farmers' elevators increasingly confronted their limits as strictly local institutions and had to meet new challenges posed by competing agricultural movements and organizations. The first decades of the twentieth century witnessed a variety of efforts to mobilize rural interests, which varied primarily according to their willingness to engage in political activity, and in the amount of importance they attached to local organizations and decentralized structures.

Those issues came to a head during the period following World War I. The wheat market fluctuated wildly and was unstable, underscoring the inabilities of local cooperatives to exert much influence on larger trends. Moreover, the agricultural depression of the 1920s created new pressures for collective action, which challenged the local orientation and decentralized nature of the farmers' elevator movement. In particular, new attempts to move into the terminal markets or to organize on a translocal basis posed significant logistical and ideological problems. The farmers' grain elevators were uncomfortable with the political solutions being advocated by some farmers' movements, and they were leery of other efforts to mobilize grain growers into centrally controlled, corporate marketing organizations, which betrayed their commitments to local autonomy and their opposition to pooling in order to control the market. Thus, the changing relationships between farmers' elevators and other agricultural movements, particularly the American Farm Bureau Federation, are critical to an understanding of the perspective of midwestern grain farmers as American society became dominated by large-scale organizations.

Two of these movements, Equity and the Farmers' Union, actually complemented the farmers' elevator movement in geographical areas where it was less prominent. The American Society of Equity had started in Indiana in 1902 as a centrally controlled effort to counter business monopolies and control grain prices, but within five years its focus shifted to state organizations and to Kentucky, where it achieved its first successes among tobacco farmers.[51] In the grain-producing states, the Equity movement split into several factions that adopted different strategies. Two organizations stressed pools or terminal facilities and were attracted to political action. The Wisconsin Society of Equity tried to form wheat pools and wool pools and became involved in the state's progressive politics as an ally of Robert La Follette. The Equity Cooperative Exchange established a cooperative terminal market in St. Paul, which eventually provided an outlet for its network of eighty elevators in Minnesota and North Dakota, and it waged a political campaign in 1915 to establish a terminal elevator owned by the state of North Dakota. That issue, in fact, was one of the most important factors in the rise of the Nonpartisan League, whose political activities, together with the exchange's own financial and managerial problems, eclipsed the older movement. In contrast, another offshoot organization, the Farmers' Equity Union, which was formed in 1910, eschewed centrally controlled pooling and price-setting efforts and believed in a more limited and gradual approach that emphasized local organizations. It promoted local cooperatives in Colorado, Nebraska, Kansas, Oklahoma, South Dakota, and southwestern North Dakota and, according to one scholar, "in its quiet fashion . . . became the most successful of the various branches of the equity movement."[52]

Although the more mainstream farmers' grain dealers' associations looked askance at Equity's political activity, especially in Wisconsin, Minnesota, and North Dakota, they agreed wholeheartedly with the Farmers' Equity Union's focus on local cooperatives, which were similar to the cooperatives in their own association and were often members as well. The differences were certainly not obvious to E.L.S. of Pike County, Illinois, when he wrote to the *Prairie Farmer* in 1918: "We want to organize and build an elevator. What do you think of the Farmers' Equity Union, or is there something better? I don't know anything about farmers' associations, but do know that PRAIRIE FARMER is O.K." Instead of endorsing the Farmers' Equity Union, however, the editor advised forming a cooperative elevator under the laws of Illinois along the same line as many farmers' elevators already operating in the state, and plugged the Illinois Farmers' Grain Dealers Association, which they could join after forming an elevator.[53]

According to a list of farmers' elevators in Illinois, Farmers' Equity Union, which had its headquarters in Greenville, Illinois, mounted an organizing campaign during this period, but it had limited success. The word "equity" first appears in farmers' elevator names in 1920, but of the 66 elevators formed that year, only 5 had it in their titles, and only 1 elevator was so labeled in subsequent years. Only 5 of the 66 did not use the word "cooperative" at all, however, signifying that the vast majority of new elevators were organized under the state's cooperative laws. Farmers' Equity Union was more successful in Ohio, where the farmers' elevator movement was newer and less established. There were only 4 farmers' elevators in Ohio before 1910, but ten years later, the state had 162 and one-fourth of these were Equity Union elevators, most of which had been organized in the previous two years.[54]

Like Equity, the Farmers' Educational and Cooperative Union was founded in 1902 and achieved its greatest influence outside its region of origin. Started in Raines County, Texas, by Newt Gresham, a former organizer for the Farmers' Alliance, the Farmers' Union ultimately became more important in the Midwest and West, especially in Kansas and Nebraska. Even though it thought of itself as the alliance's heir, the union did not espouse agricultural fundamentalism, but subscribed instead to a more limited view of farmers as an interest group, and it was most successful in the organization of local cooperative stores, elevators, and livestock shipping associations. According to one scholar, "Whatever its [Farmers' Union's] roots in the less-corn-and-more-hell aspects of Populism, it was a tacit repudiation of the Taylorian view of the universality of agriculture as a political base for the nation."[55]

In Nebraska, which was one of the Farmers' Union's strongholds, the first local chapter was organized in Antelope County in 1911, and by 1920, there were more than 1,000 locals with a membership of about 45,000. According to one study, 150 of the 400-plus cooperative elevators in the state in 1918 had been organized through Farmers' Union activity, many of which also shipped livestock and managed cooperative stores; another source counts about 600 Farmers' Union elevators for the country as a whole. These were not under centralized control, however, and, in the words of one observer, the Farmers' Union "strongly recognizes in its work the principle of local control and management. . . . In many states the locals are organized on the capital stock plan, operating as separate business entities, maintaining only a loose fraternal or social association with the larger bodies."[56]

Thus, although some of the Equity factions and the Farmers' Union subscribed to more militant rhetoric and were more active in politics than the more mainstream farmers' elevator movement, all three movements stressed the overarching importance of local cooperatives and organization, and emphasized decentralized, rather than centralized, control. In fact, ideological similarities and Equity's declining fortunes led the union to merge with the Equity Cooperative Exchange in 1926 and with the Wisconsin Society of Equity nearly ten years later. During the early 1920s, they all opposed the highly centralized plans for grain marketing promoted by the American Farm Bureau Federation.

The Farm Bureau also played an important role in the formation of farmers' cooperatives during the early 1920s and had a complex and changing relationship with the farmers' grain elevators. Although this emphasis on cooperatives represented a change from its original purpose, it proved to be the most important source of Farm Bureau's growth and popularity among midwestern farmers. At first, the bureau concentrated on local organizations, and it enjoyed a big boost in membership as well as some support from the farmers' grain elevator movement. As the American Farm Bureau Federation advocated more centralized marketing strategies that undercut those local cooperatives, it lost both the farmers' elevators' support and hundreds of thousands of members who had joined in order to form local marketing organizations in their communities. Instead, those members remained committed to a perspective that stressed the primacy of local institutions and local control.

Farm Bureaus first developed during the second decade of the twentieth century to support the extension work of the county agent, which focused on improving agricultural production but not on issues of marketing. They were often funded by local chambers of commerce and corporations such as Sears, Roebuck and Co., in addition to farmers, to provide a more conservative alternative to other agrarian movements.[57] In contrast, the Farmers' Union excluded bankers, merchants, lawyers, and anyone "belonging to any trust or combine that is for the purpose of speculating in any kind of agricultural products, or the necessities of life," and regularly led local campaigns against public appropriations for the county agent and the Farm Bureau, which they believed represented big farmers and local businessmen rather than their own membership.[58]

This distinction became even more pronounced during the Red scare that followed World War I, when the different state Farm Bureaus formed a national organization. When the Illinois Agricultural Association (the Illinois Farm Bureau) president gave the keynote address at the founding meeting of the American Farm Bureau Federation (AFBF) in 1919, he pointed out that more than three thousand strikes had occurred in the one year since the signing of the armistice and urged: "It is our duty in creating this organization to avoid any policy that will align organized farmers with the radicals of other organizations. The policy should be thoroughly American in every respect,— a constructive organization instead of a destructive organization." Consequently, established interests gravitated readily toward the Farm Bureau, allowing AFBF president James R. Howard to testify at congressional hearings two years later: "Last week two governors came to me and voluntarily paid high tribute to the work of the Farm Bureau in keeping down dangerous expressions of unrest. They declared the Farm Bureau to be the great sober, thoughtful, careful, practical organized force in the country today."[59]

By 1921, however, state Farm Bureau organizations, particularly in the Midwest, had moved away from an emphasis on relatively noncontroversial educational programs directed at improving farm production and stressed the organization of cooperatives to market agricultural products and purchase supplies; Howard's testimony, in fact, was intended to allay misgivings about these activities. At first, county agents on government payroll actually recruited members for the Farm Bureau and helped organize and operate cooperatives in conjunction with them, but opposition by affected businesses led to a 1921 memorandum of understanding between the Farm Bureau and the U.S. Department of Agriculture that put restrictions on this collaboration. The Farm Bureau continued to organize cooperatives on its own, and through the middle of the decade, this was the most dynamic part of the movement and the main source of its appeal as it operated under the slogan, "Service through cooperative marketing."[60]

Organizing efforts intensified and more farmers joined precisely because the Farm Bureau emphasized cooperative activities. "Farmer salesmen were all pepped up on the wonders that the new organization was going to accomplish," recalled longtime co-op activist W. N. Woods about the 1920 campaign in Ohio. "Memberships were sold on promises that no sensible person would ever make, and no sensible person would expect to see fulfilled." As a result, membership in the Ohio Farm Bureau Federation shot up from under

20,000 to more than 90,000, an all-time high, but this was still a minority of the state's farmers. Farmer recruiters for the Illinois Agricultural Association were equally intent; they were paid $10 a day plus expenses during the 1919 drive, which also stressed the development of cooperative marketing and netted over 40,000 members. A 1921 book about the movement claimed that, as a result of similar efforts, 135,000 of Iowa's 217,000 farms were Farm Bureau members, and that, in many counties of Michigan, Ohio, Illinois, and Iowa, fully 95 percent of the farmers called on joined the new organization. From the point of view of grassroots farmers in the 1920s, then, the Farm Bureau meant cooperatives, and "a farmers' cooperative selling and buying association" was the most common definition given in a 1930 survey of almost fourteen hundred Ohio farmers.[61]

The Farm Bureau's activities and campaigns during this period were often full of the same zeal that had initially animated the other farmers' movements, in marked contrast to its later image of stolidity. One writer remembers the excitement of a neighbor's visit to the family during a recruiting drive for the Farm Bureau in Will County, Illinois: "After supper one summer evening, Frank Grannis and a farmer from some other part of the county called at our home near Elwood. I had been reading in the farm papers and the local press about the new organization, and I was all ears as the men talked to Dad." Another Illinois farmer, who needed no convincing himself, was surprised by his supposedly "hard-boiled" neighbor, who "joined up as soon as the man told him who he was—quicker than I did. Neighbor did most of the talking in fact. He's hot under the collar. He wants to fight. He has a passion against middlemen. . . . He's mad clear through and talks vehemently about such things as 'Boards of Trade,' 'Speculators,' 'Committee of Seventeen,' 'Commodity Organizations,' 'Agricultural Banks,' 'Pooling,' 'Real Cooperation,' and so on." As one local historian from Minnesota summed up that early spirit: "You may feel that the Farm Bureau at present is a bit stodgy and conservative. Those with good memories are entitled to smile. About thirty years ago the Farm Bureau and the extension office were roundly damned for their 'socialistic' attitudes. Local businessmen faced competition from farmers' co-operatives and only the preponderance of farm trade kept them from being more vocal in their opposition to cooperatives."[62]

Some of these efforts were welcomed and supported by the farmers' elevator movement and other farmers' organizations such as the Grange. In Michigan and Illinois, for example, the state Farm Bureau Federations united with the state Farmers' Grain Dealers' Associations to promote elevators where they were needed and to establish state brokerage offices. Similarly, in Ohio and Indiana, the state Grange, Farm Bureau Federation, and Farmers' Grain Dealers' Association joined forces to establish a single statewide buying agency for farmers' supplies and equipment.[63]

The Farm Bureau, however, embodied a fundamentally different organizational philosophy than the other farmers' cooperative movements, and this ultimately limited its appeal. From its inception, the Farm Bureau movement attempted to be the overarching organization that would speak for all farmers. According to an early Michigan leader, the Farm Bureau intended "to unite under a definite head all other farm organizations" and "should not be considered just another farmers' organization added to the list but as THE ONE which . . . may assist all others to better accomplish their purposes." It also adopted a distinctly top-down mode of operation, which minimized the importance of local organizations. Although the Farm Bureau initially tried to hold regular meetings in different townships, and then in districts of three or four townships, these did not last long, and the movement failed to establish itself on the community level. Instead, Farm Bureaus operated as county organizations that were increasingly run by paid employees under the control and direction of the state and national Farm Bureau Federations, and not by local farmer leaders.[64]

Often, the agenda and methods of the Farm Bureau conflicted with established local cooperatives, even those that were more mainstream and in sympathy with its basic perspective. A 1922 editorial in the *American Cooperative Journal* urged its readers to "Stand by Your Farm Bureau" in the face of declining membership and the nonpayment of dues, but went on to complain that the movement too often set up new cooperatives that competed with existing farmers' elevators, a practice that it labeled "senseless and expensive."[65]

In one instance, the state Farm Bureau actually undermined a cooperative that had been established by a group of its own active members in northwestern Ohio. These men, who were early producers of hybrid corn seed, started a cooperative to sell and control the quality of their crop, which they typically marketed through county Farm Bureau co-ops in the region. "But,"

wrote one of the founders, "as the State Association went deeper into production of hybrid seed, pressure was put on the county co-ops to put all their
orders through the state co-op, and we lost this business." Nor was this uncommon. According to the 1930 survey of Ohio farmers, the Farm Bureau
created some of its bitterest opposition by entering into competition with locally owned farmers' cooperatives: "In the minds of many farmers, the local
business was 'theirs' and the farm bureau was the intruder and aggressor.
Failure to find out and respect such local opinions and attitudes in develop-
ing the farm bureau's work seems to have been a serious handicap to the organization in these situations." Put another way, the most frequent complaint
against the Farm Bureau by Ohio farmers was that "members by and large do
not control their organization."[66]

Problems also occurred in statewide organizations. The jointly sponsored
brokerage agency in Michigan was initially a division of the state's Farm Bureau and under its control, but tensions over that arrangement quickly led to
its reorganization as a separate business enterprise. Similarly, the Indiana
Farmers' Grain Dealers' Association withdrew from the Indiana Federated
Marketing Service that had been formed in partnership with the state Farm
Bureau because of a combination of personality conflicts and differing views
of marketing, particularly about the role of farmers' elevators.[67]

The tensions between the Farm Bureau and others advocating a local and
more decentralized approach to cooperation and farm organization reached
their peak—or their nadir—during the U.S. Grain Growers episode of the
early 1920s. Although grain farmers were already organized on a local level,
market instability was still a problem, especially in 1919, and this required
new approaches and solutions, at least as far as the AFBF was concerned.
Consequently, the Farm Bureau sponsored a general conference on grain
marketing in 1920, the first in a series of initiatives dealing with different
commodities, and this led to the Committee of Seventeen, which included
representatives from the different state Farm Bureaus, the farmers' grain elevator movement, the Farmers' Union, the Equity Cooperative Exchange,
Farmers' Equity Union, the Grange, the U.S. Department of Agriculture, and
the agricultural press. The outcome of that committee's work, the U.S. Grain
Growers, Inc. (USGG), was unveiled with much fanfare in April 1921, and,
in the words of James R. Howard, the AFBF president, it represented "the

combining of time and effort, of capital and of commodity—coopera-
tively—in 'c-o-o-p-e-r-a-t-i-o-n'—not 'corporation.'"[68]

In spite of the ballyhoo, however, the USGG began under a cloud of compromise between different interests and perspectives that was darkened
further by organizational jealousies and rivalries. On the one hand, Aaron
Sapiro, who had successfully organized commodity marketing groups in
California, gave a riveting and influential address to the Grain Marketing Conference and urged replacing small, local cooperatives with a single
large organization for each commodity that would contract with each grower
individually. After enough farmers agreed to pool their crops in this manner, this one organization could exercise much greater control over the
market than a series of local cooperatives. "Organization by commodity—
not by locality," argued Sapiro, who hoped to see a wheat growers' organization "fixing a price on production and handling it in just the same way that
the United States Steel Corporation handles steel rails." This was the so-
called big plan, and it appealed especially to the delegates from the Farm
Bureau.[69]

Others, however, were suspicious of Sapiro and his "big plan." In particular, the farmers' grain elevators and the Farmers' Union, movements of local
cooperatives, which were the most common farmers' organizations in the
grain belt, were chagrined by Sapiro's brusque dismissal of their accomplishments and resisted changes that would either bypass them or reduce them to
mere receiving and storage facilities under the centralized direction of a far-
off manager. While recognizing the need for a new translocal strategy, they
preferred a more gradual approach that relied on existing local cooperatives
and emphasized market efficiency rather than market control. The compulsory pooling of wheat, which also undermined individual freedom and local
control, was a particular sticking point, and posed an additional irony to cooperatives that had originally formed to counter pooling by the so-called
regular dealers. Thus, a proposal that would have required the compulsory
pooling of one-third of the wheat was defeated by a vote of 61 to 38 at the
conference to ratify the Committee of Seventeen's report, the farmers' elevator movement providing the strongest opposition. As one of the delegates
remarked sardonically after the vote: "We're for harmony even if we have to
fight for it."[70]

The compromise (and compromised) organization that emerged, then, satisfied neither side. Advocates of pooling and the immediate creation of a new superorganization that would dominate the grain trade felt defeated. In spite of this defeat, the farmers' elevator movement remained suspicious because the USGG board continued to be dominated by poolers. That mistrust was compounded by the decidedly corporate style and big business trappings adopted by the new organization during its first year. One board member wanted to undertake an extensive and expensive ($250,000) advertising campaign. Others proposed renting a tony office building for $70,000 a year or actually purchasing a twenty-two-story building in the Chicago Loop district to prepare for the anticipated rapid expansion of the organization. They also approved what, from the farmers' perspective, were extravagant salaries: $16,000 a year for the president, $15,000 for the treasurer, $12,000 for the secretary, and even $6,000 to $7,500 for solicitors in the field. Although these abuses and excesses were corrected at the first annual meeting, and the offending board members were replaced, the USGG seemed to spell "c-o-r-p-o-r-a-t-i-o-n," instead of "c-o-o-p-e-r-a-t-i-o-n" as Howard had promised.[71]

Those suspicions were also manifest on the local level, where individual farmers' elevators did not always embrace the new organization. In 1921, the board of directors of the Grand Ridge, Illinois, Farmers' Elevator declined to sign an agreement to handle grain for members of the USGG and passed a resolution that refused either to endorse or condemn the organization on the grounds that the plan was "incomplete, untried, and experimental." In response, the Farm Bureau threatened to call a meeting of the elevator's stockholders to vote on the issue, but the board called one instead and featured a debate between a representative of the USGG and a former speaker of the Illinois House who was a member of a nearby farmers' elevator. The USGG representative did most of the talking, however, as he was forced to defend his organization against accusations that it used strong-arm tactics against farmers' elevators in order to force them to sign, or that it contracted with private, independent elevators instead of farmers' co-ops to handle its members' grain. As the hour grew late, a quorum disappeared and no vote was taken, but the farmers' elevator movement's resentments about the USGG's willingness to coerce or bypass them and to support their competitors continued to rankle and dampened their support for the new organization.[72]

The organization was never able to overcome this bad beginning. USGG solicitors managed to sign up 50,000 members, including about 10,000 in Illinois and 8,000 in Nebraska, but this was far short of the avowed goal of 1 million and it was not enough to provide much clout in the marketplace. Moreover, only 1 percent of those 50,000 agreed to use any of the several pooling methods available. In addition, the expenses associated with its costly membership drive left the nascent organization with no money for finances and operations. In fact, the USGG appealed to county Farm Bureaus for extra funds. Although many county Farm Bureaus answered this call, especially in Illinois, it was often regarded in retrospect as the biggest and most expensive mistake in the group's early history. According to Earl Price, the first farm adviser in Kendall County, Illinois: "Perhaps the greatest blunder of all was the unqualified support given the United States Grain Growers both in funds and membership. . . . Down this went with a thud and a boom . . . and with it went the prestige and reputations of many Illinois Farm Leaders. And with it also went close to $10,000 out of the pockets of Kendall County farmers."[73]

By 1923, the USGG had failed completely. Thirty years later, Ralph Snyder, a former president of the Kansas Farm Bureau and an original member of the Committee of Seventeen, provided its best epitaph:

> We met, and met, and met. We developed some grandiose ideas. We also developed some rather bitter animosities. . . . The conflict between the group who wanted to make use of the existing grain cooperatives and those who wanted to develop an entirely new form of organization for wheat pooling developed into a battle royal every time we met. . . . However, we organized the U.S.G.G. and set out to secure members. We first tried to get the interest of the existing cooperative elevators. We got their opposition. Then we tried to go over their heads, direct to members. That failed. And, that was the end of the U.S. Grain Growers. It never did market any grain.[74]

In the wake of this failure, which the AFBF blamed on the farmers' elevator movement, the Farm Bureau no longer felt compelled to compromise and embraced a top-down perspective even more strongly in its next venture in wheat marketing, the Grain Marketing Company. This was actually proposed initially by the old grain combines, Armour et al., as a scheme to have a farmers' organization buy their facilities at what critics regarded as inflated prices. This time, however, opposition came from within the Farm Bureau's own ranks. Individual members were slow to buy stock, and county Farm Bureaus, chastened by their experiences with the USGG, refused to contribute funds. The Farm Bureau of McLean County, Illinois, for example, had ponied up $10,000 to the USGG and criticized the AFBF for not doing more to save it, but it refused to support the Grain Marketing Company in January 1925, in spite of the fact that two members of its own executive board were employed by the new company. State Farm Bureaus, particularly in Illinois and Indiana, actively worked against the new venture and caused it to cease doing business by 1926. In general, this opposition and the failures of its large-scale grain marketing schemes shifted the AFBF away from an emphasis on cooperatives and toward lobbying for McNary-Haugenism and other national farm legislation.[75]

As it retreated from the organization of cooperatives, the Farm Bureau experienced a dramatic loss in its membership. From its high of 94,211 in 1920, for example, the Ohio Farm Bureau claimed only 61,686 members in 1922, and declined steadily to just over 7,000 in 1933; and for the nation as a whole, Farm Bureau membership fell from a high of over 466,000 to only 163,000 during this same period. This decline stimulated systematic investigation. According to a 1928 survey of 1,002 farmers in Illinois, the movement's strongest state, 43 percent were members of the Farm Bureau, 30 percent had never belonged, and 27 percent were former members. Most of the former members joined during the heyday of expansion and the organization of cooperatives around 1920, but they quit after the expiration of their first membership contract and remained especially critical of the Farm Bureau because they either did not see the value of the organization or felt that it had neglected or discriminated against them. According to a similar 1930 survey of 1,372 farmers in Ohio, 32 percent were members of the Farm Bureau, 40 percent were not, and 28 percent had joined but quit. These depression-era farmers were reluctant to pay expensive dues to an organization that no longer provided tangible economic benefits such as cooperatives, and they were disaffected by the centralization and aloofness of the Farm Bureau organization.[76]

Farmers in Minnesota also did not like centralized organizations, according to a 1926 survey. They preferred federations of local cooperatives in which farmers owed their allegiance to the local organization and these, in turn, dealt with the central organization. In a centralized cooperative, by contrast, large groups of members attached directly to the central office, which set up receiving plants wherever necessary, eliminating, according to the authors of the survey, "a great deal of local autonomy."[77] Significantly, unlike the failed AFBF grain marketing ventures, the most successful large cooperatives during the 1920s were federations of local organizations, even those that involved the state Farm Bureaus. Nebraska agricultural economist Horace Filley highlighted two in his 1929 book, *Cooperation in Agriculture*: the Grain Sales Department of the Ohio Farm Bureau Federation, which served nearly 100 farmer-owned elevators, and the Michigan Elevator Exchange, which claimed 107 of that state's 120 farmers' grain elevators. As Filley put it: "After the hue and cry for 'fixed prices' and market control shall have died down, . . . practical farmers who have made possible the growth of the cooperative elevator movement will doubtless come forward and develop a plan of marketing which will carry grain from the local elevator to the consumer at a lower cost than it can be carried under the present market system."[78]

The battles over the USGG, then, reflected more than the internecine squabbles over turf and power that had often undermined attempts to organize farmers on a large scale. Rather, they revealed and symbolized a deeper struggle between the primacy of local life, its institutions and perspective, and the emergence of a new bureaucratic and organizational ethos that transcended the local community. Partly, the defeat of the USGG and the Farm Bureau Federation represented the rejection of corporate culture and the reaffirmation of more traditional small business sensibilities, which remained rooted in the localities. Yet concerns about the farm crisis of the 1920s and the initial successes of a few federated organizations also indicate the perceived need and willingness to move beyond strictly local organization, albeit in ways that minimized compromises to local autonomy.[79]

Within the larger context of the period, however, this was hardly an unalloyed victory for older values or a renaissance for local institutions. Rather, as the depression deepened, first in the countryside and then in the nation as a whole, local associations and more traditional ways of dealing with social and economic problems were severely challenged and quickly overcome by their inabilities to ameliorate worsening conditions. Instead of relying on increasingly inadequate local resources and organizations, farmers turned to direct political action and to the federal government, with results that fundamentally and permanently altered their relationship to the larger society. And, as the federal government became the most important arbiter of rural life and as the numbers of farmers declined dramatically during the second half of the century, rural people paradoxically found a new voice through the kind of highly centralized, bureaucratic organizations that they had once rejected.

Thus, during the first decades of the twentieth century, in the wake of Populism's demise and the domination of American society by large-scale organized interests, midwestern grain farmers also became organized. But they did so in ways that were consistent with time-honored values and beliefs, and so resisted the prevailing direction of American society. In one sense, they were motivated by a long-standing antagonism to middlemen, which had its roots in an earlier producers' ethic and the Grange and Populist movements, and they waged numerous struggles against abusive local merchants who cheated them and obstructed their efforts. Yet, chastened by earlier experiences, grain farmers also recognized the necessity of the middleman's role and the importance of marketing expertise and sound business practices as they set up their own business organizations.

In addition to local merchants, grain farmers also opposed large and powerful business interests from outside the community. Here their efforts were guided by concerns about centralized concentrations of power, which had their roots in a republican ideology that stressed local autonomy. But they were also informed by a small businessman's mentality, which worried about the primacy of local life in the face of outside forces of change. In keeping with these precepts, farmers at first fought the railroads, the grain trusts, and the associations of grain dealers. But after these battles, they continued to resist efforts to institute centralized control and corporate culture that were sponsored by the American Farm Bureau Federation.

Compared to the vision of earlier farmers' movements and even their more politically oriented contemporaries, the farmers' elevator movement steered a middle course, and that, in part, helps to explain the broadness of its appeal. This lack of ideological boldness, however, should not belie the intensity and zeal that accompanied the movement and animated its participants, especially during its formative years. Instead, this militance in the service of narrow goals echoes mainstream organized labor with its predominant emphasis on wages and work conditions. For grain farmers, as well as their dairy counterparts, it was also a matter of bread and butter, and their most heartfelt convictions also contained the seeds of their own limitations.

During the first decades of the twentieth century, then, both midwestern grain growers and New York dairy farmers were poised between two worlds: a past, which they remembered clearly, that had given them an appreciation of individual independence and local autonomy; and a future, which they sought to control, that threatened to undermine those values by creating a more distant and centralized society. That they continued to believe in the importance of individual freedom and the primacy of the local community and to act on those beliefs even as changing structural conditions dictated otherwise is a measure of their perspective on the second great transformation in the northern countryside.

Part III

CONSUMERS

What is that coming up from the wilderness,

    like a column of smoke,

perfumed with myrrh and frankincense,

    with all the fragrant powders of the merchant?

    — SONG OF SOLOMON 3:6

5

WITH ALL THE FRAGRANT POWDERS OF THE MERCHANT

Mail-Order Buying in the Rural North

In addition to the emergence of large-scale organizations and the centralization of power, the expansion of a consumer economy and the development of a consumer culture are also defining characteristics of the second great transformation in American society. Although we know much about northern farmers as citizens and producers during this period, the history of rural participation in a consumer society is less well understood. Yet, just as the consolidation and centralization of the agricultural marketplace and the state confronted older agrarian values of independence and local autonomy, so, too, did the proliferation of new consumer goods and new methods of selling them.

Indeed, for northern country people, this dimension of the second great transformation challenged their identities as producers and their assumptions about the moral superiority of rural life by introducing new standards of value that were defined and embodied in material possessions that emanated from and reflected urban culture. Initially, the growing need for cash in order to buy the new goods reinforced and deepened their involvement with commercial agriculture and specialized production. More significantly, the emergence of consumer society altered rural northerners' relationships to their local communities and threatened the importance of those communities in the larger society. This history has two phases: the integration of rural northerners into a growing consumer economy during the late nineteenth and early twentieth centuries, and their responses to the explosion of consumer and mass culture during the 1920s.

Rural encounters with consumer society have long been portrayed in terms of the increasing presence and dominance of the city and consumer capitalism in the countryside and of the convergence of urban and rural society and culture. This view, however, typically focuses on the larger development of a consumer society rather than on the behavior or attitudes of rural people. Instead, rural northerners dealt with the challenges of an emerging consumer society in ways congruent with their own values; they were neither passive victims of forces beyond their control nor overly eager participants in the new order.[1]

Mail-order buying was the most important manifestation of the consumer economy in the rural North during the decades after the Civil War, and in order to understand the perspectives of agrarian consumers, it is necessary to reconstruct their experiences with the catalogue houses. The first of the large mail-order businesses did not represent a new cultural departure for northern country people. Rather, Montgomery Ward's success reflected his ability to resonate in important ways with more traditional agrarian values, which dampened suspicions of him as a merchant and outsider. Rural northerners saw Montgomery Ward as a more comfortable and trustworthy alternative to their other encounters with the consumer economy, and, along with their confidence, he also gained their patronage.

Montgomery Ward's and the other mail-order firms posed a threat to the primacy of the local community, however, and this generated tensions with other rural sensibilities. Small-town merchants explicitly championed the cause of the local community and waged a multifaceted campaign against the catalogue houses as they made inroads into their businesses. Northern farmers also worried about their communities, although they were by no means the merchants' automatic allies, and they also sought an accommodation with the consumer society in which they enjoyed the benefits of mass consumption while preserving local autonomy. As a result, attitudes toward mail-order buying became a referendum on the meanings and the place of the local community in American rural society and the relationship of that community to the larger world. By the 1920s, rural northerners had to contend with new challenges to the independence and viability of their communities but were too thoroughly enmeshed in a consumer society to contain its effects.

The northern farm families that Montgomery Ward solicited after the Civil War had a long history of conflicting attitudes about consumer goods and less-than-felicitous encounters with those who sold them, a context that needs to be understood to appreciate the reasons for his success. During the first half of the nineteenth century, rural northerners had misgivings about many of the new consumer products. Items that were too fancy or frivolous did not sit well with republican principles that stressed simplicity and a lack of unnecessary adornment; imported luxury goods, whether from abroad or from the city, threatened the independence of the nation and the local community as well as the primacy of an agrarian way of life. Yet rural consumers, men as well as women, were increasingly enticed by ever-more-affordable merchandise that introduced novelty into their lives and offered greater comforts and refinements for their homes, even if these challenged more traditional sensibilities.

Country people were also leery of the sellers, for those who sold these products, whether plain or fancy, were not producers or truly virtuous members of society. Rural northerners typically bought from local merchants, peddlers, and, immediately after the Civil War, from the first mail-order magazines, and these interactions were often marked by uncertainty, antipathy, and distrust. This was the context of rural northerners' experiences as consumers before the rise of the catalogue houses, and it represented a basic clash of cultures that Montgomery Ward needed to transcend in order to succeed.

For most of the nineteenth century, rural northerners typically purchased their goods from local merchants in country stores; the storekeepers, in turn, often bought country produce or accepted it in trade. Informed by a producers' ethic, farmers resented the merchant's role as middleman and the fact that merchants performed little physical labor. They believed that storekeepers were lazy and viewed mercantile pursuits as less desirable than more "honest" ways to earn a living. The *Hampshire* (Massachusetts) *Gazette* lamented in 1817 that young men who worked and obtained some money soon found labor "irksome" and desired instead to be merchants. "Can it be more honourable to measure rum and molasses, tape and ribbons, than to follow the hardy pursuits of agriculture or manufactures?" they wondered.[2]

Besides these attitudes, the main source of tension between country merchants and their rural customers was the determination of value and the negotiation of prices, and because both parties tried to buy cheap and sell dear, conflict was inherent in their dealings. For agricultural produce such as butter and grain, farmers and merchants could refer to newspaper market reports to determine a satisfactory price, although storekeepers had to remain vigilant against such ploys as rancid butter at the bottom of the tub and other adulterations. By contrast, there were few comparable benchmarks for dry goods and manufactured items. Local competition from other merchants was often minimal, and standardized brands with set prices and national advertising did not emerge until later in the century. Even if the store's asking price for a given item remained fixed over time, variations in the quality of the goods sold meant that the price was not necessarily an accurate reflection of its worth. Far from being an orderly and trustworthy transaction, then, the process of buying and selling in a country store was a constant battle of wits under the guiding principle of caveat emptor.[3]

The spirit of these encounters has been captured most colorfully in the memoirs of P. T. Barnum, a victor in numerous battles of wits and a paragon of the new urban mass culture. Barnum began his career in the 1820s as a clerk in country stores in and around Bethel, Connecticut, because, like the young men complained about above, he also did not enjoy laboring on his father's farm. There he drove many a "sharp trade" with rural women and men who paid for their purchases with "butter, eggs, beeswax, feathers, and rags . . . hats, axe-helves, oats, corn, buckwheat, hickory-nuts, and other commodities." Each side sought the upper hand, leading Barnum to conclude that tricks and deceptions were not confined entirely to the city. As he put it with his flair for showmanship:

> It was "dog eat dog"—"tit for tat." Our cottons were sold for wool, our
> wool and cotton for silk and linen; in fact nearly every thing was different

from what it was represented. . . . Each party expected to be cheated, if it was possible. Our eyes, and not our ears, had to be our masters. We must believe little that we saw, and less that we heard. Our calicoes were all "fast colors," according to our representations, and the colors would generally run "fast" enough and show them a tub of soap-suds. Our ground coffee was as good as burned peas, beans, and corn could make, and our ginger was tolerable, considering the price of corn meal. The "tricks of the trade" were numerous.[4]

Although Barnum's entertaining exaggerations contain more than a kernel of truth, in reality local storekeepers could not afford to be excessively unscrupulous because they depended on their customers' goodwill and willingness to patronize their businesses. In many cases, merchants came from the communities they served and were related to their customers. In order to sell their goods, then, local merchants had to maintain long-term relationships with their customers and often accommodated their needs. In particular, they provided credit, at first because farmers were not comfortable with cash transactions, and later in order to compete successfully with rival businesses. Ironically, the carrying costs of that credit forced local merchants to charge higher prices. This made them more vulnerable to those who could sell cheaper, while the lack of cash flow left them more susceptible to outside market pressures when their own creditors demanded payment.[5]

Significantly, those who did sell cheaper were outsiders, and rural northerners before the Civil War also encountered the wider world of consumer goods through itinerant peddlers who sold all manner of Yankee notions, as well as watches, clocks, and books.[6] These hawkers and walkers were less constrained by the bonds of community and less trustworthy than local merchants, and, if anything, country people were even more suspicious of them. The Yankee peddler became a stereotype for a shrewd operator, and the word "Yankee" was commonly used as a verb meaning to cheat. According to Thomas Hamilton, an English observer of the American scene in 1833:

The whole race of Yankee peddlers in particular are proverbial for dishonesty. They go forth annually in the thousands to lie, cog, cheat, swindle, in short, to get possession of their neighbour's property in any manner it can be done with impunity. Their ingenuity in deception is confessedly very great. They warrant broken watches to be the best time-keepers in the world; sell pinchbeck trinkets for gold; and always have a large assortment of wooden nutmegs and stagnant barometers.[7]

Coupled with these trepidations, however, was an equally keen appreciation for the lower prices the peddler charged as well as a sense of excitement generated by his visit. The peddler's visit was an amalgam of magic, danger, and theatricality that introduced rural northerners, particularly rural women, to a new consumer culture and the transforming powers of material possessions. In contrast to the local merchant, the peddler had little overhead and, because he only dealt in cash, none of his carrying costs or credit risks. He was also free to trade in only those items that sold well or garnered big profits—the "light and fancy" articles, rather than the more mundane "necessaries of life." In addition to watches and jewelry of questionable quality, for example, peddlers distributed Eli Terry's Connecticut shelf clocks, one of the first luxury items to commonly grace northern rural homes.[8]

Local merchants tried to control or eliminate this competition by instituting licensing laws and other regulations against peddlers. With arguments that presaged later opposition to mail-order houses and chain stores, rural merchants represented themselves as "agents of the community" and acted against itinerants who paid no taxes and made no contributions to local commerce. As a result of these efforts, several states passed laws such as the Massachusetts Hawkers and Peddlers Act of 1846, which imposed stiff fines for peddling without a license. Some sheriffs made a specialty of catching unlicensed peddlers, and country newspapers, which received no advertising from the transients, often published lists of those who were licensed for the "protection" of their readers.[9]

Rural northerners, especially rural women, also encountered the world of consumption in less personal ways. If the worried reactions of writers in agricultural periodicals serve as an accurate indicator, New England young farm women began imbibing urban styles and fashions from women's magazines before the Civil War and became increasingly disenchanted with the plainness and drudgery of life on the farm, much to the consternation of their fathers and the young farm men who sought to marry them. The parlor piano was the largest and most expensive symbol of this new sensibility, but it encom-

passed a wide range of goods and activities associated with more refined urban living. Indeed, as Allan Kulikoff has suggested, rural women's desires for
domestic amenities were one of the most important causes of the integration
of the countryside into an urban economy and culture.[10]

By the end of the 1860s, the mails not only brought news of urban fashions and consumer items, but also provided the means to buy them directly
through the so-called mail-order magazines, which only increased rural suspicions of outsiders.[11] The first of these, the *People's Literary Companion*, was
founded in 1869 in Augusta, Maine, by E. C. Allen, an advertising and marketing genius who certainly did not go broke underestimating the gullibility
of the American public. Allen made his money marketing a recipe for a washing powder that used simple ingredients, which could be purchased at any
country store. He printed the forty-word formula for the National Washing
Compound on slips of paper with the legend, "Price $1.00," and sold these to
agents for $10 per hundred or $25 per thousand for resale to anyone who
promised not to reveal the secret. This scheme proved so successful that
Allen expanded his list of recipes and sold formulas for magic copying paper,
silver plating, artificial honey (produced for the "trifling" cost of ten cents a
pound), different kinds of ink, liquid mole and freckle lotion, a patent gold
and silver counterfeit detector, the best shaving soap, furniture polish, a hair-
growth promoter, a hair restorative, salves, cologne, medicines, mead, cham-
pagne cider, making cider without apples, and burning fire under water. All,
he claimed, were "useful articles which afford large profits, and which sell
readily everywhere." [12]

Rather than continue to pay thousands of dollars to advertising agents in
New York, Allen founded the *People's Literary Companion* in 1869 in order to
promote his business. Less a literary publication than a commercial tool, the
Companion was an illustrated sixteen-page magazine replete with stories,
household hints, fashions, poetry, humor, and, above all else, advertising for
his recipes and the growing number of other product that he sold. Once he
was a publisher, Allen also began to produce engravings, chromolithographs,
and oleolithographs, and he offered these to his customers as well. Nominally
priced at fifty cents per year, for all intents and purposes the *Companion* was
distributed free, and it reached a circulation of .5 million in 1870, its second
year of publication.[13]

Allen's success spawned a host of imitators and competitors. P. O. Vickery, who used to work for Allen, began publishing *Vickery's Fireside* in Augusta in 1874, and True & Co. started *Our Fireside Journal* one year later in order to advertise products that were sold by direct mail. Vickery's catalogue did not offer recipes, but "New and Attractive Novelties, Useful Articles, Books, Etc., Etc." and "The Latest, Best, and Fastest Selling Goods," which he sold in quantity at wholesale prices for resale by agents or at retail for direct purchase by the consumer. The books focused mostly on magic and fortune-telling, while the novelties included false mustaches and goatees, a "magnetic and microscopic" knife, and a noisemaker called "The Naughty French Frog"—"bushels of fun for only 15 cents."[14] A similar venture in Chicago targeted women consumers and published a catalogue entitled *The Ladies' Friend* with the following explanation: "It aids her to adorn her person, to make home brighter by the introduction of the choicest music and musical instruments, games for the amusement of old and young, books for their instruction and profit, and a thousand articles of beauty and worth, calculated to make home happier and lighten life's burdens in almost every department."[15]

While they may have lightened life's burdens, these mail-order concerns, like the peddlers, their kindred spirits and forbearers, hardly inspired trust. None of the companies guaranteed the quality of their goods, and one of their stocks in trade, watches and jewelry, were notorious sources of cheating and swindling among rural customers. In the same vein, Vickery Co. perpetrated another fraud familiar in the countryside when it offered the Tabitha Sewing Machine for only $1.65 and compared its stitch to the "much prized Wilcox & Gibbs machine," at a time when legitimate manufacturers charged more than ten times that amount and had to pay a substantial royalty per machine to the pool of companies that controlled the key patents.[16] When the publisher of *The Ladies' Friend* reassured its customers "that there is not a single article in this catalogue which can be termed 'snide,'" they also offered some cautionary advice: "Of course there are different qualities of goods, but the descriptions and price are sure guides to that. One thing, however, no reasonable person will expect the same service from a cheap article as from one costing four or five times as much."[17] Caveat emptor!

E. C. Allen's self-serving effort to reassure and entice those who would act as his agents simultaneously underlined rural suspicions as well as his business's appeal:

> We are aware that advertisements for agents are often looked upon with distrust. We are also aware that at the present day there are many humbugs hailing from all parts of the country and agents can not be too careful as to what they take hold of. . . . We do not propose to make a fortune for any one with whom we deal. But we do propose to put those with whom we deal in the way of making a fortune, and then whether the fortune is made or not depends entirely upon the Agent. If you are willing to work, not hard but perseveringly, then you are sure of success—not a bare living but abundant crowning success.[18]

From the perspective of rural northerners, then, the mail-order magazines epitomized both the allure and the danger of embracing an emerging consumer culture during the last third of the nineteenth century. Marketed to rural women, the jewelry, music, and elaborate chromolithographs represented a way to achieve a more stylish and genteel way of living. Marketed to rural men, the books on magic and other exotica opened a window to an imagined world beyond the confines of their small villages while the tricks and novelties promised to infuse their lives with new dimensions of excitement and humor. Finally, the prospect of "abundant crowning success" instead of a "bare living," and without hard work, must have represented the soul of temptation.

Those enticements, however, were coupled with the real possibility of being swindled by strangers and being left with little recourse. Nor did the appeal of these mail-order businesses sit well with more traditional agrarian values. Becoming an agent to sell suspect recipes or frivolous trinkets and tricks in order to get rich quick hardly represented the honest labor cherished by the producers' ethic. Similarly, an overemphasis on sophisticated styles and urban culture represented an implicit rejection of the superiority of country living for the more superficial and ephemeral allure of the city.

Thus, for many rural northerners, the consumer economy of the mid-nineteenth century was fraught with caveats. To satisfy increasing desires for goods, consumers had to prevail in a battle of wits against the sharp dealings of their local merchants or they had to overcome the deceptions of itinerant peddlers and the exaggerated claims of bogus mail-order hucksters. By the mid-1870s, however, country people had an alternative to dealing with the devils they did know and the devils they did not.

Although not exactly a saint, Aaron Montgomery Ward offered rural consumers a more comfortable and straightforward way to buy—one that resonated in important ways with fundamental agrarian values. In 1872, Ward started the first mail-order business that enjoyed widespread success with rural consumers. Significantly, much of his success can be attributed to his affinity with agrarian sensibilities, which was epitomized by his connections to the Grange, the leading farmers' organization of the day. In addition, Ward's honesty and aboveboard business practices as well as the quality and low prices of his merchandise provided northern country people with a much needed alternative to less salutary dealings with local merchants, peddlers, and questionable mail-order concerns. Ward also recognized the appeal of the consumer goods themselves and catered to growing rural desires for domestic refinement and amenities. Thus, what was initially embraced as an extension of unadorned, agrarian virtues soon led country consumers in other directions.

Aaron Montgomery Ward was born in Chatham, New Jersey, in 1844, and moved to Michigan with his family when he was nine. After attempts at brick and barrel making, his father's trade, he clerked in a local country store before relocating to Chicago in 1866, where he worked in the wholesale division of a Marshall Field affiliate and became a salesman for other firms in Chicago and St. Louis. As a salesman, Ward visited numerous country stores and took note of the complaints of farmers and the myriad inefficiencies of both retailers and wholesalers, and, consequently, developed an idea for a general mail-order business. This afforded important advantages: He could lower prices by bypassing the large number of middlemen normally involved: eastern distributors, state distributors, jobbers, and retailers. He could eliminate the risks and carrying costs of credit by insisting on a cash business. And his business would cater specifically to all the farmers' needs and tastes, unlike the specialized mail-order catalogues or frivolous mail-order magazines then in circulation or the urban department stores, which sold by mail only as a

GRANGERS

SUPPLIED BY THE

Cheapest Cash House

IN AMERICA.

At the Earnest Solicitation of many Grangers, we have consented to open a House devoted to furnishing

FARMERS & MECHANICS

Throughout the Northwest with all kinds of

Merchandise at Wholesale Prices.

You can readily see at a glance the difference between our Prices and what you have to pay your Retailer for the same quality of goods.

It is with great pleasure that we present you with our Catalogue. We find our business is increasing to such an extent that our present quarters are entirely too small. Our new store on Clark street will be one of the largest and best arranged in the country for shipping goods promptly. We are also prepared to make purchases of all kinds of Merchandise which we do not keep, for our customers, charging them only five per cent. on the net cost. We do this simply as an accommodation.

All goods will be sent by express (Collect on delivery), subject to examination. In this way you can see just what you pay for. Any one sending us orders will place next the number opposite to the articles they wish sent. When convenient, as many as possible should club together, ordering one order. In this way the goods can be shipped at much less expense. Samples of piece goods sent on application by enclosing ten cents to pay postage, etc.

Address

MONTGOMERY, WARD & CO.,
Box 517, Chicago, Ill.

Montgomery Ward price list, 1872. (Reprinted with permission from Montgomery Ward)

sideline to over-the-counter sales. Ward returned to Chicago to work and ac-
cumulate capital for his venture, and sent out his first price list on a single
sheet of paper in August 1872.[19]

Ward distributed this price list to forty members of the Patrons of Husbandry, or the Grange, a four-year-old organization of farmers that was
growing rapidly during the early 1870s, and he continued to cultivate this
connection throughout the early years of his operation as a way to establish
and expand his business. The earliest surviving price list from 1872 is headed
in bold, large type: "GRANGERS SUPPLIED BY THE CHEAPEST CASH HOUSE IN
AMERICA," and in his first catalogues a year later, Ward billed himself as "The
Original Grange Supply House," in part to distinguish himself from other
businesses soliciting the Grange trade. Although Ward sold to everyone at
the same price, he encouraged local Grange chapters to pool their orders in
order to save on freight expenses. He shipped to individuals by express on a
C.O.D. basis, but any Grange order with the chapter's seal affixed went out at
less expensive freight rates with payment due in ten days. And, if the local
chapter did not yet have a seal, he encouraged them to order one from S. D.
Childs, Jr. & Co., who advertised in his catalogue. By the same token, one of
the earliest illustrations in the Ward catalogue was a woodcut of the "Regulation Grange Hat," which was sold exclusively by Montgomery Ward & Company along with other Grange regalia. Ward himself advertised regularly in
the *Prairie Farmer*, an agrarian periodical with close ties to the order, and he
spoke to numerous Grange chapters in Illinois to encourage business. On
one such trip near Bloomington, Illinois, he offered Grange members an all-
expenses-paid visit to the business in Chicago if the local chapter would purchase $300 worth of orders.[20]

Ward's solicitation of the Patrons' patronage was a shrewd business move,
but it also reflected genuine sympathy for their cause and sensibilities. The
Grange actively opposed monopolies such as the railroads, and much of their
appeal was due to their promotion of cooperative purchasing and marketing
in order to eliminate other middlemen and save money for their members. To
quote from a song, "The Middle-Man," from the 1874 Granger song book,
The Trumpet of Reform:

> It is an ancient farmer-man, And he is one of three,
> He said unto the middle-man, "We have no need of thee."

This man here makes his cloth so strong, And sells it unto me;
He buys my wheat, and thus we save The slice that went to thee.[21]

In his 1874 catalogue, Ward agreed with these sentiments and echoed what he termed the "Grand Grange principle": "Do away with the middlemen as far as possible." Instead, he wrote, "We propose to occupy the 'middle' and both *sides* ourselves so far as we can." He expanded on this affinity for the Grange ethos the next year as he summarized his accomplishments to date:

> We are the Original Wholesale Grange Supply House, the Pioneers in the trade. When we introduced our system, in 1872, we were looked upon with scorn by the monopolists and suspicion by the Patrons themselves. In the short period of three years we have saved the consumers directly over *one million dollars*, and indirectly, millions, by breaking up monopolies and forcing dealers to sell their goods at fair prices. This herculean task has been accomplished through the *power* of the Grange organization.[22]

In addition to his advocacy of Grange principles, Ward took great pains to assure his customers of his honesty and trustworthiness and to differentiate himself from less scrupulous operations. On November 8, 1873, the *Chicago Tribune* ran an editorial under the heading: "GRANGERS, BEWARE! Don't Patronize 'Montgomery, Ward & Co.'—They Are Dead-Beats." Responding to Ward's circular and its "Utopian" prices, and mindful of other mail-order schemes, the newspaper warned its readers that Ward was likely to disappear after he had collected enough of their money: "If such fools would only consider how easy a thing it is to start a swindle of this kind, the dead-beats who get them up would be driven to hard work, or still better, perhaps, starvation." After an investigation, prompted most probably by Ward's complaints, the *Tribune* printed a retraction on December 24 and noted that the previous article was "grossly unjust": "The firm of Montgomery, Ward & Co. is a bona fide firm, composed of respectable persons, and doing a perfectly legitimate business in a perfectly legitimate manner." To emphasize the point, Ward reprinted the full text of this article in subsequent catalogues.[23]

The *Prairie Farmer* also distinguished between Ward and others who went after the Grange's business in a November 1, 1873, column. "Scarcely a day passes," noted the editor, "that this office is not the recipient of requests for a list of the Granges and Clubs in the Northwest. These applications are by individuals who desire to send letters, circulars, pamphlets and the like, and we presume that the offices of the different secretaries are full of all manner of printed schemes, whereby members may save money, or make money, without limit." Called upon by its readers to evaluate the merits of these different proposals, the paper offered opinions of two Chicago firms "that are the subject of a large number of inquiries." It advised readers to "give a wide berth" to Geo. B. Hodge & Co., a firm name believed to be bogus, and a business scheme that, if not "an absolute swindle," was conducted by "men below par in business circles." In contrast, the paper spoke of Montgomery Ward & Co. in "better terms": "We find them young men of considerable business tact, and bearing a reputation for honesty and promptness."[24]

Although Montgomery Ward solicited the Grange trade, he was, in 1873, also something of a competitor with the order's own efforts to promote cooperative purchasing agencies and stores. Consequently, the editorial in the *Prairie Farmer* shied away from a complete and wholehearted recommendation of Ward's firm and urged Patrons to buy from Grange agencies instead. Indeed, according to Solon Buck, the appeal of these Grange cooperatives was one of the biggest factors in the order's rapid growth during the first part of the decade.[25]

Grange cooperatives in the early 1870s were promising alternatives to more traditional ways of doing business. Typically, local chapters pooled orders, particularly for farm machinery and agricultural supplies, and these were handled by state purchasing agents who were paid a salary or a small commission of 2 to 5 percent. These efforts saved money at first, especially on big-ticket items. In Wisconsin, for example, wagons that usually sold for $110 were purchased by Grangers for $74, and $700 threshing machines cost only $560. Local Grange cooperative stores, which developed out of the purchasing agent system, also enjoyed initial successes because they could locate in communities where merchants charged excessively high prices.[26]

As these efforts evolved, however, their disadvantages became more apparent. Grange businesses lost much of their initial edge when local competitors began to lower their prices, and they sometimes engaged in price wars from which they did not recover. Attempts to branch out into other products failed as well because the margin of savings for groceries and general supplies was much smaller than that for agricultural implements and clothing. Leading manufacturers also refused to do business with the upstart Grange agencies and stores, forcing the Patrons to deal with less established firms, which either produced inferior goods or went out of business and discontinued their lines. In Iowa, for example, the Grange went bankrupt because of the poor quality of the harvesters it manufactured and sold. In addition to the Panic of 1873, Grange cooperatives were hindered by incidents of corruption and incompetence as well as a lack of business knowledge and careful planning. The Hillsboro, Ohio, local supply house, for example, was managed by a man who had failed at his own business. According to one reminiscence, "It used to be the practice in starting stores, to look around and find some man who had no business and get him to run the Grange business. The man who has no business of his own, has no business running other people's business." In the face of such problems, midwestern Grange business operations and Grange membership more generally declined rapidly after 1875.[27]

While these efforts to establish cooperative purchasing foundered, Montgomery Ward provided an alternative that was palatable to both manufacturers and agrarian consumers. As a businessman, Ward was less threatening to manufacturers and easier to deal with than official Grange operations. Indeed, village merchants may have actually preferred him initially as a less radical alternative to more direct flesh-and-blood competition from local Grange stores. From the farmer's perspective, Ward was reliable, and he identified explicitly with the Grange. Local and state Grange agents had been patronizing him since he started in 1872, and Grange publications regularly recommended his as a firm eager to do business with the order. Although not an official Grange agency, Ward offered farmers low prices, greater convenience, and enough of an attachment to agrarian ideals to satisfy their principles while saving them money.

Besides stressing his connections with and affinity for the Grange, Montgomery Ward tried to win over rural consumers who were suspicious or chastened by less salutary encounters with other mail-order businesses. In contrast to the others, Ward did not sell pinchbeck; according to the first price list: "All of the above which are marked as gold you will find as represented. The others are equal to solid gold and will wear for years." Buying from him was a comparatively risk-free proposition. Patrons were encouraged to examine their orders before paying for them, they were free to refuse the shipment if they were less than satisfied, and all errors were corrected promptly if reported within ten days of receiving the order. When certain spoons and

forks proved to be "a very cheap and unserviceable item," the Ward's catalogue ran an apology, switched to a more celebrated brand name of silver-
plated goods, and vowed to "discontinue the quotation of any article that we
do not know to be serviceable." Montgomery Ward stressed his differences
from other mail-order operators as well when he noted repeatedly that he did
not use agents or offer premiums to those who drummed up orders.[28]

Ward also appealed to the farmers' trust by pointing out his firm's familiar-
ity with rural conditions:

> One of the firm was brought up on a farm, and when of age went into a
> country store and served there in different capacities for fifteen years. The
> other served twelve years in a country store, and ten years as buyer for
> some of the largest wholesale houses in Chicago and St. Louis. We think
> our experience has been sufficient to enable us to know our business. We
> seem to offer much for little, and those who do not know us may doubt
> our ability to fulfill our obligations. To such we simply say, Look at our ref-
> erences, in back part of Catalogue.[29]

By 1875, Ward's integrity and commercial standing were well established,
and the references he referred to included the First National Bank of Chicago; Dudley W. Adams, master of the National Grange; Oliver H. Kelley,
the national secretary; and the state Grange secretaries and/or business
agents from Pennsylvania, Ohio, Indiana, Illinois, Michigan, Wisconsin, Iowa,
Minnesota, Kansas, Nebraska, Missouri, Colorado, and Oregon.[30] Even
more telling are a series of letters from local Grange secretaries and purchasing agents, which Ward reprinted as testimonials. The June 1874 note from
H. H. Velie, secretary of the Grove Lake, Minnesota, Grange, is typical: "The
goods are distributed and gave good satisfaction in quality. We will order
again soon." When Ward asked for permission to reprint that letter, Velie
responded: "I cheerfully grant your request for the privilege of publishing
my letter of June 24 or any other one speaking in praise of your goods and
your straight-forward business-like manner of dealing. We feel more highly
pleased with your goods and system of selling them than we have expressed
in any letter." According to another note from an equally satisfied Grange
secretary in Russell, Iowa, Ward sent the wrong size collars, which the writer
then sold for 25 cents per box. As if to underscore his own honesty, though,
Ward noted parenthetically, "We charged Mr. Morrison 15 cents per box; the

same collar will be found in this catalogue, No. 873."[31] To quote one historian, "At once, rural Americans came to feel that the catalogue man, Aaron Montgomery Ward, was on their side. . . . He understood perfectly the mental processes of the disenchanted folk on the outlying farms; and the goods they needed, too."[32]

As the previous statement indicates, rural consumers may have felt comfortable dealing with Montgomery Ward because of his trustworthiness and his understanding of and sympathy with agrarian values, but they also wanted the merchandise that he had to sell at the prices that he offered. At the start, A. Montgomery Ward carried a relatively simple line and based his appeal not on fashion or novelty but on price and quality. As he noted in his first price list in 1872: "You can readily see at a glance the difference between our Prices and what you have to pay your Retailer for the same quality of goods." The 163 items listed were mostly yard goods for one dollar: "12 yards best quality Prints," "5 yards Kentucky Jeans," "9 yards Spanish Dress Linen," and so on. By January 1874, Ward's circular listed 456 items, again primarily fabrics and inexpensive articles of clothing; the fanciest and costliest items were a silver hunting-case watch for $15 and a "genuine extra quality" mink muff and collar set for $18. According to the local Grange officials who wrote in, the cost of merchandise from Montgomery Ward represented a savings of one-third to one-half over their local merchants.[33]

As his business expanded, so did the catalogue; by 1876 it was a small bound booklet ($3\frac{1}{2}'' \times 7''$) running more than one hundred pages. In contrast to the price lists from state Grange purchasing agents, however, Montgomery Ward offered very little in the way of farm machinery or supplies. Instead, his merchandise targeted domestic life and the female consumer. Yard goods, clothing, and dressmaking items continued to predominate, but he now offered a wider variety of goods, including trunks and valises, kitchenware, and games and musical instruments. Ward's also began to sell more fancy goods and brand-name items such as Rogers and Bros. silver-plated flatware, shelf clocks from Seth Thomas and other companies, and watches for men and women from the Elgin and Waltham companies, with the solid gold 18 "K" Lady Elgin for $60, one of the most expensive items in the catalogue. In 1878, Montgomery Ward & Co. surpassed $400,000 in sales, more than any of the state Grange purchasing agencies at their peak.[34]

The sewing machine was the most popular single piece of merchandise that Ward sold—his big-ticket item—and it embodied the two divergent aspects of his appeal. In one sense, it reflected and reinforced agrarian values and a producers' ethic, but, in other ways, it enabled and epitomized the growing lure of new consumer goods and fashions, which eclipsed that older mentality. Ward sold sewing machines for much less than the dealers: "We offer you the same machines as sold by the Sewing Machine Companies at one-third to one-half less rates." In 1876, he sold, among others, $75 Singer or Howe machines for $52.50, an $80 Whitney for $40, and a $75 Weed machine for $37.50, $7.50 less than the Wisconsin State Grange Purchasing Agent charged for the same model.[35]

By underselling retail sewing machine dealers, Ward struck still another blow for the antimiddleman cause of the farmers, but he also connected with their antimonopolist ideology more directly by opposing the sewing machine patent pool. In 1856, a group of sewing machine manufacturers, including Elias Howe and Isaac Singer, pooled their patents in order to grant licenses and protect against infringers, and began controlling prices and collecting substantial royalties on every legitimate sewing machine manufactured in the country.[36] When Congress extended those patent rights in 1872, the Grange and the *Prairie Farmer* expressed outrage and demanded the defeat of the representatives who had voted for the measure. Isaac M. Singer was a particular target of the agrarian press, which regularly criticized his immense wealth and the "vulgar magnificence" of his lifestyle as exemplified by his castles in Europe, his divorces, his illegitimate children, and the squabbles over his will in 1875.[37] As the patents were finally due to expire in the late 1870s, the *Prairie Farmer* anticipated the event with glee: "We most heartily rejoice in this fact, and we know that every poor family and single sewing-girl will also be glad at the prospect of a release from this most oppressive burden. When a sewing machine costs but $20 or $25 there is no reason nor justice in charging $65 and $85 for them. And yet this is precisely what these great, soulless, grinding sewing machine corporations have been doing for many years."[38]

Sewing machine prices tumbled with the expiration of critical patents, and the Singer and Howe models that Montgomery Ward sold for $52.50 in 1876 cost $30 and $28 in 1880. Ward also marketed a knockoff of the Singer machine, the New York Singer, for $10 less. He was, however, still forbidden by the big companies to sell in communities where they had an agent, and this prompted him to continue his opposition to their power and to stop listing their products: "It has been the policy of most sewing machine manufacturers to sell their machines through local agents only, thus *forcing* purchasers to pay the retail prices. We have worked against this monopoly for years, and have furnished thousands of machines to our customers, at from 25 to 50 per cent. less than the retail price. We now, however, desire our customers to patronize the companies who are willing to sell their machines to any person, at any time, in any place."[39] Similarly, Ward was forced to defend the quality of his merchandise as well as his honesty against rumors circulated by his competitors that his machines were so cheap because they were secondhand. "The facts are, *we never have* sold a second hand machine," Ward retorted, "There are cheaper machines in the market, but we refuse to quote them."[40] This forthrightness and his, admittedly self-professed, unwillingness to make money selling shoddy goods offered welcomed assurances to rural consumers in a marketplace where sewing machine swindles were only slightly less common than cheats on watches and jewelry.

While Ward's marketing of sewing machines reinforced his image as an honest merchant in sympathy with agrarian sensibilities, the machines themselves facilitated the spread of new fashions and consumer culture in the countryside, which challenged those values. In contrast to men's clothing, which had been dominated by ready-to-wear goods since the standardization of sizes and the conversion of uniform manufactures after the Civil War, women's dresses continued to be made by local dressmakers who tried their best to reproduce the styles presented in *Godey's* and other women's magazines. Dressmaking was transformed during the 1870s, however, by Ebenezer Butterick and the development of the paper dress pattern industry in New York City, which greatly expanded the range of fashions available and allowed any woman with skill and a sewing machine to recreate them. Rural women and men continued to rely on local dressmakers and tailors for their very best attire, but the availability of ready-made clothing through mail order or patterns for garments that could be made at home offered them much more variety for less money.[41]

The increasing importance of fashion and style in the home is even more apparent in the burgeoning Montgomery Ward catalogues of the 1880s. Beginning at the end of the 1870s, Ward's switched to a larger format with more illustrations, which featured a greater assortment of the catalogue's usual

offerings of clothing and housewares, as well as more ornamental items—
twenty-three pages of pictures of jewelry or thirteen pages depicting fancy
silver-plated table casters and matching goblets, sugar bowls, napkin rings,
and the like. The range and decorousness of these domestic amenities grew
throughout the 1880s, and in 1889, Montgomery Ward sold almost $2 million
worth of goods from a catalogue that was over five hundred pages long and
listed everything a farm family could need or want except for groceries,
which were available from a separate special price list. The vast majority of
items continued to cater to women's tastes and their control of the domestic
sphere, but the catalogue also reached out to male consumers with twelve different styles of suits and over fifty pages of tools and hardware, as well as additional sections devoted to agricultural implements, smokers' pipes, guns
and pistols, and hunting, fishing, and sporting goods. Children, one assumes,
were content with the twelve pages of toys.[42]

Although the front cover of the 1889 catalogue still proclaimed Montgomery Ward & Co. as "The Original Grange Supply House," that document
stood in marked contrast to the comparatively humble and unadorned price
lists of the early 1870s. Rather than the sturdy agrarianism of the Grange, the
later catalogue reflected a more embellished middle-class domestic culture
and the ability of the farm family—rural men as well as women—to emulate
it. While the lures of consumer goods may have displaced appeals to more
traditional values, those earlier connections were critical factors in the business's success. Montgomery Ward's honesty and his support for the Grange's
ideals were of a piece with the sensibilities of his rural customers, and this allowed them to partake of an emerging consumer economy in a manner that
was comfortable and straightforward, even though it later led them in other
directions. In their negotiations between the producers' ethic of their past
and the consumer culture of their future, he was their middleman.

———

Rural integration into an expanding consumer economy increased greatly
at the turn of the century and was facilitated by the rise of numerous imitators and competitors of Montgomery Ward, particularly Sears, Roebuck, and
Company, which quickly surpassed the older firm both in terms of sales and
salesmanship.[43] In contrast to Montgomery Ward, Richard Sears did not em-
body or appeal explicitly to agrarian sentiments. He started in 1886 by selling

mail-order watches as a sideline to his job as a railroad freight agent in Minnesota; after he teamed up with watchmaker A. C. Roebuck, the two began business as Sears, Roebuck and Company in Chicago in 1893. In general, Sears was more of a huckster than Ward and was known, significantly, as the "Barnum of merchandising." He sold goods that were less expensive and not as high quality, and he did so in a flashier manner. While Ward's declared itself the "Cheapest Supply House in America," for example, Sears, Roebuck claimed the title of "Cheapest Supply House on Earth." At the end of the century, however, in large part because of Ward's success, rural consumers were more comfortable with mail order and less wary of such tactics than they had been in 1872. Consequently, Sears, Roebuck seized the initiative from Montgomery Ward and, in 1900, surpassed them in sales for the first time by a margin of $10 million to $8.7 million.[44]

Local merchants, however, were threatened by the new scale of mail-order buying, and, in contrast to their relatively mild reactions to Montgomery Ward in the 1870s and 1880s, they waged a dramatic and comprehensive campaign of opposition, which stressed loyalty to the local community. Although this most obviously and directly reflected their economic self-interests, it was also part of a broader array of concerns about the declining vitality and viability of rural and small-town life and the increasing centralization of American society. In order to promote localism and meet mail-order competition, however, merchants paradoxically relied on new translocal organizations as well as national advertising and brand names, further integrating the countryside into a new consumer society and further diminishing the primacy of their towns. Farmers shared some of these worries and rejected others as they, too, came to terms with their increasing integration into a national consumer economy. As a result, attitudes toward mail-order buying during the first decades of the twentieth century became a referendum on the place of the local community in the rural North as well as the larger society.

Just as cautionary stories earlier in the century served to undermine trust in peddlers by emphasizing their "outsider" status, opponents of mail-order houses generated a new but similar folklore in the form of negative rumors about the owners of the biggest companies as well as the quality of their merchandise. False stories that Montgomery Ward, his partner George R. Thorne, Richard Sears, or A. C. Roebuck were African Americans began to spread as early as 1897, most probably circulated by local merchants and traveling salesmen, and proved especially troublesome in the South. The fact that Sears's successor, Julius Rosenwald, was a Jew and an active supporter of black education also did not sit well with southern (or other) whites. As a result, Montgomery Ward ran an advertisement in 1898 under the heading, "An Infamous Lie," offering $100 for the name of the person who started the rumor that he was a mulatto. Both catalogues also featured prominent photos of their founders as proof of their racial "correctness," leading one Ward's customer to write and express pleasure at doing business with "such fine looking men." Significantly, rural black customers may have actually preferred to buy from mail-order houses, which, in contrast to the local merchants, were color-blind and treated them the same as other customers.[45]

In a different vein, the rumor mill charged that mail-order merchandise was shoddy, secretly made by convict labor, or always arrived late and broken. The numerous puns and stories featuring "Shears and Rawbuck" or "Rears and Sawbuck," "Monkey Ward," "Deuteronomy, Fraud & Co.," and others were also attempts to undermine the credibility of the mail-order business. According to one popular joke, "Rears and Soreback" offered a watch that was not only half the price but ran twice as fast as any you could get in town. In at least one case, however, the joking backfired when "Monkey Ward" became an expression of endearment rather than opprobrium for rural customers.[46]

Most of the opposition to mail-order buying took place within the more specific context of the local community. According to one Indiana farm periodical, known mail-order customers were shunned on the streets and in local stores, and "the poor fellows can not bear the pressure." Similarly, "the dealers are always on the lookout for the man who has goods shipped direct and every firm in town that he has been doing a credit business with simultaneously send him urgent duns."[47] Both Ward's and Sears recognized this potential for embarrassment, ostracism, and retribution, and assured their customers of strict confidentiality. All goods were shipped in plain wrapping without the name or address of the sender, and the merchandise itself had no tags or marks that could identify its source. This protected mail-order customers from the ire of local merchants, but it also allowed those same local merchants to order and resell mail-order merchandise, and their ability to make a profit doing so was touted in the mail-order catalogues. According to the 1903 Sears catalogue: "If you are a merchant and wish to buy goods to sell again, your customers will be unable to learn from any marks inside or outside where you bought the goods or what you paid for them. . . . While we would be glad to have our name appear on every item of merchandise and on every box and package, as a valuable means of advertising, we have learned that thousands of our customers need the protection that the omitting of our name affords. This applies especially to townspeople."[48]

The most vocal and active campaigns against mail-order buying were waged by small-town newspapers. In June 1905, for example, William A. White, the famous editor of the Emporia, Kansas, *Gazette*, wrote a series of early but typical editorials with titles such as "Mail Order Leeches," "The Dry Rot," and "Stand By Your Home," and sounded themes that would soon become quite familiar. The "mail order disease," as White labeled it, was responsible for Emporia's social and economic decline and its loss of population by draining money out of the community. "A dollar saved in Chicago," he wrote, "is lost to Emporia. . . . the mail order dollar bids good-bye to the town and its prosperity at the city limits and never comes back." In contrast to local businesses, the mail-order houses "pay no taxes here to help run the county expenses and educate your children." White also equated mail-order buying with a shirking of citizenship in nativist and racist terms: "The man who buys his goods of a mail order house, and expects his neighbors in Emporia to buy goods of him, or to buy labor of him or to buy professional service of him is economically a leech. He is sucking industrial blood out of the town and gives none back. He sends his profits out of town like a Chinaman, and has no more right to a standing in the community than a foreigner." His ultimate provocation came, however, when the local policeman started wearing a mail-order uniform: "If the editor of this paper were mayor—which Heaven forbid—Al Randolph would be fired on the spot."[49]

On the one hand, White's sentiments and those of the many other small-town editors who echoed him reflect a sincere commitment to the welfare of their communities in the tradition of local boosterism. On the other hand, however, they cannot be divorced from their own self-interests. Small-town newspapers depended on local merchants for advertising revenues and typically refused to run rival mail-order advertising as a matter of policy. Indeed, according to less sympathetic contemporary observers, country publishers may have exaggerated the whole issue of mail-order buying to frighten local

Early anti-mail-order cartoon from a small-town newspaper,
Glencoe Enterprise, *Glencoe, Minnesota, 1905.*

merchants into purchasing more advertising to compete successfully. In the words of one farm editor: "The country publishers are working from a selfish standpoint. They really do not care if people buy away from home. This gives them something with which to scare the local dealer into buying advertising space."[50]

Agrarian publications offered a somewhat different perspective on mail-order buying, in part, no doubt, because they received their advertising from mail-order companies, not local merchants. Between 1905 and 1908, however, an Indiana farm journal, the *Farmer's Guide*, ran a series of letters from its readers, unfortunately all from men, which discuss their experiences with and attitudes toward mail-order buying, and these illustrate a range of viewpoints. Of the letters that expressed a clear opinion, almost twenty favored buying by mail order, while eight expressed support for buying at home, although at least one of these was written by a local merchant.

In their letters, the advocates of home buying did not downgrade mail-order businesses so much as they stressed the positive aspects of local patronage. They noted a strong preference for seeing what they bought, and those who purchased farm machinery from a nearby dealer emphasized the importance of being able to have it repaired speedily, especially during critical phases of agricultural production. Most of all, however, they echoed their small-town editors and underscored the mutuality of interests between farmers and merchants: local merchants provide a convenient market for the farmer's produce, and a thriving town causes farm property values to increase.[51]

Conversely, mail-order supporters expressed a high degree of satisfaction with the catalogue houses: items were good quality and as represented in the catalogue, they arrived quickly, any errors were rectified in a timely fashion, and the prices were significantly lower than those charged by local merchants. According to Nelson J. Shultz of Steuben County, Indiana, who purchased "a great many articles by mail," including groceries, clothing, hardware, and furniture such as a bookcase, a writing desk, a chiffonier, a stove, and a kitchen cabinet (but not, presumably, the kitchen sink): "I would rather deal with a good reliable mail order house than with many of the home merchants as I have found their goods to be nearer the quality represented." This sentiment was reiterated by C.B.C., who contrasted the prompt delivery of the catalogue company with the more lackadaisical approach of the home merchant special ordering something not commonly used: "He will say, 'just wait, I'll get it for you.' Then you see him in a week or so and he will say, 'Oh, I forgot that; I'll send tonight; just wait.' See him again and it is waylaid or the factory is crowded with orders and you get the article after it is out of season and you have no use for it. Great satisfaction."[52]

Mail-order advocates reserved their choicest remarks for responses to local merchants' appeals to home loyalty. J. A. Miller, a farmer from Marshall

County, Indiana, originally supported home buying and "took strong ground against sending our money away from home for supplies for any reason." Within a few years, however, he changed his mind:

> But when I go to town and find the stores lined up to completion with Michigan potatoes, Manitoba flour, Swift's breakfast bacon and hams, and then go to the butcher shop and find my steak cut from the carcass of one of Armour's dressed beeves, I am inclined to think that it is time for all this sentimental "home love" to cool off a little. Two years ago I had about twenty bushels of fine pears and tried in every store to sell at some price and failed, but in a few days one of the dealers had about forty bushels ordered from Michigan that were not as good and at a higher price.

"This talk of home market," he went on, "sounds big on water, but it is political humbug with a big 'hum.'" [53]

F. S. Girard from Carroll County, Indiana, made a similar point when he questioned whether the home merchant bought all that he could from local farmers or even from canning factories in other Indiana towns. Ultimately, he supported a free market and did not blame the merchant for buying goods wherever it suited him to do so. But, he noted, "the right that we willingly grant to him we also claim for ourselves. When we send off for goods we are doing no more injury to the home town, dollar for dollar, than the merchant does to the farming community when he sends away for anything that he could buy of a farmer." Arthur A. Robey of Blackford County simply rejected appeals to forgo mail-order savings and buy locally in order to "build up" the home towns. Instead, he suggested, "let us patronize the mail order houses and save the 25 per cent on our orders and donate it in Carnegie style." [54]

At one level, these farmers' criticisms reflect their own resentments at having to compete against nonlocal agricultural producers and corporate processors and distributors of farm products and thus parallel the merchants' complaints against the mail-order houses. At another level, farmers and local merchants, in spite of their different interests, shared a common suspicion of distant institutions and forces that shaped their lives from afar. For some farmers this ambivalence even extended to the mail-order houses themselves, which were, by the early twentieth century, big, large-scale businesses. One farmer couched his opposition to their growth in terms that ironically evoke the Grange's earlier affinity for Montgomery Ward: "Surely a system of this kind would tend to build up large and powerful concerns and call them what you may, 'trusts,' 'combines,' 'corporations' or 'monopolies,' we have all seen that these are not in the interest of the individual citizen, either producer or consumer." Another farmer who bought from the catalogue houses but would have preferred to buy locally if prices were lower, articulated this dilemma: "I am opposed to supporting a monopoly and yet I will do so if it is very much to my personal interest."[55]

A common resolution, suggested by both supporters and opponents of mail-order buying, was for the local merchant to change his ways, not only to buy local produce, but to meet mail-order competition in terms of prices. According to the conflicted correspondent in the previous paragraph, "the average farmer would much rather buy at home than send away if he could get what he wants for somewhere near the same money, but the retail dealer cannot bulldoze us into paying them from 50 to 200 per cent profit on everything we eat, wear or use." O. V. Lehman of Whitley County, for example, thought that "the mail order house is doing us a great service if we get nothing more than their quotation of prices." Although he had catalogues from the largest houses, he noted with pleasure that he had not sent in an order for two years because his local merchants adjusted their prices to keep his business. "We do not wish to whip the dealer into submission," he concluded, "but wish him to humble himself to twentieth century business methods."[56]

Local retailers did adopt "twentieth-century business methods" in response to mail-order competition, but not, at first, in the humbled ways anticipated by the optimistic correspondents to the *Farmer's Guide*. Instead, small-town merchants fought the catalogue houses by forming cartels and trade associations in order to undermine their competitors and lobby for their legislative interests. As early as 1905, the *Farmer's Guide* reported on a furniture dealers' convention in Indianapolis where members were bound by resolutions not to buy from any manufacturer who also sold to the mail-order houses and not to advertise in any magazine that carried advertisements that "put the manufacturer in direct communication with the consumer." One manufacturer was even forced to relinquish a contract with a catalogue house that was worth $3,000 a month in order to maintain his clientele. Six months later, the Indiana Retail Merchants' Association issued a call for a convention in Fort Wayne in order to "wage a vigorous warfare for self-protection" against the mail-order houses; by the summer of 1907, such efforts were widespread. According to the *Farmer's Guide*: "The wholesale and retail dealers throughout the country are doing everything possible to kill the mail order concerns. . . . The dealers are organized and are working together to accomplish their plans. First, there is a national organization, then a state organization and finally each county is organized. The scheme includes every line of business, for all lines are affected by the catalogue or mail order houses."[57]

The retailers waged a particularly nasty campaign of "dirty tricks" against the Gordon–Van Tine Company of Davenport, Iowa, which sold building materials and prefabricated house kits directly to the consumer. According to both the *Farmers' Guide* and *Wallace's Farmer*, in which the company advertised, lumber dealers received an anonymous "little black book" filled with suggestions for harassing Gordon–Van Tine, "compiled from ideas offered at various conventions." Merchants were urged to send for at least two catalogues per week, in their own names as well as the names of their partners and employees and all possible family members. They should also send in weekly lists of materials and requests for estimates, requests for samples and paint color cards, and letters that must be answered, especially those requiring a specially written reply as opposed to one already printed. "By using care," the book notes, "each name will answer for five communications." Finally, dealers were encouraged to "make a practice of visiting the depots each day to see if any shipments arrive from catalogue houses, being particular to note the party's name and the kind of goods received."[58]

Opposition to mail-order buying reached a new level of organization and intensity as Congress considered the establishment of parcel post, which would permit the post office to ship parcels of up to twelve pounds at low rates. Although parcel post had been recommended as early as 1880, it was not enacted until August 24, 1912, due to opposition by the railway express companies. John Wanamaker, the department store magnate who crusaded for parcel post as Harrison's Postmaster General, noted in 1891: "there are four reasons against the establishment of parcels post: the American Express Company, the Adams Express Company, the United States Express Com-

pany, and the Wells Fargo Express Company." Indeed, the big express companies constituted a very powerful oligopoly: six of them controlled 90 percent of all express business before World War I, and the industry went un-
regulated until 1906. Two of the period's most powerful senators, in fact,
Thomas C. Platt and Chauncey M. Depew, both of New York, were the president of the United States Express Co. and one of the largest stockholders in
the American Express Co., respectively, and they kept any parcel post legislation from even being introduced in either house. By 1910, however, the defeat of the conservatives and the election of progressives as well as the support of Presidents Roosevelt and Taft led to a series of bills and hearings that
stimulated public discussion and awareness of the issue.[59]

The newly formed American League of Associations led the opposition to
parcel post. Based in Chicago and secretly funded by the express companies
even though they were not listed as official members, the league consisted of
associations and businesses that would be hurt by parcel post and the consequent expansion of mail-order trade, including the National Federal Retail
Implement and Vehicle Dealers' Association, American Hardware Manufacturer's Association, Illinois Retail Merchants Association, National Association of Retail Druggists, National Association of Retail Grocers, National
Retail Hardware Association, Wholesale Dry Goods Association, Paint Manufacturers Association of the United States, Marshall Field and Co., and Butler Brothers Store, which was a wholesale, as opposed to a retail, mail-order
house that supplied small-town merchants.[60]

Significantly, the biggest potential beneficiaries of parcel post, the retail
mail-order firms, Ward's and Sears, kept low profiles during the debate and
insisted publicly that since most of their shipments were large and went by
express, the new system would have little impact on their operations. Instead,
farmers' organizations such as the Grange, the Farmers' National Congress,
and the Farmers' Union were the most vocal advocates of the new legislation.
Farmers did not support parcel post as a way to facilitate mail-order buying
and undermine the local merchant, however, but saw it as an extension of
rural free delivery, which would allow them to bypass other middlemen and
ship their produce directly to urban consumers. Even more important, parcel
post would free them from the monopolistic practices of the express companies, whose excessive profits, arbitrary pricing, high-handed treatment, and

indifferent service had long been sources of irritation and complaint in the agrarian press.[61]

Ironically, the opponents of parcel post turned this antimonopoly sentiment on its head when they raised the specter of a huge "mail-order trust" that would be fostered by the new legislation. Almost all the arguments against parcel post, including this one, were variations on the older theme of the need to preserve and protect the local merchant and the local community, but the invocation of a mail-order trust resonated with particular concerns about the increasing centralization of American society and the power of large-scale organizations. George H. Maxwell, who represented the jobbers' interests before Congress, began his affidavit: "The centralization of trade in the great cities of the country resulting from the growth of the mail-order business is a national menace of far-reaching proportion." Maxwell then went on to lament the replacement of the small-town merchant, characterized by "self-reliance" and "sturdy individuality," by urban employees who were "mere machines, fitting like cogs into one great wheel with which they must day after day revolve."[62]

Whereas a defense of small-town independence coming from a national lobbying organization may seem somewhat incongruous, the contradictions of the merchants' opposition became even more apparent between 1908 and 1917 as local campaigns against the mail-order houses intensified. Small-town editors continued to exhort local readers to buy at home and sounded familiar and similar themes. Many of the editorials were, in fact, actually the same, for in contrast to the initial writing against mail-order buying epitomized by William A. White, it was not unusual for later columns to be syndicated or boilerplate productions from a central office or organization. One author, Thomas J. Sullivan of Chicago, published a book in 1914 entitled *Merchants and Manufacturers on Trial*, with the lengthy subtitle: *A complete survey of the illegitimate methods employed by the Retail Catalogue House System, with suggestions of modern means for preventing its further practice and growth. A logical and sane defence of local communities, local Retail Merchants and the Middlemen.* In fact, the seventy-eight chapters of the book were so many editorials ready for reprinting in local newspapers, complete with headlines and subheads, with titles such as "The Farmers' Market His Local Town," "They Deceive with Pictures," "Mail Order Buying an Unfair Practice," and "A Woman's Sorry Experience."[63]

Along with newspaper editorials, local merchants relied on editorial cartoons to get their message across. A 1909 cartoon in the *Lismore Leader* from Nobles County, Minnesota, for example, has the caption, "On Which Side Are You Sawing?" and depicts a farmer sawing off the same branch of a tree that he is sitting on. The branch is labeled "Local Institutions & Industries"; on the saw is written "Mail Order Patronage"; and his seeming fate below is the "Excessive Tax Mud Hole."[64] While most early anti-mail-order cartoons were probably local products of varying degrees of artistry, they, too, began to be produced professionally and distributed from the big cities. By 1916, newspapers throughout the upper Midwest and West began running a series of anti-mail-order cartoons featuring Buster Brown and his dog, Tige, drawn by the creator of the famous character and one of the originators of newspaper comics, R. F. Outcault. Buster Brown was already familiar to rural readers because of the popularity of the comic strip, one of the most influential examples of that genre, so, again, the use of a paragon of national mass popular culture as an icon of localism poses a paradox. But the choice of Buster Brown was not random, because he was also known in small towns as a brand of shoes, which were advertised regularly in local newspapers and sold only by local retailers and not available by mail order.[65]

In one of the cartoons, Buster is igniting a mail-order catalogue with a match, saying, "I'll just burn this thing up," a not-too-subtle reference to a particularly dramatic phase of the merchants' campaign. Anti-mail-order efforts reached a nadir of sorts when local papers and merchants offered rewards to residents who turned in their mail-order catalogues and then staged a public burning of them in the town square. Members of the Cedar Falls, Iowa, Commercial Club, for example, paraded through town in 1912 on the way to their bonfire, accompanied by a marching band and holding banners that announced "Cedar Falls makes good" and "We thought we were buying cheaper, but we know better now." In other cases, every child who brought in a catalogue got free admission to the motion pictures in town. One woman in Kansas hoped to win $50 for collecting the greatest number of catalogues and collected three hundred after assuring her neighbors that the catalogues would be returned after the contest. When they were burned instead (and she failed to win any prizes), she wrote to Ward's and asked them to please send her three hundred books at her expense so that she could honor her promise to return them.[66]

Anti-mail-order cartoon featuring Buster Brown, Glencoe Enterprise, *Glencoe, Minnesota (date unknown).*

Anti-mail-order cartoons featuring Buster Brown, 1916, from Frank B. Latham,
1872–1972, A Century of Serving Consumers: The Story of Montgomery
Ward *(Chicago: Montgomery Ward & Co., 1972), p. 41. (Reprinted with*
permission from Montgomery Ward)

The most comprehensive and vivid account of catalogue burnings is a 1933 short story, "The Catalogues," by George Milburn. Although it is a work of fiction set a decade or so after the wave of public burnings, "The Catalogues" amplifies the earlier historical record. The main character, R. W. E. "Swede" Ledbetter, editor of the Conchartee County *Democrat*, publishes a classic buy-at-home editorial, the full text of which is part of the story, and urges the local Lions Club to mount an anti-mail-order campaign, which he will promote in his paper, and offer a dollar in trade for each catalogue collected, to be burned at a "big Home Town Industry Jubilee." The day of the "Jubilee" is something of a small-town carnival, with music from the local band, sack and potato races, and hundreds of area farmers and their families milling about town. By evening, the crowd thinned and consisted primarily of townspeople, and only the "bustling Lions" mustered much enthusiasm for the actual burning of the catalogues. The story ends the next day in the post office, where there is a run on postal cards and a rush of mail canceled in time for the 5:45, all addressed to the mail-order houses requesting another copy of the fall-winter catalogue. As one of the cards put it: "we want to order some things from you and our other catalogue was made away with."[67]

As Milburn's story indicates, these displays of small-town loyalty, however theatrical, were also exercises in futility. Local "patriots" typically redeemed old editions of the catalogue, or they sent in requests for new catalogues on the day after the bonfire. More important, the parcel post system that began on January 1, 1913, was an immediate success at the rate of 250 million to 300 million packages per year and a great boon to the mail-order business. In the system's first year, Sears, Roebuck and Company received five times the number of orders it had received in 1912, swamping the company's shipping department; by World War I, revenues had more than doubled. At the local level, the *North Loup Loyalist* reported that during October 1913 nearly three hundred parcel post packages passed through the railroad depot in Ord, Nebraska; several years later, mail carriers delivered an average of 1.8 packages per family on the four routes operating out of the village.[68]

Although local merchants continued to campaign against the mail-order houses throughout the decade, they increasingly adopted other strategies to meet mail-order competition. Most of these efforts can be summarized by the aphorism "If you can't beat 'em, join 'em," and resulted in changes in the way small-town retailers did business and related to their customers. These various strategies were delineated in textbook fashion in the 1922 publication, *Meeting Mail Order Competition*, which reiterated suggestions from numerous articles in trade journals and national magazines to advertise more, spruce up and modernize store displays, deal with customers more openly and cheerfully, and either do away with credit entirely or charge lower prices for cash customers. Small-town retailers also began to carry more brand-name merchandise and entered into exclusive cooperative arrangements with the manufacturers like Buster Brown, who, in turn, advertised nationally. This allowed local merchants to offer their customers well-known and desirable products that they were not able to get from the mail-order houses, but it also strengthened their connections to a national consumer culture that transcended and later eclipsed the local community.[69]

One local merchant urged his colleagues to build up their own businesses and quit tearing down the mail-order houses and expressed regret about earlier tactics: "Our object was to prevent the farmers and townspeople from sending their orders away, but we did nothing to show why they ought to trade with us." His solution was to reorganize his store and display and sell comparable mail-order goods right next to his regular stock. When a customer wanted an item that he did not carry, he offered to order it from the catalogues and sell it at the mail-order price, plus shipping. Increasingly, though, customers inspected his line before buying or ordering mail-order goods, and before long he realized that he was able to sell his own goods at the same price, allowing his customers to see their purchases ahead of time and save on shipping costs and delays. "After two years of careful competition," he reported, "we had about ended the sending away of mail orders from our town."[70]

Such changes were consistent with the earlier hopes of farmers who wanted to be able to trade at home, and they were applauded in the agrarian press. According to the editor of the *Farmer's Guide* in 1921:

A few years ago there was much talk among country merchants about the menace of the mail order houses. . . . We do not hear so much of this nowadays. The mail order catalogue is no longer referred to as the farmers' bible. But the change is not due to any boycotting or intimidation of the

farmers, such as was attempted in a few scattered instances. The change
was due to a return to reason on the part of the local retailers. They found
ways to adjust their own management to meet the mail order competition.
They found the farmer would rather trade at home, other things being
equal or nearly so.[71]

Although this statement reflects a common desire to preserve the local
community in the face of larger, outside forces of change, by the 1920s worries about mail-order competition were becoming increasingly anachronistic
and hopes for local autonomy increasingly difficult to fulfill. Instead, rural
northerners confronted new technologies and pressures that drew them out
of their communities and into different economic and cultural arenas to an
even greater degree. The automobile was the most obvious and direct agent
of change in this respect, and the greater mobility afforded by the car as well
as the rise of chain stores in the larger towns created new sources of competition that lessened both the appeal and the threat of mail-order buying.
Significantly, merchants fought against chain stores in the 1920s and 1930s in
ways that echoed their earlier campaigns against the catalogue houses, but
these were no more effective than they had been before. Rural northerners
also moved beyond their communities or reconfigured them in different
ways when they went to the movies or turned on their radios and, like their
urban counterparts, became more thoroughly enmeshed in a burgeoning
mass culture.

By the 1920s, northerners on the farms and in the small towns were more
thoroughly integrated into the consumer economy that was a hallmark of
twentieth-century American society, and mail-order buying had played a central role in this process. In particular, Montgomery Ward made it possible for
rural consumers to participate in ways that lessened their trepidations and
suspicions and minimized the tensions between their traditional values and
the lures of the new goods.

That participation, however, eventually led to other conflicts with their
commitment to localism and their desire to preserve the independence of
their communities. Although these concerns were first raised by small-town
merchants, their strategies for meeting mail-order competition ultimately
contradicted their dedication to the primacy of the home town. As retailers

participated in translocal organizations or relied on brand names and images promoted by national advertising and mass culture, they, too, became more thoroughly integrated into the new translocal order. Thus, rather than finding common ground and triumph under the banner of the local community, rural northerners after 1920 would have to find other ways to accommodate to the newer dimensions of consumer culture and the second great transformation in the countryside.

She looks well to the ways of her household,

and eats not the bread of idleness. . . .

Give her of the fruit of her hands;

and let her own works praise her in the gates.

— PROVERBS 31 : 27, 31

6

NOT THE BREAD OF IDLENESS

The Rural North and Consumer Culture in the 1920s

Mail-order buying during the late nineteenth and early twentieth centuries helped to integrate rural northerners into an emerging consumer *economy*, but the full flowering of a consumer *culture* in American society did not occur until the 1920s. Characterized by new goods and technologies and new modes of advertising and sales, this consumer culture represented a dramatic shift from a social ethos that emphasized individual autonomy and personal identity based on production to a culture that stressed mass consumption and defined personal satisfaction in terms of the purchase of commodities. At the same time, new forms of mass entertainment and leisure created a national popular culture that transcended older boundaries of community and added momentum to the desire to consume.

For rural northerners, who remained small producers in small communities well into the twentieth century, these cultural transformations posed a daunting array of challenges to more traditional agrarian sensibilities. As with their earlier encounters with mail-order buying, however, rural northerners interacted with the new consumer culture in ways that initially reinforced rather than diverged from those values. Cosmopolitan advertisers and university-based agricultural extension agencies were the leading promoters of a more "urban" and "modern" society based on consumption, but this is not necessarily what country people "bought" when they purchased the new goods. Rather than serving as the passive and obedient recipients of outside appeals, rural northerners tempered their participation in consumer culture with an ethos of practicality and a continued ambivalence toward what they perceived to be city ways. Rural men and rural women had different perspectives and experiences with respect to this consumer culture, however, which also widened the gap between older and younger generations in agrarian communities.[1]

What began in ways that were comfortable and consistent often entailed consequences of a different sort. Far from perpetuating an old-fashioned rural life, the negotiation of consumer culture in the northern countryside helped construct a new translocal rural society and culture, which remained distinct from and, at times, opposed to the more urban mainstream. Encapsulated in such seemingly mundane affairs as Saturday night trips to the county seats and market towns, the WLS *Barn Dance* radio show, and appeals in the *Rural New Yorker* to buy Listerine, this hybrid culture grew out of rural people's encounters with some of the major innovations of the period. In particular, the automobile, electricity and the radio, and the transformation and proliferation of brand-name advertising were some of the critical components in the development of a rural consumer culture in the northern countryside during the 1920s.

———

Although the automobile was the most common and the most costly manifestation of consumer culture in the countryside during the 1920s, farmers earlier in the century had vociferously opposed the "devil wagons" and their urban pleasure riders. Country people regularly complained that automobiles spooked horses, hit and killed livestock, stirred up dust, and forced them off their own roads, and they resented motor tourists trespassing to picnic on their property. Farmers in Ohio threatened to boycott any merchant who bought a car, and rural inhabitants near Evanston, Illinois, formed the Farmers' Anti-Automobile League to "mete out justice to reckless chauffeurs" after a local woman was injured by a speeding motorist. Many rural communities imposed unreasonable speed limits and other restrictions on cars and their drivers, and, in several instances, local residents horsewhipped or shot offending motorists. According to one scholar, farmers did not object to the new technology per se, but felt that automobiles were urban vehicles that had no place in rural society.[2]

After the development of the Model T in 1908, however, rural inhabitants embraced the new technology in record numbers. The number of automobiles on U.S. farms shot up from 85,000 in 1911 to 2,146,512 in 1920. In 1930, 58 percent of American farms had at least one car, and the 9,724,950 cars registered from farms and towns with populations under 1,000 represented about half of the total passenger car registration for that year.[3] Rural standard of living surveys from the late 1920s indicate the even greater ubiquitousness of the automobile in the northern countryside. Studies of Vermont, upstate New York, Ohio, Iowa, and Wisconsin report car ownership in 80 to 95 percent of farm families, tenants as well as owners.[4] The editor of the *Indiana Farmer's Guide* pondered this dramatic shift in 1918: "Time is a great worker of changes. Today farmers are among the largest owners of cars. Seventy percent of all the automobiles sold during the last five years have gone to farmers. . . . The automobile is no longer thought of as a menace to the rural community but as its greatest friend."[5] The farmers' adoption of the automobile did not necessarily imply an acceptance of the culture of urban consumers, however, particularly the pleasure riders whom they scorned. Instead, rural consumers had their own perspective on the automobile, which differed from that of city folk.

The individual most responsible for bringing the automobile to the countryside, for example, was not perceived as an agent of urbanity but as someone who had deep roots in an agrarian way of life. Henry Ford was the quintessential poor farm boy who made good, but unlike other self-made men from the countryside, he continued to espouse agricultural fundamentalism and express deep concern for the well-being of rural society. Ford himself stated in 1922 that "Farming is and always will be the foundation on which the economic growth of our nation depends." The agrarian press also professed great admiration for Ford, and farm journalists regularly visited his seven-thousand-acre farm in Dearborn to write articles that celebrated his simple but virtuous childhood on the farm and applauded his efforts to both preserve that rural heritage and modernize American agriculture.[6]

From the outset, the Model T was designed for and marketed to rural consumers. Early advertisements proclaimed "Ford, the Farmer's Car" and "Your Harvest is Incomplete without a Ford," and rural consumers responded to such appeals. According to a 1926 survey of 167 farmers in Pickaway County, Ohio, of the 90 percent who owned cars, over half owned Fords. Similar data gathered in upstate New York in 1929 also shows Ford as the leading make of automobile, although by this date three farmers were driving the newer Model A, which replaced the Model T in 1928.[7] After Fords, the most popular makes were the Model T's competitors, especially Chevrolet, Dodge, and Buick, which were all low- or mid-priced cars that cost less than $1,000.

Farmers who wrote to agricultural periodicals took pains to distinguish their ownership of these modest and practical vehicles from what they saw as more frivolous urban priorities. In an article in the *Indiana Farmer's Guide*, "The Auto for Business," A.V.D. pointed out that most urbanites buy cars solely for pleasure. "Here it is," he noted, referring to the city, "that the dealer sells the high-priced electrics and twin sixes, real palaces on wheels. On a recent Sunday I counted 30 machines passing a given corner in 10 minutes in a small city. There was not a single 'flivver' in the first 15, and only 4 in the whole number counted. The majority of the others cost on an average over $1,000." By contrast, he claimed, the farmer "can get the most out of his 'tin lizzie' or moderate priced four or six in a hundred ways during the week, and then load the family into the same car at any convenient time for a pleasure spin."[8] R.G.K. claimed that the use of the term "pleasure car" discouraged farmers from purchasing an automobile because "joy riding" does not appeal to a busy farmer. Instead, "a real profitable investment on a farm can be a source of pleasure but it must also be a factor in the improving of the business. . . . More farmers will wish to own automobiles when they can think of them as investments in their business."[9]

Reflecting similar priorities, in "Horse vs. Motor Car," T.F. found that when all things were considered, "We find a motor car cheaper to operate . . . than the upkeep of a horse." In the same vein, H.H.F. reported the costs and benefits derived from his $700 automobile under the title: "Young Farmer Saves $120 a Year by Use of a Car, Makes 17 Per Cent on the Purchase Price." Finally, according to one contemporary observer, automobile advertising in farm papers "indicates that the manufacturer is appealing to the farmer with the argument that the auto is to be considered a business proposition." Thus, while rural spokesmen did not deny the pleasurable benefits of automobile ownership, these took a backseat to more practical considerations. Cars were pieces of agricultural machinery used primarily to transport farm produce and supplies and enabled the farmer to travel more widely in order to get the best prices on necessary items.[10]

Although it was touted primarily as a "modern" and practical farm implement, the automobile meant different things to younger and older generations and to rural men and rural women, and not everyone in the farm family thought of it in utilitarian terms or had equal access to its benefits. Older farmers, in particular, reacted against the pleasurable uses of the automobile by their youngsters, especially on Sunday. To quote Ruth Suckow's 1924 novel, *Country People*:

> August had kept his hands on other things, but he couldn't keep the boys from using the car. . . . They went out on Sunday afternoons when they felt like it. August would go out and find the car gone again. It was no use trying to stop them. Emma thought it was dreadful for the boys to "pleasure-drive on Sunday," against which the Richland Methodist Church was making a last futile stand, as against cards and dancing; but both she and August got used to it. All the young people seemed to do it. But one thing August said: if he ever heard of his boys driving to a Sunday baseball game, they would never have the car again.[11]

The automobile was also controlled primarily by farm men. Many rural women did not learn how to drive and continued to depend on their husbands and sons to take them to town. Laura Drake of Parke County, Indiana, remembered the restrictions on her father's car in the 1920s: "Nobody touched that but him." Newlywed Eunice Houze in Ohio County was learning to drive her family's car until her father-in-law objected. "You better keep her out of there," she remembers him saying to her husband, and "I never touched that thing again."[12]

Of the 40 farm women in Jerusalem Township, Yates County, New York, who were interviewed in 1929, only 5 knew how to drive, and all of them were highly educated. The percentage of driving homemakers near Lockport, New York, was higher, however; one-third of the 81 women surveyed could operate (25) or were learning to operate (2) the family car. In both communities, though, women who did not drive depended on others. When asked when she did her shopping, one sixty-year-old wife replied, "Saturday night, whenever the men can go," while others went "when husband takes" or "whenever taken."[13]

The farm women who did drive tended to be significantly younger than those who did not, adding to the generational differences brought on by the new technology. The average age for women drivers in the New York survey was around 37, as opposed to 50 for nondrivers. Put another way, the experience of driving was a relatively common one for younger farm women: 70 percent of the homemakers near Lockport who were 45 or younger knew how to drive, but only 43 percent of those over 50 could take the wheel of the family car. This was also the case in the tight-knit and ethnically homogeneous German Lutheran community of Block, Kansas, where older farm wives did not drive, but fathers taught all of their adolescent children, girls as well as boys, how to operate the new family car. They did this, in the words of a recent historical study, not to "instill independence (which it certainly did)," but to enable daughters "to run errands to town for fathers and brothers who could continue to work in the field until the necessary items arrived." In her recent reminiscences, septuagenarian Hoosier homemaker Della Ackerman also pointed out this generational divide when she noted that her mother never did learn to drive, and that this made a major difference in their lives.[14]

Whatever its own merits as a useful farm implement or an enjoyable consumer good, the automobile increased rural access to consumer culture and had a dramatic impact on the economic geography of rural society. In general, the automobile led to the decline of many smaller village centers and the increasing centralization of commerce in larger towns and cities. The most immediate and obvious effect, of course, was the demise of horse-related businesses and the rise of enterprises to sell and service automobiles, as blacksmith shops and livery stables throughout the North were replaced by automobile dealerships, garages, and service stations.[15]

More important, however, the automobile facilitated longer and more frequent shopping trips and increased the number of communities within the reach of the rural consumer. According to numerous sociological and business studies of rural areas during the 1920s, farm families with cars traveled farther to buy consumer goods, particularly stylish items such as dress clothing and shoes. Farmers in Union County, Ohio, for example, typically went twelve to fifteen miles for finer clothing, which they could have bought closer to home, and 75 percent of them went outside of the county because no store stocked enough to suit all of the different preferences. Similarly, a survey of over 3,600 country families in Wayne County, New York, showed them traveling an average of 14.6 miles to buy women's dresses, and 14.3 miles for men's suits. Rural families traveled shorter distances for groceries and everyday items, but even for these goods they were increasingly drawn away from the general store in the local villages and toward the new chain stores in the larger towns where the prices and selection were better.[16]

Besides going farther, the automobile also allowed farmers to journey to town more often. Instead of once a week, which was the custom during the horse-and-buggy era, 88.5 percent of the country families in Wayne County, New York, traveled to their marketing centers an average of four times a week, and they ventured thirty miles to the big city of Rochester once a month. A present-day historical geographer has found similar changes in his analysis of one family's diaries from Ogle County, Illinois. During the first decade of the twentieth century, Hugh Ray and his family made trips to the larger cities of Rockford or Dixon once or twice a year, but they made 8 trips to Rockford between 1911 and 1913 because they went with friends who had a car. The real change came after they purchased their own automobile in 1916. Between 1917 and 1919, the family traveled to Rockford 45 times and made 23 trips to Dixon—several times a month instead of several times a year.[17]

This greater mobility worked to the advantage of larger towns and to the detriment of smaller village centers, with general stores as a particular casualty. According to "The Influence of Automobiles and Good Roads on Retail Trade Centers," a 1927 study of southeastern Nebraska conducted by the state university, that region experienced a 25 percent decline in general stores between 1903 and 1925. Even general stores that stayed in business saw their trade diminish, in the words of a sociologist surveying Wayne County, New York: "The old-time general store is rapidly disappearing and instead of handling 'everything from a needle to a threshing machine' the paying merchandise has been reduced to a very few lines." One cross-roads grocer there reported that his business consisted of just three commodities—gasoline, candy, and tobacco—while another who had been in business in the same village for more than thirty-five years managed to stay afloat only by running a delivery service into the surrounding countryside four times a week. Merchants in a village of three hundred in nearby Yates County had similar problems: one's annual business had decreased from $25,000 to $15,000 in the past nine years, and another's inventory had fallen off 25 percent since 1920.[18]

General store merchants who were interviewed in Illinois in the 1920s believed that they could compete with the larger centers in terms of price, except, perhaps, for "Saturday specials" and other items that were deliberately sold at a loss in order to lure customers. "Larger towns do not undersell," claimed a general store owner in an Illinois village of 500 who was 10 miles from two towns of 2,000 and 42 miles from·a city of 50,000. Style and selection, however, posed more difficult challenges, as the study noted: "Some of the dealers reported that their customers demand the latest styles as soon as do the people in the cities. This increases their difficulties, for with full assortments and limited sales it is hard to turn their stocks fast enough to buy the newest lines as soon as they are available."[19]

The need to keep up with changing styles posed particular problems for village specialty businesses, which sold furniture, jewelry, shoes, and dress clothing. According to the Illinois study, "It is especially hard to carry what people want in shoes. Styles of shoes change so fast now that it is hard on the small dealer." In Wisconsin, increasing amounts of rural trade went to the urban centers because "a surprising number of women explained that they could not be fitted and still have sufficient range of selection in the local town store." Specialty stores in Nebraska declined markedly in places with populations under a thousand, and jewelry and silverware, which formerly were purchased in the home town by 43 percent of the families interviewed were now purchased locally by only 14 percent. In general, the report notes, "only goods with little style element and lower prices are carried in the smaller villages."[20]

Although merchants in larger towns benefited from the farmers' new mobility, it was a mixed blessing. On the one hand, cars brought in customers who had previously shopped in smaller places, and they lessened the appeal of the merchants' old nemesis, the mail-order catalogue. On the other hand, successful town merchants now had to contend for the first time with competition from chain stores in their own communities and from merchants in other cities and large towns within driving range. In both of these cases, local merchants again resorted to the familiar refrains of community loyalty that they had honed in earlier campaigns against the mail-order houses. But spatial conceptions of the community were changing because of the automobile, and as local merchants began to woo new customers from outside their communities in order to survive, the contradictions inherent in their appeals to buy at home became even more obvious, and older ideas of local loyalty became increasingly anachronistic.

By the end of the 1920s, northern farmers were less tempted to buy by mail because they could shop around in their cars for the best prices and the greatest variety, and what had once been a major thorn in the side of the local merchant became only a minor irritant. Illinois merchants in the 1920s, for example, expressed few worries about mail-order competition because farmers' mail-order purchases declined during this period and consisted primarily of low-cost standard items such as work clothes, underwear, and linens. According to a 1925 survey of 167 farm families in Pickaway County, Ohio, only 61 families bought clothes and dry goods from the catalogues and spent an average of $41, which represented 7.7 percent of the total spending for these types of goods; 21 families, typically those who lived more than ten miles from the major shopping town of Circleville, were the only ones to order mail-order furniture; and fewer than 10 families purchased farm equipment or groceries by mail.[21]

Instead of mail-order houses, chain stores emerged as a new threat to local businessmen. Originally an urban phenomenon dating from the late nineteenth century, grocery and variety chain stores began appearing on small-town Main Streets in the wake of the automobile in the 1910s, and their numbers exploded during the 1920s. In Yates County, New York, for example, local groceries declined by almost 40 percent, from 39 to 24, between 1900 and 1929, whereas the number of chain groceries increased from none in 1915 to 23 in 1929, including 9 in Penn Yan, the county seat and major marketing center. Nationally, the Atlantic and Pacific Tea Company expanded to more than 15,000 stores during this period and generated over $1 billion in sales in 1929. Between 1919 and 1929 chains increased their share of national retail sales from 4 percent to 20 percent and expanded from the Middle-Atlantic into the South and the West and into new lines of merchandise such as dry goods, shoes, drugs, and automobile accessories.[22]

This rapid growth and the dominance of chain stores in certain lines of goods prompted local merchants to wage a multifaceted campaign against them. Invoking familiar rhetoric, merchants raised the specter of a chain store "menace" that threatened to siphon money out of the community and subject hometown commerce to outside control, and they formed "independent merchants'" associations and "allied businessmen's" associations to wage a new round of trade-at-home campaigns. These efforts were strongest in the South and reached a peak as the fortunes of all retailers declined and tensions increased during the early years of the Great Depression, culminating in the passage of special taxes on chain stores in twenty-eight states, as well as a related federal law, the Robinson-Patman Act, which Congress enacted in 1936.[23]

As was the case with the earlier campaigns against the catalogue houses, these efforts had little effect on rural consumers. A 1930 survey of 2,940 rural families in Genesee County, New York, showed that 57 percent bought most of their groceries at independent stores, while 43 percent shopped mostly at chain stores, but the survey does not indicate how many families patronized both kinds of stores.[24] By contrast, the more detailed 1929 survey of 40 farm families in Jerusalem Township, Yates County, New York, shows that 28 (70 percent) shopped at chain groceries in nearby Penn Yan or Bridgeport, 6 traded primarily at general stores, and only 3 relied exclusively on independent grocers in the larger centers. When asked for their reasons, farm wives overwhelmingly stated that the chains were cheaper, more reasonable, and had more sales, and that the goods were fresher, and a few even noted that they liked the manager. Conversely, most of those who went to the independent Penn Yan groceries instead of the chains did so because they extended credit or took eggs and produce in trade, and those who shopped at village general stores stressed convenience or their friendship or kinship with the owner. Only two homemakers commented explicitly that they did not patronize chain stores. Another had initially refused to buy at the chains, but not out of any sense of home loyalty. Rather, she avoided the chain stores because they only stocked house brands instead of nationally advertised ones, and when they began carrying items such as Ivory soap and Del Monte canned goods, she took her business there.[25]

Local merchants were also keenly aware of competition from rivals in other towns and cities, and they mounted trade-at-home campaigns and promotional activities in order to counter it. As Hugh Ray and his neighbors began driving to Rockford with its population of over 80,000, and subscribing to its daily paper to keep abreast of the sales and other events, local merchants in Oregon, Illinois, a county seat of just over 2,000, were forced to respond in kind. They ran advertisements and editorials advocating trading at home and staged their own "dollar days" and other specials to keep their old customers and attract new ones. To compete with the vaudeville house in Rockford, for example, they started a "be-entertained-at-home" campaign and established the Oregon Community House, which featured games and dancing. In the same vein, local voters finally passed a city ordinance allowing Sunday movies in 1927 after two previous defeats in 1919 and 1925, responding, in part, to an appeal in the local paper the week before the vote:

> If Oregon had no farmer neighbors, no working people, or young folks, or if Oregon did not have to compete with surrounding towns connected by good roads, then there would be no serious reason for having Sunday pictures here. Rockford, Dixon, Rochelle, and Polo have Sunday movies. Yet they are acknowledged to be better church towns than Oregon. . . . Why not let Oregon have an equal chance with our surrounding towns? We must keep up with the times or go backwards. . . . Good roads through "dead towns" result in business failure. . . . Oregon's good roads are serving more as an outlet to trade than as an inlet.[26]

By the same token, local boosters began promoting tourism, and Oregon businesses and hotels began catering to the same Sunday drivers touring the Rock River valley from Rockford, Dixon, and Chicago who had been scorned earlier in the century.

Although merchants in Oregon and similar towns continued to appeal to local pride, hometown loyalty, and the need to keep money in Oregon so that it would continue to be "a place on the map," their success paradoxically depended more and more on their ability to lure new customers who were outsiders. In other words, Oregon merchants wanted their own people to heed the cry of localism, but they did not want anyone else to, and their older spatial conceptions of community became increasingly contradictory and anachronistic because of the automobile.

Rather than heed the mixed messages of local boosters, however, farmers defined their own communities and used their automobiles to reconfigure them over a larger territory. After the rise of the automobile caused local stores in the German Lutheran community of Block, Kansas, to go out of business, for example, the village's German-speaking farm families simply drove seven miles to the larger town of Paola, where they continued to patronize other German-owned businesses. According to Mary Neth's recent study of the rural Midwest, the automobile did not disrupt traditional forms of rural social life, but may have actually facilitated the informal visiting that was the glue of the rural community by allowing intimate relations with more distant neighbors. This perspective is confirmed by a 1927 survey of a rural consolidated school district in southeastern Pennsylvania, which found that country people used their cars most frequently first for shopping trips and second for visits to friends and relatives.[27]

Also, the automobile extended the reach of more organized community activities. After the automobile came to Oregon and Ogle County, Illinois, for example, new intertown organizations met monthly, as opposed to the older county associations, which typically met only once or twice a year. Similarly, local band concerts drew from a wider area, and people drove to the county fair from a sixty-mile radius, revitalizing an event that had devolved into nothing more than a program of horse races. Autos were also a boon to intertown high school athletic competitions, allowing the teams to meet each other more easily and increasing the number of fans who came to the games. This was certainly the case in the predominantly Danish community of Askov, Minnesota, in 1926, where "one or another of public meetings, dances, moving-picture shows, or other entertainments [brought] to the village some member of most households for at least one or two evenings in the month," and where the community's baseball team won eleven straight games in the county league and its basketball team made it to the district tournament.[28]

In particular, Saturday night, or "farmers' night" as it was known in many marketing centers, became an important component of rural social life during the automobile age, and provided an occasion for farm families from different towns to visit as well as to shop. According to the study of Askov during the 1920s, "ample parking spaces often show their flocks of cars at leisure; for the village is neither unvisited nor fled from of an evening." Penn Yan, with a population of just over five thousand, had the only two movie houses in the county and its stores stayed open on Saturday night, so instead of going to the nearest village, area farmers went there. One rural sociologist counted seven hundred cars parked in the center of town on two separate Saturday nights in the summer of 1929; and according to a survey of rural homemakers who lived in nearby Jerusalem Township, almost half indicated that they regularly went to Penn Yan to shop on Saturday night. Conversely, three women made a point of stating that they deliberately avoided Saturday night in Penn Yan, including one farm wife who did not like crowds and another who lectured for the Woman's Christian Temperance Union.[29]

For the vast majority who did come to town, Saturday night did not represent the lure of city lights or a new consumer culture so much as an opportunity for some old-fashioned socializing. According to a study of Circleville, the county seat of Pickaway County, Ohio, with a population of over seven thousand, "Not every farm family goes every Saturday night, of course, but enough do go to give such trips recognition in a study of town and country relations." The author, too, counted the cars parked in town and tallied about one thousand with an average of three passengers apiece, and wondered, "What were these three thousand people doing while in town?" The theaters, confectioneries, restaurants, and poolrooms were crowded, and the grocery stores and meat markets usually had a very active trade, but "on many occasions the investigator went into clothing, shoe, dry goods, and hardware stores between eight and ten o'clock in the evening and counted more clerks than customers." The sidewalks, by contrast, "were always busy with sightseers and friendly visitors," crowds of farm families visiting with town friends and each other or "window shopping" and taking in the scene on the street. A similar observation of the smaller community of Ashville counted fewer people, but evoked the same social atmosphere: "Here, as at Circleville, the people were mostly standing on the corners, walking about, or sitting in their automobiles or on chairs and benches along the sidewalk provided by the business men. There was a great deal of visiting among friends from neighboring farms or friends from other parts of the community who came to 'town' largely for the purpose of such visits."[30]

One Iowa man had comparable memories of "farmers' night" during the 1920s from the other side of the counter where he was a teenage clerk in a Main Street grocery store:

> The sidewalks and stores were packed with people milling around, comparing notes on the crops and neighborhood gossip. At the store the early evening rush lasted until about nine o'clock. Then there was a lull until about eleven o'clock when the second show at the Plaza Theater let out. Then we were rushed again for the next half hour. At first I thought that it was inconsiderate of these late shoppers. Why couldn't they shop before the second show so that we could close earlier? But the answer was simple and reasonable. Most cars at that time were not enclosed and had no trunks. People had no way of locking up their groceries when they were at the show.[31]

The best evocation of "farmers' night" is from a 1939 anthropological study of an Iowa corn belt county. Farm families arrived in town after supper and split up according to age and gender:

> The women go to their favorite stores to shop and chat. Aside from the trading which is done, everyone has a chance to talk to friends. . . . As the people move about, groups of acquaintances form on the sidewalks. Girls parade by, arm in arm, and are shouted at by the loitering groups of boys. This results in isolating acceptable double or triple couples of "dates" who later go off in cars. Conversation groups are continually forming, dissolving, and reforming. Friends from over a very wide radius are thus thrown together, and the expanded community does not have to be utterly dependent upon the "personal" columns of the newspaper for grist for its gossip.[32]

Farmers, then, used their cars primarily to go to marketing centers rather than the big cities and metropolitan centers. There they found an environment that catered to them and in which they felt comfortable, and where they could pick and choose among activities that were both new and old in ways that resonated with and reinforced their values instead of threatening them.

Significantly, much of what transpired on "farmers' night" represented a continuation of older patterns of socializing that integrated country people over a broader area rather than new cultural departures.

As the foregoing descriptions indicate, going to the movies was a common activity on farmers' night in addition to visiting on the streets, and may have represented more of a break with older patterns of rural socializing. According to a survey of town-country relations in Union County, Ohio, the larger towns each had a motion picture theater, and these were filled to capacity on Saturday night. During the summer, local merchants gave out tickets with each dollar's purchase that could only be used on two evenings during the week, and the theaters were crowded on these nights as well. In the words of the author, "A good share of the audiences was made up of country people as was shown by the number of persons coming to and going from the theaters in automobiles." As Pearl Sollars of Tippecanoe County, Indiana, recalled: "Now on Saturday night we went to town; we went to the free shows in Reynolds. We went to buy our groceries, and that was your one big night out, on Saturday night." [33]

The growing importance of movies is also evident in the rural press. Paramount Pictures regularly advertised its latest productions on the first page of the *Country Gentleman*, and the *Farm Journal*, which was the most widely read farm magazine in the country, had a special columnist, C. F. Stevens, who reported on movies and movie matters. Several times a year Stevens gave brief summaries of the current crop from Hollywood and ranked the films in five categories: "Superb!," "Recommended," "Better than Most," "At Your Own Risk!," and "Junk." Stevens took the high road culturally, he did not mince his words or pull any punches in his reviews of bad films, and he had high hopes for the edifying influence of talkies on rural society. "I hope I can make you realize the tremendous difference this is going to make on dwellers on the farms and in the small towns," he wrote in his column describing the advent of talking motion pictures. "What Broadway or The Place de l'Opera sees and hears, Macon, Ga., Cimmaron, Kans., Ypsilanti, Mich., Swampscott, Mass., and Wenatchee, Wash., will see and hear in exactly the same renditions, about the same time, and probably at much less cost." [34]

In spite of the crowded theaters and the coverage in farm papers, moviegoing was by no means universal among rural northerners, and country people who did go went less often than their urban counterparts. Only 36 percent of the nearly three thousand farm families surveyed in Genesee County, New York, in 1930 ever went to the movies, for example, and the large majority of them went only once a month or less. Similarly, just 38 percent of the families in and around Marathon, in Cortland County, patronized movie theaters, and over half of these also went only sporadically. Conversely, 74 percent of the country, as opposed to the village, families, did not go to the movies at all. Edna Winter of Pulaski County, Indiana, remembered going to the movies with her family as a singular event after a day's outing at the lake: "And we went to the movies—just once in the summer. . . . And we got to go that one night. That was our summer recreation."[35]

Younger people, however, were much more likely to attend movies and to be influenced by them than their elders. In Marathon, even though only 26 percent of farm families ever went to the movies, the families who attended were families with children. Whether with their parents or not, teenagers went to the movies the most and were more affected by the images emanating from the screen. The 1927 survey of the Unionville School District in Chester County, Pennsylvania, shows that while half of the adults did not attend movie theaters, almost three-fourths of their teenage sons and daughters did, and averaged 35 movies per year. According to a Wisconsin survey, farm families went to the movies an average of 11 times per year. The farmer and his wife went 6 times, but the other members of the household went more often: 20 times for other males, and 16 times for other females. This was still lower than comparable figures for urban youth, though.[36]

In one sense, going to the movies was simply a more commercialized way for rural teenagers to spend time with their friends. But, in the words of a recent study, "although attendance at movies fit into existing visiting patterns," they also "introduced new images of leisure and consumption." That kind of exposure had an impact, according to a history of Jefferson, a town of 3,400 that was the county seat of Greene County, Iowa: "Movie stars were clearly becoming role models for Jefferson adolescents. One Jefferson woman recalled that local clothing and hairstyles followed Hollywood leads." As with their urban counterparts, then, these encounters with mass culture helped to distinguish rural youth from their parents' generation.[37]

In addition to going to the movies, rural youth also relied on the automobile to indulge in other, newer forms of recreation and leisure. In particular, the automobile altered patterns of courtship in rural society and gave young people the opportunity to date people from a wider area. Double, triple, and even quadruple dates were common because not every family had a car, and young men who had access to one often invited their friends. This "progress" came at a price, though, according to one fond reminiscence of youthful romance in a horse and buggy: "I liked the buggy the best because you could tie the reigns [sic] to the dash and let the horses run wherever they want[ed], whereas in the automobile, you always had to steer."[38]

Young people from the countryside also made frequent trips to town for school athletic competitions, church youth group activities, and dances, which had long been a staple in rural social life but became bigger and more frequent with the advent of the automobile. Although the devout German Lutheran children of Block, Kansas, probably did not spend too much time in the movie theaters or at other frivolities, the automobile lessened the religious and geographical isolation of their community and facilitated more contact with non-Lutheran society, and a similar change occurred among third-generation German Lutheran and Norwegian youth in Hardin County, Iowa. Still, though rural teenagers went to town more often than their parents had when they were young, those newer activities continued to coexist with more traditional forms of visiting and socializing, and did not supplant them.[39]

For most rural northerners, the almost universal adoption of the automobile did not necessarily signal an embrace of a new consumer culture and a rejection of older agrarian precepts. Rather, cars fit into their lives quite easily. They were marketed as practical pieces of farm machinery and were used primarily for the business of running the farm and the farm household. Although younger rural women were more likely to drive than their mothers, that access did not automatically alter traditional gender relationships because rural men still exercised primary control over the new technology. Finally, even though village merchants bemoaned the sight of their former customers speeding off in their Model Ts, farm families neither shared those concerns nor acted in accordance with them. Rather, they used their automobiles to extend older patterns of socializing and to reconfigure their communities over a wider area. The one major exception to this overall picture of continuity, perhaps, was the younger generation. For them, the automobile was an important means of access to leisure and the new forms of popular culture emanating from the city. It was a vehicle in more ways than one.

Rural northerners during the 1920s also confronted and negotiated the new consumer culture in their homes. In particular, farm families made decisions about whether to "modernize" their homes with electricity, new heating systems, and indoor plumbing, and whether to purchase any of the many domestic appliances that came on the market during this period, including power washing machines, electric irons and vacuum cleaners, new gas and electric cookstoves, refrigerators, and radios. In addition, they made countless smaller decisions about more mundane consumer goods when they chose among different brands of food, clothing, and sundries, or whether to choose any brand at all. Although none of these decisions was as momentous or as expensive as the purchase of an automobile, farm families also approached them primarily in terms of the pragmatism that informed much of their lives rather than any overweening desires to embrace a different lifestyle. In the case of home improvements and appliances, however, that pragmatism was also informed by the undervaluation of women's work that led farm families not to buy the new goods.

In contrast to their counterparts who lived in urban apartment buildings, middle-class suburban homes, or the larger marketing centers that served them, farm families could not take certain basic domestic amenities for granted. In Nebraska, for example, a 1926 study by the General Federation of Women's Clubs found that between 75 and 90 percent of the homes in Nebraska towns and cities had electricity, as opposed to only 17 percent of the more than 3,000 farm homes surveyed; and most of the farm homes with electricity got their power from home generators. In the same vein, fewer than 40 percent of those farm homes had running water, including homes with an indoor hand pump, whereas more than 60 percent of homes in towns and over 80 percent of the homes in cities were so equipped. The disparities between rural and urban toilet facilities were even more pronounced; as one agricultural leader recalled his boyhood home in rural Indiana during this period, "we had six rooms and a path."[40]

Other surveys also illustrate the relative absence of domestic comforts in the countryside. A 1925 study of 357 Minnesota farm families, many of them immigrants or the children of immigrants, found only 50 percent with modern lighting, 38 percent with central heating, and 15 percent with indoor toilets. Significantly, farm income rather than ethnicity had more of an effect on these consumption patterns. Elsewhere, 62 percent of the farm families surveyed near Marathon, New York, did not have any modern equipment at all and only 11 percent of the homes were equipped with all of these conveniences. Nor did farm families accept such disparities as an inevitable part of country life. When asked what improvements they looked forward to making as soon as circumstances permitted, 118 Ohio farm families surveyed in 1926 expressed the greatest preferences for electricity, running water, and indoor plumbing, in that order. Although these conveniences were somewhat more common in Ohio than in Nebraska, they were still not ubiquitous, and over 50 percent of the many families who did not already have them ranked them high on their wish list.[41]

In the 1920s, before widespread rural electrification, these were expensive propositions. Home and farm electric power plants cost hundreds of dollars, and the extra components needed to operate electric lights or pump water for indoor plumbing represented significant additional expenditures. As with the automobile, these electric plants were marketed in terms of their practical benefits and their ability to fit in smoothly with farm life. Unlike the automobile, however, farm women rather than farm men were the primary targets of these appeals, which focused on women's work on the farm and the quality of domestic life. A 1928 advertisement for the Westinghouse farm electric plant, for example, shows a farm woman in a room with an electric light cheerfully pouring milk into an electric cream separator with the caption, "I wish other women knew what I know about this new light plant." In the same vein, Delco addressed one of its advertisements "To Women on the Farm," and depicted a farm wife using indoor plumbing to wash dishes and bathe her child.

Other advertisements, though, played to rural women's desire for a more comfortable home life and stressed electricity as the way to achieve an urban middle-class lifestyle on the farm. Three generations of a farm family dressed in their finest clothing sit down to a Thanksgiving dinner in another Delco-Light solicitation, which wondered how much more thankful the original Pilgrims would have been if they also had push-button electric lights at the first such meal. Another competitor, Fairbanks-Morse, made this domestic bliss an everyday occurrence and depicted a well-dressed man reading a book while his wife, who is wearing hose and heels, sews and their two children play—all illuminated by an electric table lamp. Under the caption, "Those golden evening hours," the copy reads: "Evening hours . . . precious hours . . . life's richest reward for a day's work well done . . . but robbed of their glory in thousands of farm homes by feeble, flickering kerosene lamps." Although Fairbanks-Morse advertisements also mentioned a full line of electrical generators, water plants, and even feed grinders, all of which had numerous practical applications on the farm, its illustrations evoked urban rather than rural living.

These expensive new household conveniences created tensions between rural men and rural women, which are best captured (if not resolved) in a 1929 short story that was published in the *Farm Journal*. Written by Walter Prichard Eaton, an accomplished writer and urban drama critic, "Everything Electrical" is the story of Bessie Hughes, who was brought up in "the movie and bathroom belt" in a small city replete with bathrooms, washing machines, electric lights, and electric irons, and "knew as little about hauling water from a pump as her grandmother did about radio kilocycles." After graduating from the State Normal School she took a job teaching in a rural district as something of an adventure, fell in love and married a local farmer, Bart Sherrill, and moved into the ancestral farm home.[42]

Although it was full of charm and antique furniture, the Sherrill home had no modern conveniences other than spring water running to the kitchen sink, the single innovation that Bart's mother had been able to introduce in the sixty-five years of her life. Bart himself had only recently come to the conclusion that farm machinery, cow testing, and blooded stock were good investments, and failed to see the need for modern equipment in the home. "Money spent on a tractor meant money actually saved on horse feed and hired help. But money spent on a washing-machine or bathroom—well, you just couldn't see the profit in dollars and cents." Although Bessie used her own savings to put in a pipeless heater, Bart drew the line at a new bathroom regardless of who paid for it.

Instead, Bessie began imagining the home improvements that she could not have and wrote articles describing them in great detail, which she sent to a farm magazine. After writing about the bathroom, she wrote a second article in which her husband dammed the stream and installed an electrical generator to run a milking machine as well as a washing machine. The magazine accepted these pieces, paid her handsomely, and asked whether she had installed other electrical or labor-saving devices that their women readers would like to hear about. In subsequent articles she fictitiously wired the house for electric lights and bought a vacuum cleaner, an electric range, and a refrigerator. But she also wanted a toaster, a coffee percolator, an electric iron, a bedwarmer, and a fan, and she wrote about these in turn.

Bessie kept all of these articles hidden from her husband even though she longed to show them to him and make him understand her point of view. She did leave out the magazine that contained her first article and casually brought it to his attention without admitting her authorship: "He glanced through it, snorted a trifle, and remarked that if people couldn't get along without luxuries like bathrooms they'd better quit farming and move to the Waldorf-Astoria. After that, Bessie gritted her teeth and said nothing. She'd have that bathroom anyhow! If he'd only go away for two weeks, so she could install it while he was gone."

The story came to a climax when the dean of the State Agricultural College, a few home demonstration agents, and several of their students paid a surprise visit to see this model farmhouse firsthand. Although Bessie was mortified and embarrassed at being found out, when Bart learned that she had made $200 writing articles, he realized how much these improvements meant to her. As she said: "Oh Bart, it isn't that I want the bathroom so terribly—or, anyway, the electric things—I *do* need the bathroom, and the hot water; it's just that I want you to understand why, and to be just a little bit sorry that I haven't got 'em. I know we love each other, Bart. I know you love me. But sometimes you don't realize I'm a woman, and I'd like not to be so tired, and to be clean and look pretty, and to—to make you glad to see me and—and want to kiss me!"

Bart did kiss her, "with ardor," and the story ends with his telling Bessie to save her money while he makes plans to install a power plant—after the bathroom is finished, that is.

Although it underscores the often gendered tensions between rural women's desires for urban amenities and men's resistance to such appeals,

"Everything Electrical" is not an accurate depiction of life in agrarian society. Few rural families could afford the whole range of improvements depicted in the story, least of all a newlywed couple just getting started, and financially constrained farmers were not willing to spend money on home improvements at the expense of measures that would increase the productivity of the farm. Similarly, the resolution of the tensions between Bessie and Bart has a fairy-tale quality, which emphasizes the centrality of physical beauty and movielike romantic love instead of the working relationship typical between farm men and farm women. In reality, the home power plants were also not the deus ex machina that the story and the advertisements depicted, and, according to reminiscences by Indiana farm wives, their batteries rarely stored enough power to run the lights and more than one appliance, and needed constant recharging by a noisy gasoline generator.[43]

Almost 40 percent of the farm families surveyed near Penn Yan and Lockport, New York, in 1929 received the issue of the *Farm Journal* with this story in it (it was the single most popular magazine in the survey), but it did not reflect their lives either. Only 29 percent of the 121 homes had electricity, and these were typically farmers who lived within five miles of the two towns, which each had a local electric company. Although a few already had them, no one installed a home electric plant that year, and only one family, which already had electricity, "fixed the bathroom." Instead, outlays for surgical operations, doctor and dental bills, and even funerals were far more common, and just as expensive.[44]

Sixteen of the thirty-five farm families with electricity did buy new appliances, but no one quite matched Bessie Sherrill in fact or fiction. One family spent $140 on a McCormick-Deering cream separator, which they thought the best brand after having tried others and looked at the advertising, but domestic household appliances were much more common purchases. Five families bought washing machines, four purchased vacuum cleaners, three bought irons, two acquired refrigerators (a "great advantage," according to one), two got electric stoves, and one farm wife bought a hot plate ("nice for summer," she commented). Very few farm families were willing to go into debt to buy this equipment by making installment payments, an increasingly common strategy among urban consumers during the 1920s. According to the home economist who conducted the survey, "The rural families in general seem to be averse to instalment buying or to buying any article until a cash payment can be made for the full amount at the time of purchase. Rather than buy by means of instalment credit, they prefer not to have the equipment."[45]

The two women who came closest to the short story's ideal, significantly, were both members of the Home Bureau, an extension organization for women that promoted home economics and domestic technology in the countryside and to which only a handful of the other women in the survey belonged. Mrs. K. was a thirty-five-year old mother of two and wife of a German American farmer, who lived five miles from Lockport and was considered by the bread deliveryman to be the "best farmer on the whole road." During 1929, she fixed up her bathroom and spent $225 for a Kelvinator refrigerator and $200 for an RCA Radiola, the first all-electric radio. The other, Mrs. W., was close to sixty, and had dropped out of the Home Bureau because she and her husband spent the four winter months in Florida while their son and daughter-in-law ran the farm and household, complete with a new Kalamazoo stove, a $100 ironer from the Montgomery Wards in Elmira, and a $145 Atwater Kent radio.[46]

For a variety of reasons, then, rural northerners did not completely embrace the vision of a fully equipped, modern, middle-class home that was promoted by advertisers and extension agents, especially if that meant going into debt. First and foremost, technological constraints made it too expensive. Until electricity became more widely available in the countryside, the expense and the inadequate service provided by home and farm generators did not warrant their adoption. That seemingly pragmatic decision also embodied other considerations, however. While electricity and indoor plumbing may have made life more pleasant for everyone, they had a much greater impact on women's work than on men's and were marketed in those terms. In the gendered calculus of the farm family's economy, that meant that these improvements were worth less, and usually not enough.

Farm families, however, were more willing to buy radios, which, according to the Cornell Home Economics survey, were the most common big-ticket item that farm families purchased for the home. Thirteen families bought sets in 1929: seven who had electricity in their homes, and six without power who, presumably, bought battery-operated units.[47] Like the automobile a decade earlier, radios spread rapidly in northern rural households during the second half of the 1920s. One 1923 survey in rural Iowa did not even bother to note radio ownership even though it counted all other appliances, and data from Nebraska for the same year reports that less than 1 percent of farm households in that state had a radio. Surveys after 1925, however, demonstrate a dramatic increase in radio ownership. In Tompkins County, New York, for example, 10 percent of the rural families and 16 percent of the village families had radios. "Radio ownership is very recent," noted the surveyor. "The data indicate, however, that families in the open country are buying radios relatively as rapidly as those in the villages and in the hamlets." Rates of ownership increased quickly throughout the rural North, from 18.5 percent in Pickaway County, Ohio, in 1926, to 34 percent in a five-county survey in Iowa in 1928, to 45 percent of all Nebraska farm families in 1930, and 70 percent in Walworth County, Wisconsin, where most sets had been purchased in the previous five years and the radio was now "accepted as necessary equipment in a majority of the farm homes of the county."[48]

Like the automobile, the radio was embraced by rural consumers because it offered practical benefits, and, like the automobile, it helped to reconfigure and redefine the rural community and rural culture in ways that they did not anticipate. From the point of view of farming operations, the radio provided, among other things, reports about crop conditions and daily weather and market reports. According to one social scientist who interviewed farmers in Ohio during the early phase of radio adoption in 1926, when fewer than 20 percent owned the new technology:

> Several farmers said that before the days of the radio, hog and cattle buyers, who kept in touch with the latest trend of the markets, had frequently taken advantage of the farmer's ignorance. One man said that whereas formerly there were several buyers along his road each week looking for livestock, at the time this study was made there was scarcely one in a month. Members of his family listened in whenever he had any stock to sell and so he knew what the market situation was. He said that often his neighbors who did not have receiving sets in their homes either came to his house or called on the telephone at times for the market reports.[49]

Publicly owned stations began broadcasting out of state universities and agricultural colleges and provided useful information as well as home and farm extension lessons for rural listeners. By 1926, twenty-four agricultural colleges had their own programs, and in 1928, the U.S. Department of Agriculture, in conjunction with the land grant colleges and several private agricultural organizations, began broadcasting the *National Farm and Home Hour* everyday at noon on NBC affiliates.[50]

As they did with the automobile and other appliances targeted for rural consumers, manufacturers advertised the radio in terms of its utility and its compatibility with more traditional agrarian sensibilities. Atwater Kent urged the readers of the *Country Gentleman*: "Buy your radio just as you buy your farm machinery," and showed two farmers watching another plow a field with a gasoline tractor, while the text drew parallels between buying a tractor and buying a radio. RCA Radiola adopted a softer sell that also emphasized the radio's congruence with rural life. In one scene, the younger farm family welcomes the older generation into the family parlor, which now has a radio at its center rather than a hearth, as the copy expounds on the benefits of crop, market, and weather information as well as musical entertainment, notable speeches, inspiring sermons, and helpful talks on household problems. In addition to ensuring familial continuity, RCA also evoked the endurance of communal ties in another advertisement as a group of farmers gathered around the radio in the local barber shop and listened, stroking their whiskers while their compatriot was having his shaved, a picture seemingly at odds with the textual descriptions of the brand's superior technological virtues.

Indeed, one reason for the radio's rapid adoption in spite of its expense was the fact that it could be adapted to rural life without much disruption. Farm families tuned in while they ate dinner at noon, and they sat in the parlor during the evening and listened to the radio instead of (or in addition to) reading. A 1930 survey of nine hundred farm families in Wisconsin found that they spent an average of 200 hours per year listening to the radio and 292 hours per person reading. Near Marathon, New York, 10.5 percent of the families had their radios on five or more hours per day.[51]

Farm women in particular listened to the radio while they did their domestic chores. In her 1928 article in the *Farm Journal*, "Mother and the Radio," Ethel Morrison-Marsden described a typical farm wife's daily routine in terms of the programs that were being broadcast on the radio—from weather and household hints at breakfast, news and entertainment all afternoon, to music and a travel lecture at night. According to Katherine Jellison's study, letters to Elizabeth C. Wherry, who wrote a column on radio for

ATWATER KENT

RADIO

Buy your radio just as you buy your farm machinery . . .

WHO MAKES IT—and how? Is it simple. and easy to keep in order? Will it do its job— and keep on doing it?

Aren't these the questions you want answered before you invest your money in a tractor and everything else you use on the farm?

It's the same way with radio. Here's an instrument your family will depend upon for years and years. You want to know it's always ready to go.

Atwater Kent Radio comes from the largest manufacturer. It is made of better materials than are ordinarily thought necessary. So strictly is its reputation guarded that one out of every eight workers is a tester or inspector—and every set has to pass 222 tests before it can leave the factory.

So, when an Atwater Kent comes into your home, it is absolutely dependable—and it stays

so. You do not have to fuss and tinker and apologize...If Atwater Kent makes it, it's right—tone, volume, range—everything. More than 2,000,000 owners know it.

House current or battery sets— your choice

Quality Atwater Kent Radio—first choice of rural families everywhere—is offered in two forms: 1. For all-electric operation direct from the same house current

that lights your home; you merely plug in. 2. For operation from batteries.

Either way, you get plenty of power for long-range reception, sweet, mellow, natural tone, and instantaneous program selection with the FULL-VISION Dial. There are several all-electric models and two battery models. Let an Atwater Kent dealer advise you as to which is best for your locality. See him now!

Battery Sets, $49—$68

Solid mahogany cabinets. Panels satin-finished in gold. FULL-VISION Dial. Model 48, $49; Model 49, extra-powerful, $68. Prices do not include tubes or batteries.

Model 56 (Electric)

The new all-in-one set that fits so beautifully anywhere. FULL-VISION Dial. For 110-120 volt, 50-60 cycle alternating current. Requires 6 A.C. tubes and 1 rectifying tube. Without tubes, $97.

On the air— every Sunday night— Atwater Kent Radio Hour—listen in!

Prices slightly higher west of the Rockies

Model 40 (Electric), $77

For 110-120 volt, 50-60 cycle alternating current. Requires 6 A. C. tubes and 1 rectifying tube, $77 (without tubes).

ATWATER KENT MANUFACTURING COMPANY . . . A. Atwater Kent, President . . . 4714 Wissahickon Avenue, Philadelphia, Pa.

Advertisement for Atwater Kent Radio, Country Gentleman, *1929.*
(Courtesy of Farm Journal*)*

Advertisement for RCA Radiola, Country Gentleman, *1929.*
(Courtesy of Farm Journal*)*

Wallace's Farmer, showed that midwestern farm women preferred entertainment and music programs (they did not even mention the *National Farm and Home Hour* or the extension lessons from the university), and rearranged their work schedules in order to catch their favorite broadcasts, listening to the radio while they churned butter or made beds. To quote Jellison and one of these letters, "That women could perform some of their chores while listening to their favorite broadcasts was, in the words of one of Wherry's readers, 'the beauty of radio.'"[52] This is borne out indirectly by the surveys, which show that farm wives listened to the radio more than any other member of the farm family.[53] As one farm wife near Penn Yan said simply about her new Silvertone radio, "it's wonderful."

The radio quickly became a part of contemporary rural culture and rural folklore. During the early days of radio, rural inhabitants made a game of receiving faraway stations. One man reminisced about radio in rural Iowa during the 1920s, "So down at the store, the next morning, the conversation would go, 'I got KDKA (Pittsburgh) real good last night,' or, 'That Florida station really came in strong.'" *Radio News* called this phenomenon "the radio itch," most newspapers called it "DX-ing," and local papers regularly listed the number of stations received by their readers. According to one historian, this fascination with annihilating distance led some country people to also ignore time and stay up listening all night when radio reception was better.[54]

The vagaries of battery power were also a peculiarity of radio in the countryside. These were immortalized by an announcer at KNAX in Yankton, South Dakota, in a poem entitled "When the Juice Runs Out":

Oh, I love an easy rocker close beside the radio,
With peppy music on the air, plug in and let 'er go:
That it makes me sort o' lazy, I haven't any doubt,
And it drives me plumb distracted, WHEN THE JUICE RUNS OUT.
I've an arm around my speaker on a sunny afternoon,
When there isn't any static, tho it's the month of June:
Now the score is tied and waiting and I hear the umpire shout
That the Babe is coming homeward—THEN THE JUICE RUNS OUT.
'T'was that day last September, final meet for Gene and Jack,

I've no trouble to remember, recollection brings it back:
But it wasn't any fault of mine we didn't hear that bout,
For when the referee said, "Nine"—THE JUICE RAN OUT.[55]

As the poem's references to Babe Ruth and Dempsey and Tunney suggest, the radio brought rural men as well as rural women into more direct contact with the mainstream of American popular culture, and in addition to agricultural news and serious programming, country people listened to sporting events, comedy shows, and all forms of music. The 1928 presidential election between Herbert Hoover and Al Smith also garnered new rural listeners and became a key selling point in manufacturers' advertisements: "Of course you're going to hear Hoover and Smith," asserted the 1928 Atwater Kent advertisement in the *Rural New Yorker*. Radio, then, provided a new common frame of reference. According to Carl Hamilton's memories of the period in rural Iowa: "Shortly people on both coasts and all points in between were listening to the same programs and telling and retelling the same jokes. The country was bound together as never before by such names as Amos 'n Andy, Fibber McGee and Molly, the Charlie McCarthy Show, the Cliquot Club Eskimos, the Atwater Kent Hour, and Ma Perkins."[56]

As country people started tuning in, however, they stopped doing other things, and, just as the automobile led to the demise of such venerable country institutions as the general store, so too did radio curtail older forms of rural entertainment and socializing. Various observers, for example, weighed the relative merits of listening to sermons on the radio instead of going to the local church. On the one hand, radio put rural believers in touch with the most popular preachers in the country and allowed them to be transported spiritually when they could not go physically on snowbound Sundays. On the other hand, local ministers from established denominations bemoaned any new factors that lessened membership, including the automobile as well as the radio, and all mainstream Protestants worried about the appeal of Aimee Semple McPherson and other airwave evangelists.[57]

In the same vein, several rural sociologists noted the decline of more old-fashioned village entertainments as more people stayed home to tune in. Edmund deS. Brunner even suggested that radio cut into moviegoing and automobile travel, and that the money saved on theater admissions could help pay for the new technology. The Chautauqua meeting, which started in the late nineteenth century as weeklong mixtures of sermons, self-improvement lectures, and musical entertainment, was a particular casualty of both radio and the automobile. In spite of efforts to boost its entertainment content at the expense of more virtuous endeavors during the 1920s, what was once a common institution in many rural communities could not compete with the newer forms of popular culture and became extinct. According to one small-town newspaperman who covered the annual Chautauqua week for years in Estherville, Iowa: "The inhabitants had become preoccupied with riding in their automobiles or listening to 'Amos and Andy,' 'Fibber McGee and Molly,' and other classics on the radio. They forgot about improving their minds and their morals."[58]

As well as drawing farm people closer to a national popular culture, many radio stations catered specifically to country audiences and helped create a new translocal and transregional popular culture that was distinctly rural. WLS, which broadcast from Chicago, was the largest and most significant of these stations and provided a model that was emulated by others on a smaller scale. Originally owned by Sears, Roebuck (the call letters WLS stood for "World's Largest Store"), which used the station for programming by its Agricultural Foundation rather than its own advertising, WLS began broad-casting in 1924 and was a huge success. In 1928, Sears sold the station to the influential Illinois farm periodical, the *Prairie Farmer*, which continued to tar-get the rural audience and expanded the station's influence. A 1928 survey conducted by the paper showed that 59 percent of the farmers in Illinois, In-diana, and southern Wisconsin called WLS their favorite radio station, and it received 69 percent of the votes in a presumably more impartial 1938 U.S. Department of Agriculture survey of midwestern farmers, where the next largest vote was only 5 percent. By 1930, the station was receiving over 600,000 letters per year. It affiliated with NBC in 1933 and began broadcast-ing some of its programs coast-to-coast.[59]

The most popular program on WLS was the *National Barn Dance* on Satur-day night, which was one of the pioneering programs in country music and the progenitor of numerous others, including the *Grand Old Opry*. Its first big star, Bradley Kincaid, was not a professional entertainer, but a college stu-dent from Kentucky who was studying in Chicago for a career as a YMCA secretary. Kincaid, whose radio persona embodied wholesomeness and sincerity, played the guitar and sang sad, beautiful folk ballads such as "Barbara Allen" or religious songs such as "The Legend of Robin Red Breast." In addition to Kincaid, other early regulars included Tommy Dandurand and his Barn Dance Fiddlers, ballad-singer Walter Peterson (the Kentucky Wonder Bean), banjoist Chubby Parker, and Luther Ossenbrink from Missouri, who was billed as Arkie the Woodchopper and knew a wide variety of mountain, country, and cowboy ballads. Gene Autry began appearing in 1930 as the Oklahoma Yodeling Cowboy, and the Little Cowboy, thirteen-year-old George Goebel, made his debut in 1933, the same year that Alka Seltzer began sponsoring a nationally broadcast one-hour version of the *Barn Dance* on NBC.[60]

In a cultural sense, the WLS *Barn Dance* introduced millions of midwestern listeners to mountain and cowboy music from the South and the West. It took a broader musical view than other country shows, however, and also featured orchestral numbers, hymns, "heart songs," and standard sentimental favorites, such as "Down by the Old Mill Stream," which were familiar to midwestern farm folk as the songs of their youth. In the first show, country-style fiddlers alternated with the Isham Jones dance band, and fiddle bands and balladeers regularly appeared in conjunction with performers of old-time pop and standard melodies. Grace Wilson from Owesso, Michigan, for example, came from musical comedy and vaudeville and became the longest-running *Barn Dance* star, singing her biggest hit, "Bringing Home the Bacon," every week from 1924 to 1960, and receiving over a million fan letters during her career.[61]

Significantly, the WLS *Barn Dance* was almost canceled after its first broadcast in 1924 when a Sears vice president who loved classical music listened in and was appalled at the down-home tunes instead of the more refined fare he was used to. Although he urged that the broadcast be stopped, the station received hundreds of approving telegrams, letters, and cards: "The Barn Dance brings happy memories of our youth"; "Mother and I pulled up the carpet and danced for the first time in years"; "Why, I'd never heard that song since I was a little girl." These comments reflected the tastes of those who bought from the Sears catalogues rather than those of their company executives, so the *Barn Dance* was kept on the air.[62]

Forging a new transregional musical sensibility among its rural audience, WLS also used the airwaves to create a new sense of rural community that went beyond the individual locality. After the *Barn Dance*, the station's most popular and enduring program was the *RFD Dinnerbell* program from 12 to 1 P.M., which became a daily ritual throughout the Midwest from the 1920s to the 1950s. RFD, a play on Rural Free Delivery, stood for "Radio Farmers Democracy," a name that had been chosen in a contest among the listeners, and the program was an amalgam of homespun delights, best replicated (and affectionately parodied) in our time by Garrison Keillor's *Prairie Home Companion*. After several dinner bells were rung (the station had seventeen, which had been donated by listeners), and the live orchestra played the national anthem, the host, Arthur Page, began reading the mail or interviewing his guests, usually farm leaders of one kind or another. Page also greeted and congratulated newlywed farm couples who were visiting the station on their honeymoons (after the orchestra gave its rendition of a wedding march, that is), and he recounted reports of "good neighbors" in different communities throughout the Midwest who helped families dealing with sickness, injury, or other troubles. In addition to reporting on others' neighborly deeds, WLS developed its own tradition of charitable relief and led a dramatic appeal after a 1925 tornado in southern Illinois, which collected over $200,000 from radio listeners.[63]

According to one historical study, Page "always tried to conduct his work in the spirit of a pastor. In that spirit he wanted programs which could 'belong to the family' in every rural community of the midwest." Not surprisingly, *Dinnerbell* also featured a real clergyman, Dr. John Holland, who came to radio after twenty-eight years on the pulpit as a Methodist preacher and ten seasons on the Chautauqua circuit, and who quickly became one of the station's most popular and appealing personalities. In addition to his sermons on *Dinnerbell*, Holland had his own Sunday religious program, the *Little Brown Church of the Air*, which was nonsectarian and did not solicit donations. Even though he was a Methodist preacher, he got one-third of his mail from Catholics.[64]

Given radio's fatal impact on Chautauqua, Holland's prior experience on the circuit seems, at first glance, to pose something of an irony. At another level, however, it symbolizes many of the basic continuities that characterized the rural embrace of the new medium. *Dinnerbell* was nothing if not a kind of Chautauqua meeting on the air, and through this program, the *Little Brown Church of the Air*, the WLS *National Barn Dance*, and their numerous imitators on other stations, radio allowed country people to partake of a new rural popular culture that was larger than the regions and communities they lived in. Just as the automobile allowed country people to reconfigure their communities and continue traditional patterns of visiting and socializing over a larger area, so too did the radio promote old-fashioned virtues in a different context. It institutionalized localistic values of homeliness and neighborliness in ways that transcended the particular community, and it helped to define a more general culture that celebrated localism without being directly tied to the culture of any one locality.[65]

In addition to facilitating a new translocal rural culture, the radio was also a vehicle for selling national brand-name products, another defining feature of the emerging consumer culture that affected country people. Before the late 1920s, radio broadcasters eschewed direct advertising and relied instead on sponsored programming. RCA, the Maytag Company, Maxwell House coffee, White House coffee, Montgomery Ward, the E. R. Squibb Co., and Palmolive, to mention only a few, all sponsored regular radio broadcasts, which featured music, entertainment, and informational programming. Although radio ownership did not automatically lead to the purchase of new items in the same way that electricity did, these radio programs did have an influence, and at least two of the farm wives in the 1929 surveys near Lockport and Penn Yan, New York, for example, reported that they bought products as a result of them, in their cases, Ipana toothpaste and Palmolive soap.[66]

Magazines were a much more important source of advertising than the radio. In rural Illinois, according to a 1928 study, "New styles spread with greater rapidity than ever. . . . and the distribution of newspapers and magazines by rural free delivery have contributed to this end."[67] Similarly, the 1929 survey in rural New York reveals that many women were influenced directly or indirectly by magazine advertising when they gave their reasons for buying a certain brand. In general, pictorial and textual representations of products and their virtues, which had roots in the mail-order catalogues of the nineteenth century, were much more familiar and long-standing than radio advertisements. Magazine advertising changed dramatically during the 1920s, and manufacturers embraced nonrepresentational images and subjective themes that were not directly related to their products in order to sell

them. Historians have written extensively about the contours of this advertising as paragons of a new and more modern consumer culture during the
1920s, but the actual connections between it and the behavior of the consumers remain more elusive. Because the 1929 New York survey notes which
magazines farm families read, which brands they purchased, and their reasons for doing so, however, it is possible to consider more precisely how
rural people negotiated this aspect of an emerging culture of mass consumption. As with the automobile, home appliances, and the radio, country people
chose products and brands in ways that were consistent with their own priorities instead of rejecting those values for supposedly more modern or glamorous ones.[68]

In general, magazine subscriptions were very common in northern rural
households during the 1920s. In Cedar County, Iowa, for example, 87 percent of nearly 400 farm households surveyed took farm periodicals, 81 percent took daily papers, 53 percent took other magazines, and 44 percent got
all of the above. Of nearly 450 farm families in Boone, Story, and Sac Counties in Iowa, over 50 percent took at least one local paper, one daily, one farm
journal, and one general magazine, and only 8 percent took no magazines at
all. Likewise, among farm families near Marathon, New York, 73 percent received an average of two farm journals, and in Livingston County, south of
Rochester, New York, 87 percent took at least one farm journal, and 78 percent took at least one general magazine.[69]

The data from around Penn Yan and Lockport, New York, also conform
to this pattern. Only 6 of the 121 farm households surveyed received no
magazines or newspapers, and households in both areas averaged about
four subscriptions each. The fifty-nine-year-old woman who lectured for
the Woman's Christian Temperance Union in Penn Yan received the largest
number of periodicals, eleven, and presumably spent her Saturday nights
reading them at home since she refused to go to town. Farm magazines were
the most widely read, particularly the *Farm Journal* (43), the *Rural New Yorker*
(33), the *American Agriculturalist* (30), the *Farmer's Wife* (19), which later
merged with the *Farm Journal*, and the *Country Gentleman* (14). Although more
general magazines did not claim the same level of readership in these communities, the most popular were all mainstream, middle-class, women's publications such as *Woman's Home Companion* (18), *McCall's* (16), *American Maga-*

zine (15), *People's Home Journal* (14), *Ladies' Home Journal* (12), and *Pictorial Review* (12).[70]

The farm wives who were interviewed exhibited varying degrees of brand awareness and integration into consumer culture, which correlated positively with the number of magazines they took. Significantly, the number of magazines was not correlated with wealth, and poorer families were just as likely to buy brand-name items as their wealthier neighbors. The minority who were educated beyond the district school, typically with one or two years of high school, took more magazines and bought more brand-name items, however.[71]

Consider the contrast between two dairy farm households in Royalton Township, near Lockport, New York: Mrs. W., who was fifty-three years old and had attended normal school, received seven farm and women's magazines and bought thirteen food items according to brand. She bought Campbell's soups; Del Monte canned peas, because they were smaller and sweeter and because it was "too much bother to can" her own vegetables; Hall's white bread, because it was wrapped and cleaner, although she liked homemade bread better; Wesson oil, because the Home Bureau used it; and Red Circle coffee, because she liked it. In addition, she used Colgate toothpaste because of its taste, Listerine, Feenamint laxative, because you could chew it like gum, Jonteel powder, and Palmolive soap—all items that she had seen advertised in her magazines. Mrs. W. was also an earnest shopper: she compared prices, made shopping lists, and shopped on Saturday nights when she went to town, or she made special trips to other stores in different communities.

Mrs. B., on the other hand, had a district school education and received just two magazines, *Dairymen's League News* and *Farmer's Wife*. She indicated a preference for only two brand-name food items: Red Circle coffee, the A&P house brand, because it was cheaper, and Rosebud flour, a local brand that she used out of habit. She could not remember what brand of bread she bought, although she typically baked her own bread because she liked it better and because it was cheaper. In the same vein, she did not buy canned vegetables, probably because she put up her own. She and her husband also used several products that were not advertised widely but were familiar to rural consumers: Dr. Hinkle's cascara, which was good for digestive regulation, and Watkin's liniment, which could be used on cows as well as people and was sold door-to-door by local agents who were typically neighbors or relatives. They did not use any toothpaste, but they also bought Palmolive soap, which they liked even though it did not last. But, because Mrs. B. had a supply of beef fat, she also made her own soap, which, presumably, lasted longer. Unlike Mrs. W., Mrs. B. did not make any special shopping trips, nor did she make a shopping list. Rather, she did her shopping in town in the morning when her husband delivered the milk. While the rest of the women surveyed fell somewhere in between these two ends of the spectrum, all of them bought some nationally advertised brand-name products and, conversely, chose not to buy others.

Thus, farm families during the 1920s were increasingly dependent on the larger consumer economy for their food. According to various surveys, farms in the Northeast typically supplied just over half of the farm family's food, down from over 60 percent a decade earlier, while comparable figures for midwestern farms during the 1920s ranged from 62 to 69 percent. In general, dairy, meat, poultry, and eggs came from the farm, and flour, fruits, cereal products, fats, and sweets were purchased at the store. Nor was direct purchase from nearby farmers a common alternative. According to the surveys near Penn Yan and Lockport, farm families sometimes bought butter from their neighbors, particularly if, as dairy farmers, they had to sell all their milk and could not make their own. Similarly, local farmers were only an infrequent source of meat, poultry, fruits, and vegetables. In Mrs. B.'s case, however, she bought peaches, tomatoes, and potatoes from farms in the neighborhood.[72]

Mostly, the surveyed farm families bought their food at the groceries in town, where they purchased brands that were widely advertised in both agricultural and general magazines. Morning might start with a breakfast of Quaker oats or Kellogg's cereal, Swift's bacon, Sunkist oranges, and Eight-O'Clock coffee (even though it was probably much earlier). The noonday meal could have featured an Armour ham, Campbell's soup, and a pineapple-upside-down cake made with Del Monte or Hawaiian pineapple and Gold Medal, Pillsbury, or Swansdown flour, while a light supper of sandwiches made with Kraft cheese and Hellman's Blue Ribbon mayonnaise rounded out the day's repast.

Rural consumers did not follow such advertising blindly, however. Coffee was one of the most common food items purchased by farm households, and almost all of the 121 households surveyed indicated a specific brand preference. Although the survey listed dozens of brands of coffee, Red Circle, the house label for A&P groceries, was the overwhelming favorite and was used in 34 households even though it was not advertised in national periodicals. Many of those who chose Red Circle did so because it was cheap, but more justified their preference because of the coffee's flavor. "Flavor best, have tried many others," stated sixty-two-year-old Mrs. M., who had seen all of the competitors' advertising in the eight women's magazines that she read. Mrs. VanB. liked Red Circle so much that she made special stops at the A&P to get it, because it was the only thing that she bought there. The second most popular brand of coffee, Eight-O'Clock, had 12 customers who also used it because it was inexpensive and because they liked the flavor. By contrast, Maxwell House and White House coffees, who sponsored their own radio shows but whose print advertisements featured testimonials from the wives of millionaires or elegant formal dinner parties, had only 9 and 5 customers, respectively, even though they were the next most popular brands. In terms of coffee, then, rural families chose on the basis of price and practicality rather than in response to images of glamour and sophistication.

The limited appeals of such urbane elegance are also evident in the choices of soap, which was one of the most heavily advertised and frequently consumed brand-name items in the survey. Indeed, only one of the households asked expressed no preference for any brand of soap. Palmolive and Ivory were the two leaders, with 43 homes using the former, and 39 homes using the latter, although in some cases a single family used both brands.[73] The 1929 advertisements for Palmolive emphasized the product's olive oil content and its ability to protect the face against "modern dangers to skin beauty"; under the motto, "Keep That Schoolgirl Complexion," it was aimed at middle-aged as opposed to younger women. Ivory focused on hands and showed pictures of slender hands washing dishes and clothing by day and lighting dinner candles by night under its slogan, "Protection for fair hands (all day long)," in addition to its usual mottos: "Kind to everything it touches," "99–44/100% pure," and "'It Floats.'"

When asked why they chose their brands, rural homemakers offered a range of responses. Many simply said "habit," or "good," or "like it"; others liked the low price: "cheap," they said. Quite a number, however, noted that they had seen or heard the advertising and several appropriated themes from those advertisements in their reasons. For some, Palmolive was preferred because it was "very nice for skin," or "more oily," and one woman even stated that the soap allowed her to "keep that schoolgirl complexion!" By the same token, Ivory was "best and pure," or "pure and children like it," or it "swims," and it "keeps hands soft," or is "good for dishes and hands."

As country consumers bought Ivory and Palmolive, they declined to buy other soaps that were the same price and whose advertisements appeared in the same magazines. Like Palmolive, Woodbury's soap also stressed its ability to produce beautiful skin and ran extensive advertising in the *Farmer's Wife* as well as more general magazines such as the *Ladies' Home Journal*. As opposed to Palmolive, which touted nice skin for its own sake and showed a mature woman looking at herself in a mirror, Woodbury's advertisements stressed beautiful skin as the way to lure and keep a man, and pictured tuxedo-clad men adoring fair-skinned women under the caption, "Youth and Love." But such an appeal was not effective with rural consumers, and only three households in the survey used this product. In the same vein, relatively few farm households responded to Lux soap's advertising campaign, which emphasized Hollywood and featured numerous film stars, including Clara Bow and Joan Crawford, touting the product's virtues. "Nine out of ten screen stars keep their skin lovely with Lux Toilet Soap," went the ad, but barely one out of ten farm families were buying it.[74]

Toothpaste was also widely used and frequently advertised. Two families used old-fashioned, homemade dentifrices like charcoal or baking soda, and at least two elderly households did not use anything because they did not have any teeth. For the rest, though, Colgate and Listerine were the overwhelming favorites, and were used by 37 and 28 households, respectively. The next most popular brand, Forhan's, was marketed primarily as an effective agent against pyorrhea, or gum disease, and 5 of the 9 families that used it gave that reason. None of the other nationally advertised brands, Pepsodent, Ipana, or Squibbs, had more than 6 customers.

New York farm families used Colgate primarily because they liked its taste and its price, not because they responded to its advertising. Typical comments included "habit," "cheap," "good for money," "large bottle, tastes good," and "whole family likes it." In addition, one farm woman bought Colgate because the ten-cent store carried it, while another noted that it was stocked on the market wagon that came around to the farms. Only one interviewee directly acknowledged Colgate's advertisements, and no one gave reasons that indirectly incorporated themes from those advertisements, which were fairly nondescript.

By contrast, a number of those surveyed noted that they paid attention to advertisements for Listerine, and others justified their choice of the product in terms that were highlighted by those advertisements. This is hardly surprising, because Listerine owed its success to its advertising and budgeted $5 million for it in 1928. Initially marketed as a general antiseptic, it became a mouthwash after the company exhumed the term "halitosis" from an old medical dictionary and used it to play on people's insecurities about bad breath. This success led the company to promote new uses for the product as a cure for dandruff, an aftershave tonic, a cure for colds and sore throats, an astringent, a deodorant, and more, and to create Listerine toothpaste and shaving cream, which brought even more financial returns.[75]

Most Listerine advertisements featured Listerine antiseptic rather than Listerine toothpaste or shaving cream, although the other products were often mentioned in a separate box in the text. Advertisements specifically for Listerine toothpaste appealed to the practical and stressed Listerine's low price compared to other dentifrices, a savings that allowed one woman to buy a pair of galoshes, according to a pitch in the *Woman's Home Companion.* The vast majority of Listerine advertisements, however, adopted what came to be known as the "halitosis style" or the "halitosis appeal," which presented a surrogate for the consumer as the protagonist and offered sympathy and advice to readers who, in the words of one scholar, faced "those intrusive, impersonal judgments of their skin, teeth, figure, clothes, furniture—even their choice of car polish and house paint—that modern life occasioned."[76]

As in its advertisements in general periodicals, Listerine relied on this "halitosis style" in numerous ads for farm periodicals targeted specifically at rural consumers. One series, which appeared in winter issues of the *Country Gentleman* and the *Farm Journal,* depicted an elderly farmer or an elderly farm wife worried about sore throats and catching a cold as they did farm chores outside in inclement weather. Although Listerine advertisements in more mainstream periodicals also focused on sore throats and colds, these

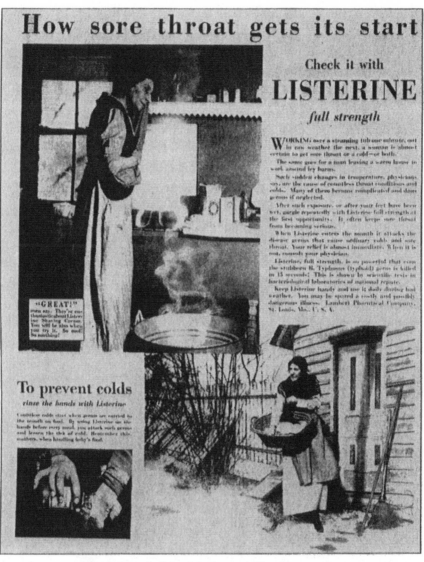

Advertisement for Listerine, Country Gentleman, *1929.*
(Courtesy of Farm Journal*)*

featured much younger models in urban settings. Another ad in the *Rural New Yorker* raised the specter of dandruff within the context of the rural community, in this case, a country church. Under the caption "In church the truth comes out," a picture shows the backs of a small congregation at Sunday services with text describing how noticeable dandruff is in church, "with only heads to look at." "Don't let dandruff humiliate you," went the blurb, use Listerine.

The most poignant Listerine advertisements, however, featured a young farm girl who cannot get or keep a boyfriend because she has bad breath. In an advertisement in the *Farmer's Wife*, she looks dejected as she leans against a sign announcing a dance on Saturday night: "Bring your best girl!" "Not invited because of halitosis," and "You can't be welcome when you have halitosis," proclaims the ad. The same model appears for Listerine in the *Rural New Yorker*, where she is outside at the clothesline sharing a letter that she has just received with her mother. Her expression is pained and her mother is somber because the letter announces that her beau is calling off their affair. "The romance wrecker," reads the headline; "Halitosis a handicap to popularity and a bar to marriage." This image also communicates an unspoken message: because the bad news comes in a letter, we assume that the lost suitor is not from the same community, and maybe not even a farmer. Likewise, the contrast between the mother, who is overweight and unattractive, and the daughter, who still has her youthful good looks (and even a touch of makeup), signals that, if she does not use Listerine, she will never leave the farm (which the author of the ad assumes is her desire), and she will wind up looking like her mother.

Even though they reflected the urban advertising agents' assumptions and biases about rural society, these appeals resonated with some of the consumers in the survey. Several of the respondents noted directly that they had seen Listerine advertised and that they were influenced by those advertisements. One woman stated that she had heard about Listerine from a friend and attributed the fact that she had not caught any colds to the product, while another talked about Listerine as having "healing" properties. Three farm wives indicated that they bought Listerine because their daughters preferred it, and in their cases the daughters were all of marriageable age but not yet married. One of these families, whose thirty-year-old daughter was still single, actually received the issue of the *Farmer's Wife* that depicted the girl

Advertisement for Listerine, Rural New Yorker, *1928.*
(Courtesy of American Agriculturalist*)*

Advertisement for Listerine, Farmer's Wife, *1928. (Courtesy of* Farm Journal*)*

with halitosis and without a date to the dance. Given such appeals, Listerine was particularly popular in households with eligible unmarried children. Seventeen of the forty households in the Penn Yan survey, or 42 percent, contained unmarried children who were of marriageable age, and 70 percent of those households used Listerine, representing three-fourths of all the families in the township that used the product.

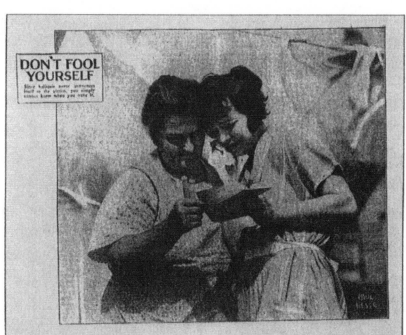

The romance wrecker

*Halitosis (unpleasant breath) a handicap
to popularity and a bar to marriage*

MANY a love affair is nipped in the bud simply because either the man or the woman has halitosis—and is not aware of it.

Don't fool yourself that you never have this all-too-common ailment. Since it never announces itself to the victim, you simply cannot know when you have it. But others know—and are offended.

How foolish to risk such offense when, by simply using Listerine systematically, you can put yourself on the safe side—and the polite side.

Listerine ends halitosis quickly. Being antiseptic, it attacks bacteria that usually cause odors. And, then, being a powerful deodorant, it overcomes the odors themselves. Even the strong odors of fish and onion yield to it.

You need only to rinse the mouth with Listerine to eliminate the risk of offending. You'll find it a precaution worth taking. Keep a bottle handy in your bathroom or on your dressing table. Lambert Pharmacal Co., St. Louis, Mo., U. S. A.

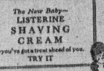

The New Baby—
**LISTERINE
SHAVING
CREAM**
you've got a treat ahead of you.
TRY IT

LISTERINE
The safe antiseptic

READ THE FACTS
If you had halitosis
68

Advertisement for Listerine, Rural New Yorker, *1928.
(Courtesy of* American Agriculturalist*)*

In contrast to the success of appeals based on price and practicality or the particular health concerns and social anxieties of life in a rural community, toothpaste advertisements that stressed glamour, sophistication, and appearance evoked less of a response among rural consumers. Pepsodent touted its abilities to remove the film that is to blame "when smiles lose fascination," and Squibb's protected the smile's beauty by attacking "the danger line" where the teeth meet the gums, but neither product was very popular. Although two of the women surveyed bought Ipana because of its radio program, its print advertisements featured drawings of a very chic and formally attired crowd at a city nightclub in the style of Toulouse-Lautrec, and failed to lure other rural customers.

Farm women also related to consumer culture as producers of food and clothing, and their skills as cooks and seamstresses as well as the superiority of their products gave them another vantage point from which to negotiate the larger culture. The majority of farm women made their own soups, for example, which they preferred to the canned variety: "can't eat the other kind, like home-made better," noted sixty-three-year-old Mrs. T. Likewise, a number of farm women canned their own vegetables, and many of those who bought canned goods did so only because they did not have any corn or peas of their own to put up.

Bread, however, was the most common product that could be made at home or bought in the store, and about half of the farm women in the survey baked all or most of their own bread. Economy was an important reason for making bread at home, and this was especially true in larger households— "cheaper for large family," stated one thirty-nine-year-old mother of seven. Taste and preference were more common reasons than cost, though, and frequent remarks included "like homemade better," "family likes better, never think of buying," "don't like baker's bread," or "husband likes better."

Conversely, the farm women who relied on store-bought bread typically stressed its convenience rather than its superior quality: "easier" and "don't have time to bake" were the most common expressions. Others thought that it was "just as cheap" as homemade, and women in small households felt that it did not pay to bake for a small family. One woman considered store-bought bread better than her own, which typically got hard, while another woman bought her bread because her family scolded her when she did her own baking (Let them eat cake, and make it themselves!).

Whether women took pride in their skills or only grudgingly acceded to their husband's demands, home baking and canning provided a measure of insulation from consumer culture, and women who pursued these activities bought fewer brand-name items than those who did not (they obviously did not buy bread or canned vegetables). Younger women under forty were much more likely to buy their bread than to bake it, either because they lacked the time to bother or felt more comfortable serving bread that was mass-produced; older women who presided over an empty nest often also bought bread rather than go to the trouble of making it. For all of these women, however, homemade bread provided the standard by which to judge the store-bought item, not the other way around. As one elderly Indiana woman recalled about her farm mother during the early twentieth century: "We had thirteen at the table. . . . It was nothing for her to bake every day, bread, and make six loaves at a time. Great big loaves—you can't beat such bread today." [77]

Similar considerations shaped farm women's decisions about clothing. In addition to preparing food, farm women also made clothing for themselves and their families: over 90 percent of the farm women near Penn Yan and Lockport made at least some of their family's clothing, and fewer than 10 percent either bought all of it ready-made or had it made by a tailor or dressmaker. As was the case in the nineteenth century, the farm women in the survey usually did not make men's clothing, although a few did sew their husbands' shirts, especially if they were large men who were difficult to fit. Relatively few women made their own tailored coats, their fanciest wool or silk dresses, or sewed their children's best clothing. Everyday cotton dresses, aprons, and children's regular clothes, however, were typically made at home.

Although economy was the most common reason given for making clothes at home, many women also thought that homemade clothes were better in addition to being cheaper. One forty-one-year-old mother of three complained that bought dresses were very poorly made and that she had to sew them over again, while another farm wife criticized ready-made garments for buttonholes that were not well made, seams that often needed sewing, and hems that came out. Another younger farm wife made her own dresses because it was hard to get the right size; she usually had to alter ready-

made dresses, whose material was hard to sew, and there was no extra material for making small repairs. Getting a good fit was a more common problem
for older women who were stout (like the mother depicted in the Listerine
advertisement), so they also made their own dresses or went to a dressmaker
instead of relying on ready-made merchandise.

If cost, quality, and fit were the main reasons for making clothes at home,
convenience and style led farm women to buy their garments at the store.
Mrs. S., for example, bought her wool dresses because they had "more snap
and style" than the ones she made at home. Considerations of style were especially important for younger farm wives or families with marriageable
daughters. In the Lockport survey, women who gave style as a reason for
buying ready-made dresses and coats were, on average, over ten years
younger than those who did not. Given that other surveys show that rural
consumers were willing to drive the greatest distances to buy women's dress
clothing, it is also significant that eight out of ten of these women also drove.
Even farm women who made all of their own everyday clothing and most of
their better dresses still bought an occasional wool or silk dress for its style or
because they "liked it." These patterns are confirmed by cost-of-living surveys in other rural areas, which show the highest expenditures for ready-
made clothing and the lowest for homemade clothing among single women
and young farm wives.[78]

For rural women in the 1920s, then, navigating among the myriad brand-
name items characteristic of an emerging consumer culture was a complicated and contradictory process. While none of them lived entirely outside of
the consumer culture and could ignore it completely, they were able to exercise some control and act in accordance with their own predispositions when
picking and choosing among brand-name items. From the advertisements
and the survey data it seems that they chose their products on the basis of
practical considerations such as price and utility rather than in response to
images that celebrated a more glamorous lifestyle. Yet they also responded to
more subjective appeals and nonrepresentational advertisements that were
directed at rural consumers, even though these embodied assumptions about
farm life that they may not have shared. Their participation in consumer culture, then, was tempered by both the realities of farm life and their psychological distance from the glitter and supposed sophistication of the big city.

Part of that distance was the result of their roles as producers of food and

clothing for the farm household. The ability to make products that were seen
as superior to those available in the stores provided both economic and emotional insulation from the imperatives of mass consumption. As with so
many other aspects of the integration of the countryside into the larger society, however, that distance was much more prevalent among the older generation than the younger; and even as their mothers continued to make clothes,
bake bread, and put up fruits and vegetables, younger farm women were increasingly more comfortable with more costly, convenient, and stylish ready-
made alternatives. For them, the products of mass consumer culture were a
better fit, literally and figuratively.

Rural northerners became integrated into an emerging consumer culture
during the 1920s, but they did so largely on their own terms. Rather than embrace the more modern or sophisticated lifestyles being promoted by the
land-grant universities and Madison Avenue, country people picked among
the new products in ways that were consistent with their own values and priorities. Their cars were humble Model Ts or other modest makes whose purchase was justified primarily in terms of their practical uses in the farm enterprise rather than as pleasure vehicles. In the same vein, the radio became
increasingly popular toward the end of the decade because it was useful as
well as enjoyable and did not disrupt the workings of the farm household.
Rural consumers also affirmed the practical and rejected appeals to glamour
in more modest ways when they bought certain brand-name items and chose
not to buy others, a perspective that was reinforced by farm women's own
skills as producers of food and clothing. Utility was a gendered concept,
however, and it did not extend to home electrical plants and other appliances
and home improvements, which affected only women's work and were much
less widely adopted, in part, for that reason.

Although rural consumers exercised some control and discretion over
what they bought, the consequences of those purchases led in directions they
did not anticipate. The universal adoption of the automobile dealt an almost
fatal blow to the small village economy and reconfigured the economic and
social geography of the northern countryside on a much wider scale. While
much that farmers and their families did in their cars continued and expanded older patterns of interaction, the new spatial context lessened the
significance of the smaller communities in their lives. In the same vein, the

radio provided a new frame of reference that also transcended the older local community. Yet the rural culture instituted on the airwaves paradoxically celebrated old-fashioned virtues of localism and neighborliness even as it rendered the specific communities more marginal culturally. So, too, did rural consumers, especially the young, come to see themselves in images from afar that flickered across the screen or were created specifically for them by the manufacturers of Listerine and other products.

Much of the integration of the northern countryside into the consumer culture of the 1920s, then, fostered a hybrid rural version of that culture rather than a replication of more mainstream patterns. Institutionalized in farmers' night in the market towns, the WLS *Barn Dance* and the *RFD Dinnerbell* shows, and the portrayals of older farm women and dateless country girls in national advertising directed at rural consumers, this culture catered to and continued more traditional sensibilities even as it put rural life on new translocal and transregional footings. This paralleled and reinforced other nationalizing tendencies in the countryside, particularly the political mobilization that culminated in the farmers' New Deal. It also offered an alternative to urban culture and a critique of urban society, which informed rural folk who moved to the cities as well as those who stayed in the countryside. In significant ways, then, rural encounters with consumer culture during the 1920s simultaneously helped to unify and homogenize northern agrarian society while adding to its more general ambivalence about modern life.

CONCLUSION

After the Civil War, the United States experienced a second great transformation in which new forces of change refashioned the contours of American life. Spearheaded by the rise of big business and the emergence of a new corporate mentality, this transformation was led by a new middle class of managers and professionals heeding bureaucratic imperatives and criteria of efficiency. It received additional momentum from the spread of new consumer goods and the expansion of mass culture.

Country people were particularly challenged by these changes, which threatened both their core assumptions and their place in American society. The centralization of political authority and the consolidation of economic power jeopardized their control over important local institutions as well as the independence they enjoyed as agricultural producers and small businessmen. Likewise, an emerging consumer culture had the potential to usurp more traditional sources of meaning, eclipsing the significance of their communities as arbiters of value and shaking their long-standing faith in the superiority of rural, as opposed to urban, life. In myriad ways, then, the second great transformation signaled a troubling shift in the center of gravity of American society, away from the countryside and its communities and toward the state, the corporation, and the city.

As rural northerners struggled with these challenges between 1870 and 1930, they fought to maintain autonomy in an increasingly corporate and translocal society and to preserve an older vision of the virtues of agrarian life that was bounded by the local community. They resisted those aspects of the second great transformation that posed the most direct affronts to these sensibilities, especially the high-handed efforts of outside reformers and corporations to restructure and control local life. But when they sent off to Montgomery Ward, or listened to the WLS *Barn Dance*, or started their own cooperatives, they also embraced other elements of the new order in ways that were consistent with their values, and, initially at least, even strengthened them.

In these ways, then, the second great transformation in the rural North yielded a mixed harvest, and northern country people in 1930 still enjoyed a significant measure of distance from the new order as well as an alternative point of view. On the local level, for example, they had stymied efforts to consolidate rural schools, acting in the name of the community and the individual, and, within their households, they rejected the appeals of a burgeoning consumer culture based on urban glamour and sophistication. More generally, with respect to the nation as a whole, new kinds of rural institutions and organizations as well as new forms of rural culture continued to stand outside of the mainstream and to voice opposition. Thus, the second great transformation in the countryside remained incomplete.

In the course of their negotiations with the forces of the second great transformation, however, the "way of life" that northern country people struggled to maintain had changed, often in ways that they did not anticipate, and they found themselves in a much different relationship to the larger society than earlier. Jefferson's voice, which had resonated so loudly in their thoughts and actions only a few decades before, was reduced to a whisper. Consequently, their future ability to maintain their distance from and opposition to the new order was much more uncertain.

Like their forbears, northern agrarians in 1930 continued to criticize the urban and corporate directions of American society, but they did so increasingly as organized interest groups in a new political economy. Politically, that trajectory transcended older regional divisions and led to the Farm Bloc and later to the farmers' New Deal, which fundamentally restructured relationships between country people and the state and added still other sources of authority in rural life that came from beyond the local community.

Northern farmers were also organized in new ways as producers and as small businessmen. But the appeals to independence and localism that helped shape these efforts had already revealed their limitations and would soon face even greater pressures for economic centralization during the Great Depression, World War II, and the postwar period. These were reinforced by the government's expanded role in agrarian society and accelerated by new farm technologies, the ever-shrinking number of farms and farmers, and the more recent rise of agribusiness.

As consumers, rural northerners had also acted at first in ways that were of a piece with time-honored values and attitudes. In part, new technologies allowed them to extend older forms of community over wider areas and to celebrate localism and other agrarian sensibilities in different media. Much in this hybrid rural consumer culture remained critical of the larger society, but, in the end, the medium undercut the message and integrated the countryside more closely. And, as it became detached from any specific community, country life itself became reified as a commodity that was "consumed" by both rural people and their kin and neighbors who moved to the city. This was less true of their children, however, who were drawn increasingly to the mainstream, aided by the automobiles and hard roads that their parents and grandparents had initially opposed.

The story of the second great transformation in the rural North, then, is one of resistance and accommodation and of change as well as continuity, and it represents a mixed harvest for both the countryside and the nation as a whole. In the end, though, harvests, whether mixed or otherwise, also produce seed for the next crop, and for rural northerners after 1930, this meant still other changes in their roles as citizens, producers, and consumers. How they negotiated these new challenges and whether those efforts also yielded mixed results, however, must remain questions for another season.

NOTES

INTRODUCTION

1. Hubert G. Schmidt, *Rural Hunterdon: An Agricultural History* (New Brunswick, N.J.: Rutgers University Press, 1946), pp. 166–68; and James J. Flink, *America Adopts the Automobile, 1895–1910* (Cambridge, Mass.: MIT Press, 1970).

2. Frank B. Latham, *1872–1972, A Century of Serving Consumers: The Story of Montgomery Ward* (Chicago: Montgomery Ward & Co., 1972), p. 41.

3. Helen Bull Vandervort, interview, typescript, 1964, Division of Rare and Manuscript Collections, Cornell University Library, pp. 69–72.

4. See Alfred D. Chandler Jr., *The Visible Hand: The Managerial Revolution in American Business* (Cambridge, Mass.: Harvard University Press, 1977); Robert Wiebe, *The Search for Order, 1877–1920* (New York: Hill and Wang, 1967); Louis Galambos, "The Emerging Organizational Synthesis in Modern American History," *Business History Review* 44 (1970): 279–90; and Galambos, "Technology, Political Economy, and Professionalization: Central Themes of the Organizational Synthesis," *Business History Review* 57 (1983): 471–93.

5. See the essays by Theda Skocpol in Peter B. Evans, Dietrich Rueschemeyer, and Theda Skocpol, eds., *Bringing the State Back In* (New York: Cambridge University Press, 1985), pp. 3–37, 347–66; and Stephen Skowronek, *Building a New American State: The Expansion of National Administrative Capacities, 1877–1920* (New York: Cambridge University Press, 1982). On the rise of consumer culture, see Richard W. Fox and T. J. Jackson Lears, eds., *The Culture of Consumption: Critical Essays in American History, 1880–1980* (New York: Pantheon, 1983); William Leach, *Land of Desire: Merchants, Power, and the Rise of a New American Culture* (New York: Pantheon, 1993); and T. J. Jackson Lears, *Fables of Abundance: A Cultural History of Advertising in America* (New York: Basic Books, 1994).

6. Olivier Zunz, *Making America Corporate, 1870–1920* (Chicago: University of Chicago Press, 1990); Lizabeth Cohen, *Making a New Deal: Industrial Workers in Chicago, 1919–1939* (New York: Cambridge University Press, 1990); and Kenneth Cmiel, "Destiny and Amnesia: The Vision of Modernity in Robert Wiebe's *The Search for Order*," *Reviews in American History* 21 (1993): 352–68.

7. Lawrence Goodwyn, *Democratic Promise: The Populist Moment in America* (New York: Oxford University Press, 1976); Robert C. McMath Jr., *American Populism: A*

Social History, 1877–1898 (New York: Hill and Wang, 1993); Don S. Kirschner, *City and Country: Rural Responses to Urbanization in the 1920s* (Westport, Conn.: Greenwood Press, 1970); and Wiebe, *Search for Order*, p. 301.

8. William Cronon, *Nature's Metropolis: Chicago and the Great West* (New York: W. W. Norton, 1991); Zunz, *Making America Corporate*, pp. 149–73; William L. Bowers, *The Country Life Movement in America, 1900–1920* (Port Washington, N.Y.: Kennikat Press, 1974); David B. Danbom, *The Resisted Revolution: Urban America and the Industrialization of Agriculture, 1900–1930* (Ames: Iowa State University Press, 1979); and Grant Mc-Connell, *The Decline of Agrarian Democracy* (New York: Atheneum, 1969).

9. Good examples of each of these perspectives are, respectively, Christopher Clark, *The Roots of Rural Capitalism: Western Massachusetts, 1780–1860* (Ithaca: Cornell University Press, 1990); and Winifred B. Rothenberg, *From Market Places to a Market Economy: The Transformation of Rural Massachusetts, 1750–1850* (Chicago: University of Chicago Press, 1992).

10. For recent studies that add new dimensions to the "social" perspective, see J. Ritchie Garrison, *Landscape and Material Life in Franklin County, Massachusetts, 1770–1860* (Knoxville: University of Tennessee Press, 1991); and Sally McMurry, *Transforming Rural Life: Dairying Families and Agricultural Change, 1820–1885* (Baltimore: Johns Hopkins University Press, 1995).

11. Jeremy Atack and Fred Bateman, *To Their Own Soil: Agriculture in the Antebellum North* (Ames: Iowa State University Press, 1987), pp. 12, 272–73.

12. See Hal S. Barron, *Those Who Stayed Behind: Rural Society in Nineteenth-Century New England* (New York: Cambridge University Press, 1984); Paula Baker, *The Moral Frameworks of Public Life: Gender, Politics, and the State in Rural New York, 1870–1930* (New York: Oxford University Press, 1991); Nancy Grey Osterud, *Bonds of Community: The Lives of Farm Women in Nineteenth-Century New York* (Ithaca: Cornell University Press, 1991); and Jane M. Pederson, *Between Memory and Reality: Family and Community in Rural Wisconsin, 1870–1970* (Madison: University of Wisconsin Press, 1992).

13. For an insightful discussion of these values and attitudes, see Paul H. John-stone, "Old Ideals versus New Ideas in Farm Life," in *Farmers in a Changing World*, U.S. Department of Agriculture Yearbook (Washington, D.C.: U.S. Government Printing Office, 1940), pp. 111–70. See also McConnell, *The Decline of Agrarian Democracy*.

CHAPTER ONE

1. See William L. Bowers, *The Country Life Movement in America, 1900–1920* (Port Washington, N.Y.: Kennikat Press, 1974); David B. Danbom, *The Resisted Revolution: Urban America and the Industrialization of Agriculture, 1900–1930* (Ames: Iowa State Uni-

versity Press, 1979); Wayne Fuller, *The Old Country School: The Story of Rural Education in the Middle West* (Chicago: University of Chicago Press, 1982); and James H. Madison, "Reformers and the Rural Church, 1900–1950," *Journal of American History* 73 (1986): 645–68. For a discussion of rural opposition to reform efforts in a different region, see William A. Link, *The Paradox of Southern Progressivism, 1880–1930* (Chapel Hill: University of North Carolina Press, 1992); and Jeanette Keith, *Country People in the New South: Tennessee's Upper Cumberland* (Chapel Hill: University of North Carolina Press, 1995).

2. John R. Stilgoe, *Common Landscape of America, 1580 to 1845* (New Haven: Yale University Press, 1982), pp. 128–29. Roads in the newer western states were straight, not crooked, and followed section lines regardless of hills, streams, or swamps, to the consternation of long-distance travelers.

3. The obvious exceptions to this generalization are private turnpikes and military roads on the frontier. After their heyday in the early nineteenth century, however, many turnpikes (especially the unprofitable and poorly maintained ones) reverted to public ownership and control by local government; the same fate befell military roads as the territories became settled.

4. Frederick G. Howes, *History of the Town of Ashfield, Franklin County, Massachusetts, from Its Settlement in 1742 to 1910* (Ashfield, Mass.: The Town of Ashfield, n.d.), p. 112; Wisconsin critic quoted in Brian W. Beltman, "Rural Renaissance in an Urban Age: The Country Life Movement in Wisconsin, 1895–1918" (Ph.D. diss., University of Wisconsin, 1975), p. 361.

5. Isabel S. Mitchell, *Roads and Road-Making in Colonial Connecticut* (New Haven: Yale University Press, 1933), pp. 31–32.

6. Stilgoe, *Common Landscape*, p. 131.

7. *Country Gentleman*, April 14, 1892, p. 284.

8. Quoted in George S. May, "The Good Roads Movement in Iowa," *The Palimpsest* 36 (1955): 20.

9. Robert R. R. Brooks, ed., *Williamstown, The First Two Hundred Years, 1753–1953* (Williamstown, Mass.: McClelland Press, 1953), pp. 135–39; Hubert G. Schmidt, *Rural Hunterdon: An Agricultural History* (New Brunswick, N.J.: Rutgers University Press, 1946), p. 164. See also chap. 2, "Demands for Better Roads," in Joseph A. Durrenberger, *Turnpikes: A Study of the Toll Road Movement in the Middle Atlantic States and Maryland* (Valdosta, Ga.: Southern Stationery and Printing Co., 1931), pp. 26–44; and Edward C. Kirkland, *Men, Cities, and Transportation: A Study in New England History, 1820–1900* (Cambridge, Mass.: Harvard University Press, 1948), vol. 1, pp. 32–37.

10. The inclusion of these top treatises in the annual report of the Massachusetts Board of Agriculture as well as their publication in a separate volume ensured an audience and an influence beyond the borders of the Commonwealth. See Massachu-

setts Board of Agriculture, *Annual Report, 1869–1870* (Boston, 1870), pp. 202–311. In its next session, the legislature commissioned a detailed survey of road administration in each township and city in the state to be conducted by Charles L. Flint, the secretary of the Board of Agriculture, and this, too, was published in the board's annual report. See Charles L. Flint, "Roads and Road Making," in Massachusetts Board of Agriculture, *Annual Report, 1870–1871* (Boston, 1871), pp. 20–82. Both the essays and the report continued to be cited as authoritative statements in discussions of road matters in other states until the end of the nineteenth century. The top essay, "The Science of Road Making," by Clemens Herschel of Boston, for instance, was revised in 1877 and published in *Engineering News*, which also reissued it in a small book in 1894.

11. On the professional culture of civil engineers, see Daniel H. Calhoun, *The American Civil Engineer* (Cambridge, Mass.: MIT Press, 1960); Monte A. Calvert, *The Mechanical Engineer in America, 1830–1910: Professional Cultures in Conflict* (Baltimore: Johns Hopkins University Press, 1967); and Raymond H. Merritt, *Engineering in American Society, 1850–1875* (Lexington: University of Kentucky Press, 1969).

12. Massachusetts Board of Agriculture, *Report, 1870*, p. 74.

13. Flint, "Roads and Roadmaking," pp. 20–82.

14. These were typically published in the annual report of the state board of agriculture. See Connecticut State Board of Agriculture, *Annual Report* (Hartford), 1875–76, pp. 31–79, 204–15; 1886, pp. 316–27; 1887, pp. 147–94; Illinois State Department of Agriculture, *Transactions* (Springfield), 1865, pp. 677–79; 1874, pp. 140–63; Ohio State Board of Agriculture, *Annual Report, 1882* (Columbus, 1883), pp. 532–37; Maine State Board of Agriculture, *Annual Report, 1870* (Augusta, 1871), pp. 223–57; Michigan State Board of Agriculture, *Annual Report* (Lansing), 1875, pp. 364–68; 1876, pp. 286–88; 1880, pp. 153–56; 1884, pp. 103–9; 1886, pp. 151–54; 1887, pp. 348–52; 1888–89, pp. 381–93; 1889–90, pp. 367–69; New Hampshire State Board of Agriculture, *Annual Report, 1872* (Manchester, 1872), pp. 397–408; New Jersey State Board of Agriculture, *Annual Report* (Trenton), 1886, pp. 225–35; 1887, pp. 107–39; 1890–91, pp. 195–218; Pennsylvania State Board of Agriculture, *Agriculture of Pennsylvania* (Harrisburg), 1877, pp. 252–56; 1886, pp. 113–23; 1889, pp. 336–87; 1890, pp. 113–82; Vermont State Board of Agriculture, *Biennial Report* (Montpelier), 1873–74, pp. 650–64; 1891–92, pp. 242–68; Wisconsin State Agricultural Society, *Transactions, 1885* (Madison, 1885), pp. 206–21.

15. Maine State Board of Agriculture, *Annual Report, 1870* (Augusta, 1871), p. 253.

16. Moses Humphrey, "Making and Repairing Roads," in New Hampshire Board of Agriculture, *Second Annual Report, 1872* (Manchester, 1872), pp. 397–408.

17. Pennsylvania State Board of Agriculture, *Agriculture of Pennsylvania, 1890* (Harrisburg, 1890), p. 115.

18. Michigan Board of Agriculture, *Twenty-Third Annual Report, 1884* (Lansing, 1884), pp. 103–9.

19. Pennsylvania State Board of Agriculture, *Annual Report, 1890* (Harrisburg, 1890), pp. 113–53, 118; *Country Gentleman*, August 27, 1891, p. 694.

20. C. O. Parmenter, *History of Pelham, Massachusetts from 1738 to 1898* (Amherst, Mass.: Press of Carpenter and Morehouse, 1898), p. 211.

21. Although these changes happened more frequently in the 1880s after the introduction of new road machinery, laws allowing the adoption of a cash tax were typically already on the books. In 1873, for example, the New York Legislature provided that any town might adopt the money system. Apparently, though, some towns that tried it wanted to switch back, because in 1879, the legislature allowed towns that had changed to the money system to return to the labor system. See W. M. Curtiss, "Development of Highway Administration and Finance in New York," Cornell University Agricultural Experiment Station, *Bulletin* 680 (1937): 22.

22. On the introduction of road graders, see Howard Rosen and Joel Mendes, eds., *One Hundred Years of Public Works Equipment: An Illustrated History* (Chicago: Public Works Historical Society, 1986), pp. 8–9.

23. Connecticut State Board of Agriculture, *Twenty-First Annual Report, 1887* (Hartford, 1887), p. 192; Pennsylvania State Board of Agriculture, *Agriculture of Pennsylvania, 1889* (Harrisburg, 1889), p. 365.

24. Connecticut State Board of Agriculture, *Twentieth Annual Report, 1886* (Hartford, 1886), pp. 316–27.

25. Howes, *Ashfield*, pp. 112–14.

26. Although advocates argued (not always convincingly) that maintaining a stone road actually cost less than keeping up more ordinary roads, the initial costs of construction were staggering, ranging from $1,000 to $10,000 per mile depending on local conditions, most typically about $2,000 per mile.

27. Joseph B. Doyle, *Twentieth Century History of Steubenville and Jefferson County, Ohio* (Chicago: Richmond-Arnold Publishing Co., 1910), vol. 1, pp. 215–16.

28. One example of this is the 1870 defeat of a $90,000 tax in Rush County, Indiana, to finance the construction of the Toledo & Louisville Railroad through Rushville. This came after bitter experiences with three other railroads. Quoting the local *Rushville Republican*: "The people had been 'done' too often to favor a tax of this kind." See A. L. Gary and E. B. Thomas, *Centennial History of Rush County, Indiana* (Indianapolis: Historical Publishing Co., 1921), pp. 102–7. This was also common in rural New York; see Paula Baker, *The Moral Frameworks of Public Life: Gender, Politics, and the State in Rural New York, 1870–1930* (New York: Oxford University Press, 1991), pp. 103–8. Battles over railroad bond indebtedness were particularly fierce in Missouri after the Civil War; see David P. Thelen, *Paths of Resistance: Tradition and Dignity in*

Industrializing Missouri (New York: Oxford University Press, 1986). Significantly, according to Baker, these issues were largely nonpartisan, and state or national party politics did not shape local politics.

29. According to Gary A. Tobin, the vast majority of LAW members were clerks, businessmen, and professionals from the eastern seaboard and the urban centers of Ohio and Illinois. The bicycle craze was widespread: the president of the LAW estimated in 1896 that there were 2.5 million cyclists in the country, and over 1.2 million bicycles were produced in 1896 alone. See Tobin, "The Bicycle Boom of the 1890s: The Development of Private Transportation and the Birth of the Modern Tourist," *Journal of Popular Culture* 7 (1974): 838–49.

30. Predictably, when Congress established the Office of Road Inquiry within the Department of Agriculture in 1893 to study road problems and disseminate information, it was staffed by wheelmen. League officials wrote the office's leading circulars, and the ORI used its postal frank to distribute good roads materials published by the LAW to a mailing list of 300,000 farmers that it also provided. The LAW also gave the office financial aid to supplement the limited government budget; at one point when the federal appropriation ran short, it paid the salary of one of the staff. Philip P. Mason, "The League of American Wheelmen and the Good-Roads Movement, 1880–1905" (Ph.D. diss., University of Michigan, 1957), pp. 83–206.

31. Quoted in May, "The Good Roads Movement in Iowa," p. 16.

32. Pennsylvania State Board of Agriculture, *Agriculture of Pennsylvania, 1890* (Harrisburg, 1890), p. 141.

33. New Jersey passed the so-called Union County Law in the 1880s, allowing counties to issue bonds in order to finance macadam roads designated as county roads, and subsequent legislation allowed townships to do the same on a more local level. Similar legislation by 1895 in Indiana, Michigan, Minnesota, New York, and Pennsylvania gave counties the option of organizing highway commissions, floating bonds, and assessing road taxes, while other laws in New Hampshire, Vermont, and Wisconsin allowed the elimination of subdistricts and made the township the smallest unit of road administration. Still other acts raised statewide caps on township and county highway taxes and lowered the special assessments against those who abutted the improved roads. In spite of these changes, without outside funding, relatively few counties and even fewer townships undertook the financing and construction of permanent roads. See Mason, "Wheelmen," pp. 207–37; Edward Burrough, "State Aid to Road-Building in New Jersey," U.S. Department of Agriculture, Office of Road Inquiry, *Bulletin* 9 (1894): 8–9; and Roy Stone, *New Roads and Road Laws in the United States* (New York, 1894), pp. 139–66.

34. The 1891 New Jersey law, which was the first program of state aid and provided a model for some of the other states, gave local residents rather than the state the power to plan, construct, and maintain improved roads funded by cost sharing

between the state (33.3 percent), the county (56.7 percent), and abutting property owners (10 percent). In Massachusetts, the state exercised more authority but still deferred to the localities in initiating road improvements. Elsewhere, rural inhabitants forced revisions in state aid programs to suit their needs, and Vermont, New Hampshire, and Maine changed their laws in order to give poorer towns a disproportionate share of state monies, which they used for gravel rather than macadam roads.

35. Schmidt, *Rural Hunterdon*, pp. 166–68.

36. Maurice O. Eldridge, "Public-Road Mileage, Revenues, and Expenditures in the United States in 1904," U.S. Department of Agriculture, Office of Public Roads, *Bulletin* 32 (1907); James E. Pennybacker Jr. and Maurice O. Eldridge, "Mileage and Cost of Public Roads in the United States in 1909," U.S. Department of Agriculture, Office of Public Roads, *Bulletin* 41 (1912). See also Stone, *New Roads and Road Laws*, pp. 139–66; Mason, "Wheelmen," pp. 229–31; Peter J. Hugill, "Good Roads and the Automobile in the United States, 1880–1929," *Geographical Review* 72 (1982): 332–34; and U.S. Department of Transportation, Federal Highway Administration, *America's Highways, 1776–1976: A History of the Federal-Aid Program* (Washington, D.C.: U.S. Department of Transportation, Federal Highway Administration, 1977), pp. 43–44.

37. *New York Times*, February 12, 1896; March 18, 1896; February 18, 1898; February 22, 1898.

38. *New York Times*, February 21, 1898; March 4, 1898; and March 17, 1898.

39. *Country Gentleman*, April 28, 1898, p. 325; and Curtiss, "Highway Administration and Finance in New York," pp. 22–28.

40. *Country Gentleman*, April 28, 1898, p. 325.

41. Cortland County Board of Supervisors, *Proceedings, 1900* (Cortland, N.Y., 1901), p. 127; quoted in Baker, *Moral Frameworks*, p. 107. According to Paula Baker, the new state funds were also attractive to rural residents because they allowed residents to resolve local conflicts over road issues at the state's expense.

42. *Country Gentleman*, November 12, 1908, p. 1077; November 26, 1908, pp. 1125–26; December 3, 1908, pp. 1149–50; and Eldridge, "Public-Road Mileage," p. 79; *Good Roads Yearbook, 1917* (Washington, D.C., 1917), pp. 28, 475; and J. L. Tennant, "The Relationships between Roads and Agriculture in New York," Cornell University Agricultural Experiment Station, *Bulletin* 479 (1929): 42–43.

43. Still, rural opposition continued. Farmers in the wealthier dairying counties in the east and southeast had already improved nearly half of their roads, in part so that their milk would not churn into butter while it was being transported, and they resented paying for similar improvements in other parts of the state. On the other hand, representatives from hilly areas with little gravel worried that the new state road standards would actually be too expensive for their constituents. Ballard Campbell, "The Good Roads Movement in Wisconsin, 1890–1911," *Wisconsin Magazine of History* 49 (1966): 273–93; and Beltman, "Rural Renaissance," pp. 355–400.

44. See Beltman, "Rural Renaissance," pp. 384–95.

45. Norman Moline, *Mobility and the Small Town, 1900–1930: Transportation Change in Oregon, Illinois*, University of Chicago, Department of Geography, research paper no. 132, Chicago, 1971, pp. 79–93; American Highway Association, *Good Roads Yearbook, 1916* (Washington, D.C., 1916), pp. 46–51; and David R. Wrone, "Illinois Pulls Out of the Mud," *Journal of the Illinois State Historical Society* 58 (1965): 54–76. Originally, the Tice Act required permanent brick roads (in part because of lobbying by Illinois brick manufacturers), even though the selection of routes (for better or worse) and the actual construction were left to the counties. After pressure from rural areas, though, the legislature amended the law in 1915 and allowed the county board to choose the type of road. Before this change, only 115 miles of roads were built with state assistance, but afterward, many more counties passed bond issues in order to participate in the state aid program, and they built earth roads.

46. See Rodney O. Davis, "Iowa Farm Opinion and the Good Roads Movement, 1903–1904," *Annals of Iowa* 37 (1964): 321–38; May, "The Good Roads Movement in Iowa," pp. 1–64; and Samuel C. E. Powers, "The Iowa State Highway Commission," *Iowa Journal of History and Politics* 29 (1931): 42–103. See also papers on roads presented at Iowa farmers' institutes that were published in the Iowa Department of Agriculture, *Annual Yearbook* (Des Moines), 1905, pp. 818–27; 1906, pp. 593–99; 1909, pp. 603–12.

47. George S. May, "The King Road Drag in Iowa, 1905–1920," *Iowa Journal of History and Politics* 53 (1955): 247–72; and Henry Wallace, *How to Make Good Dirt Roads: The Split Log Drag* (Des Moines, 1905), pp. 1–24.

48. May, "King Road Drag," pp. 259–60; Wallace, *Dirt Roads*, p. 18.

49. May, "King Road Drag," pp. 263–72. Iowa legislation in 1911 set aside one mill of township road taxes for a dragging fund, but this law relied on written contracts with individual farmers, and these were often not adhered to.

50. Wayne E. Fuller, *RFD: The Changing Face of Rural America* (Bloomington: Indiana University Press, 1964), pp. 177–98; Fuller, "Good Roads and Rural Free Delivery of Mail," *Mississippi Valley Historical Review* 42 (1955): 67–83; N. J. Bachelder, "The Demand of the Farmers for National Aid for Highway Improvement," Iowa Department of Agriculture, *Ninth Annual Year Book, 1908* (Des Moines, 1909), pp. 744–47.

51. Fuller, *RFD*, pp. 193–98, 195; U.S. Department of Transportation, *America's Highways*, pp. 84–89.

52. The creation of state highway departments after 1916 was a thorny and divisive issue in some states: despite this state authority, the real power over public roads remained with the counties. See Mary Rowland, "Kansas and the Highways, 1917–1930," *Kansas History* 5 (1982): 33–51; May, "Good Roads in Iowa," pp. 24–31; and William P. Corbett, "Politics and Pavement: The Formative Years of the Oklahoma

State Highway Department," *Red River Valley Historical Review* 6 (1981): 94–111. Even earlier limited federal involvement created tensions between the different levels of government; see Wayne E. Fuller, "The Ohio Road Experiment, 1913–1916," *Ohio History* 74 (1965): 13–28, 70–71.

53. In 1917, the Army ordered 30,000 trucks from factories in the Midwest, which had to be driven to ports on the East Coast because of a shortage of open-top rail cars. The ensuing convoy got mired in bad roads and destroyed many of the good ones. In Delaware, a single truck with a gross load of eleven tons broke up a light macadam road from end to end; in New York, traffic of only thirty trucks per day undid relatively durable bituminous-macadam roads, which cost $11,000 per mile to build in 1912 and $32,000 to repair in inflated 1918 prices. Consequently, states began to regulate trucking for the first time, and they switched to other hard road surfaces, especially concrete, that were even more expensive than macadam but were capable of withstanding the impact of motor vehicles. See U.S. Department of Transportation, *America's Highways*, pp. 90–99.

54. Iowa, which had steadfastly opposed any bonded indebtedness, allowed counties to float bond issues for the first time in 1919. Pennsylvania passed a $50 million issue in 1918 that had been defeated by a wide margin in 1913; Maine approved $10 million in 1919; Michigan passed $50 million during the same year; Minnesota voted $75 million in 1920; and Illinois voters approved $60 million in 1918 and $100 million in 1923. See W. Stull Holt, *The Bureau of Public Roads: Its History, Activities, and Organization* (Baltimore: Johns Hopkins University Press, 1923), pp. 13–30; American Highway Association, *Good Roads Yearbook, 1916* (Washington, D.C., 1916), pp. 167–71; and American Automobile Association, *Highways Green Book, 1922* (Washington, D.C., 1922), pp. 235–38.

55. The AAA was joined in these efforts by the National Highway Association, a consortium of good roads groups and automobile and highway manufacturers, and by different groups of boosters promoting specific highway routes, such as the Lincoln Highway Association founded in 1913, and over one hundred other similar organizations. These highway associations were themselves lobbied by groups of merchants and community boosters who wanted to make sure that the proposed route went through their town. See the description of the squabbles in the Marshall County, Illinois, Waubonsie Trail Association in Maud E. Uschold, *This Is the Place* (Lacon, Ill.: Marshall County Historical Society, 1968), pp. 77–79.

56. See Bruce E. Seely, *Building the American Highway System: Engineers as Policy Makers* (Philadelphia: Temple University Press, 1987); Seely, "Engineers and Government-Business Cooperation: Highway Standards and the Bureau of Public Roads, 1900–1940," *Business History Review* 58 (1984): 51–77; Seely, "The Scientific Mystique in Engineering: Highway Research at the Bureau of Public Roads, 1918–1940," *Technology and Culture* 25 (1984): 798–831.

57. Quoted in Rowland, "Kansas and the Highways," p. 39.

58. Ironically, the farmers' car of choice, the Model T, was actually better suited to dirt and gravel rural roads than concrete highways. On smooth roads, the Model T's suspension caused it to sway, pitch, and roll, prompting Ford to replace it with the Model A as concrete roads became more prevalent. See Hugill, "Good Roads," pp. 330–40.

59. Good roads, especially from farms to rail terminals, enhanced the railroad's business, so different lines offered special rates to shippers of road materials, sponsored good roads trains that preached the gospel of better roads throughout the countryside, and in some cases actually financed the construction of the roads themselves. See Mason, "Wheelmen," pp. 181–206; and Roy V. Scott, *Railroad Development Programs in the Twentieth Century* (Ames: Iowa State University Press, 1985), pp. 41–43.

60. U.S. Department of Transportation, *America's Highways*, pp. 108–13.

61. *Prairie Farmer*, December 28, 1918, p. 1163.

62. Ibid., May 31, 1919, p. 941.

63. John J. Lacey, *Farm Bureau in Illinois: History of Illinois Farm Bureau* (Bloomington: Illinois Agricultural Association, 1965), p. 59; *Prairie Farmer*, May 22, 1920, p. 1365; Don S. Kirschner, *City and Country: Rural Responses to Urbanization in the 1920s* (Westport, Conn.: Greenwood Press, 1970), pp. 183–202.

CHAPTER TWO

1. Joseph Butler, *History of Youngstown and the Mahoning Valley, Ohio* (Chicago: American Historical Society, 1921), vol. 1, pp. 524–25.

2. Massachusetts Board of Education, *Report*, 1859 (Boston, 1860), p. 75.

3. George H. Martin, *The Evolution of the Massachusetts Public School System: A Historical Sketch* (New York: D. Appleton and Co., 1894), pp. 94–95.

4. Massachusetts Board of Education, *Report*, 1859, p. 76.

5. Martin, *Evolution*, pp. 93–94.

6. Ibid., p. 95.

7. Ibid., pp. 92, 94.

8. Quoted in ibid., p. 164.

9. The following discussion is based on Martha Coons's study, which is part of Martha Coons, John W. Jenkins, and Carl Kaestle, "Education and Social Change in Two Nineteenth-Century Massachusetts Communities," in Carl F. Kaestle and Maris A. Vinovskis, *Education and Social Change in Nineteenth-Century Massachusetts* (New York: Cambridge University Press, 1980), pp. 139–85.

10. Coons, Jenkins, and Kaestle, "Education and Social Change," p. 160.

11. Martin, *Evolution*, pp. 206–7.

12. Massachusetts State Board of Education, *Report*, 1917–18 (Boston, 1919), pp. 36–38.

13. Coons, Jenkins, and Kaestle, "Education and Social Change."

14. For example, at least 16 of the 26 townships in Franklin County voted to go back to the district system. See Massachusetts State Board of Education, *Report*, 1872–73 (Boston, 1874), p. 87.

15. Massachusetts State Board of Education, *Report*, 1871 (Boston, 1872), pp. 63, 109; *Report*, 1872 (Boston, 1873), p. 109.

16. Although based on New York, Paula Baker's work is particularly instructive on this point. See "Gender Differences and School Politics in Late Nineteenth Century New York State" (paper presented at the Annual Meeting of the Organization of American Historians, Reno, Nevada, April 1988); and Baker, *The Moral Frameworks of Public Life: Gender, Politics, and the State in Rural New York, 1870–1930* (New York: Oxford University Press, 1991), pp. 74–81.

17. Ruth Zinar, "Educational Problems in Rural Vermont, 1875–1900: A Not So Distant Mirror," *Vermont History* 51 (1983): 197–220; Chelsea Town Records, Vermont Department of Public Records, microfilm. In New Hampshire, laws allowing the voluntary abandonment of the district system also had little effect, so an 1885 law mandated the creation of a township system with a three-person school board, but gave towns the option of returning to the district system after five years by a majority of votes. Maine erased district lines in 1893, at a time when only 162 of 433 rural towns had already voluntarily adopted the town system and there were still almost 3,000 school districts in the state. See Everett S. Stackpole, *History of New Hampshire* (New York: American Historical Society, 1916), vol. 3, pp. 214–15; U.S. Bureau of Education, "Consolidation of Schools in Maine and Connecticut," *Rural School Leaflet* 4 (May 1922): 5.

18. Town of Corinth History Committee, *History of Corinth, Vermont, 1764–1964* (Corinth: The Town, 1964), pp. 153, 154.

19. On the problem of rural depopulation, see Hal S. Barron, *Those Who Stayed Behind: Rural Society in Nineteenth-Century New England* (New York: Cambridge University Press, 1984); Stackpole, *History of New Hampshire*, pp. 214–15.

20. Massachusetts Department of Education, *Report*, 1871, p. 23.

21. Martin, *Evolution*, p. 203.

22. Coons, Jenkins, and Kaestle, "Education and Social Change."

23. Martha M. Frizzell, *A History of Walpole, New Hampshire* (Walpole: Walpole Historical Society and Town of Walpole, 1963), vol. 1, pp. 489–97.

24. Consolidation was enabled by an 1869 Massachusetts law that allowed towns to pay for the transportation of public school students, particularly high school students, and started first on the outskirts of Boston before spreading to other parts of the state.

25. William L. Eaton, *An Account of the Movement in Massachusetts to Close the Rural Schools, and to Transport Their Pupils, at Public Expense, to the Village Schools* (Boston: Nathan Sawyer & Son, 1893), p. 4. This is an eight-page circular from the Massachusetts Educational Exhibit at the World's Columbian Exposition in Chicago in 1893.

26. Massachusetts State Board of Education, *Report*, 1893–94 (Boston, 1895), pp. 208–15.

27. According to one reformer, George A. Walton, an agent of the state's board of education, "The consolidation in Concord, Bedford, and Lexington is as creditable a part of our school history as their stand in colonial days is of the history of the nation." Ibid., pp. 164–65.

28. Eaton, *An Account of the Movement in Massachusetts.*

29. Coons, Jenkins, and Kaestle, "Education and Social Change."

30. Massachusetts State Board of Education, *Report*, 1904–5 (Boston, 1906), pp. 83–90; and *Report*, 1917–18, pp. 44–47.

31. A. C. Monahan, *Consolidation of Rural Schools and Transportation of Pupils at Public Expense*, U.S. Bureau of Education, Bulletin 604, No. 30 (Washington, D.C., 1914), p. 22.

32. David B. Danbom, "Rural Education Reform and the Country Life Movement, 1900–1920," *Agricultural History* 53 (1979): 462–74; and Wayne E. Fuller, *The Old Country School: The Story of Rural Education in the Middle West* (Chicago: University of Chicago Press, 1982).

33. Clayton S. Ellsworth, "The Coming of Rural Consolidated Schools to the Ohio Valley, 1892–1912," *Agricultural History* 30 (1956): 119–28; Fuller, *The Old Country School*, pp. 228–33.

34. U.S. Bureau of Education, *Report*, 1898–99 (Washington, D.C., 1899), pp. 526–29, 528; also *Report*, 1900–1901 (Washington, D.C., 1901), pp. 161–72.

35. *Ohio Farmer*, March 17, 1898, p. 229.

36. Ibid., April 21, 1898, p. 333; May 17, 1900, p. 427.

37. Ibid., December 14, 1899, p. 468.

38. Ibid., October 27, 1898, p. 312.

39. Ibid., April 23, 1903, p. 438.

40. Ibid., April 14, 1898, p. 315; August 7, 1902, p. 92.

41. Ibid., March 3, 1898, p. 181.

42. The survey was reprinted in U.S. Bureau of Education, *Report*, 1900–1901 (Washington, D.C., 1901), pp. 186–204.

43. Ibid., pp. 187–88.

44. Ibid., p. 192.

45. Ibid., pp. 197, 201.

46. Indiana State Department of Public Instruction, *Report*, 1905–6 (Indianapolis, 1906), pp. 617–26.

47. Iowa State Superintendent of Public Instruction, *Report*, 1901 (Des Moines, 1902), pp. 30–76, 56.

48. In addition to Fuller, *The Old Country School*, see Danbom, "Rural Education Reform"; Ann M. Keppel, "The Myth of Agrarianism in Rural Educational Reform, 1890–1914," *History of Education Quarterly* 2 (1962): 100–112; and David B. Tyack, "The Tribe and the Common School: Community Control in Rural Education," *American Quarterly* 24 (1972): 3–19.

49. George W. Knorr, "Consolidated Rural Schools and Organization of a County System," U.S. Department of Agriculture, Office of Experiment Stations, *Bulletin* 232 (Washington, D.C., 1910), p. 27.

50. Nell J. Sullivan and David K. Martin, *A History of the Town of Chazy, Clinton County, New York* (Chazy: Authors, 1970), pp. 252–56.

51. For the different laws promoting rural school consolidation, see Monahan, *Consolidation of Rural Schools*, pp. 26–43.

52. In the aftermath of the subsequent repeal of the township system law in 1918, the bureaucrat most directly involved, Deputy Commissioner of Education Thomas E. Finegan, compiled a massive documentary history of the subject, including what appears to be every column and letter published in small-town newspapers and every local grange resolution that discussed the issue. Would that other historians could be so well served by similarly frustrated bureaucrats! See Finegan, "The Township System: A Documentary History," New York State Department of Education, *Report* (Albany, 1921), vol. 1.

53. Editorial, *Amsterdam Recorder*, December 22, 1917, in Finegan, "Township System," p. 24.

54. *Ogdensburg News*, October 26, 1917, in Finegan, "Township System," pp. 203–4.

55. Finegan, "Township System," pp. 350–51, 215–16.

56. Ibid., pp. 314–15.

57. Ibid., p. 355.

58. Ibid., p. 279.

59. In this vein, it is significant that John J. Dillon, the editor of the *Rural New Yorker*, provided an active forum for the repeal of the township law just as he campaigned against other changes in rural society that minimized the role of local organizations and institutions.

60. Finegan, "Township System," pp. 168–69.

61. Ibid., p. 263.

62. Ibid., pp. 252, 319.

63. Ibid., p. 352.

64. Ibid., pp. 354, 366.

65. Ibid., p. 400.

66. Ibid.

67. J. F. Abel, "Consolidation of Schools and Transportation of Pupils," U.S. Bureau of Education, *Bulletin* 41 (Washington, D.C., 1923), pp. 41–58.

68. Timothy Covert, "Rural School Consolidation: A Decade of School Consolidation with Detailed Information from 105 Consolidated Schools," U.S. Office of Education *Pamphlet* 6 (Washington, D.C., 1930), pp. 3–4.

69. H. E. Stone, *Consolidated Schools in Iowa* (Des Moines: Iowa Department of Public Instruction, 1926), pp. 10–35; Viggo Justesen, "Is the District School Doomed?," *Wallace's Farmer*, February 8, 1930, p. 233.

70. *Rural New Yorker*, January 14, 1928, p. 61; David M. Ellis, *A Short History of New York State* (Ithaca: Cornell University Press, 1957), p. 591.

71. James H. Madison, "John D. Rockefeller's General Education Board and the Rural School Problem in the Midwest, 1900–1930," *History of Education Quarterly* 24 (1984): 181–99.

72. Thomas C. King, "The Process of School District Reorganization, Facilitating and Impeding Factors" (Ph.D. thesis, Harvard School of Education, 1950), pp. 116–23; Alan Peshkin, *The Imperfect Union: School Consolidation and Community Conflict* (Chicago: University of Chicago Press, 1982); James H. Madison, *The Indiana Way: A State History* (Bloomington: Indiana University Press, 1986), pp. 247–53; and Steven J. Buss, "Public School District Reorganization and Consolidation in Adams County, Nebraska, 1949–1989," *Nebraska History* 72 (1991): 89–98. For an example from New England, see Polly Welts Kaufman, "The School Consolidation Movement on the Coast of Maine: A Fresh Look at an 'Old' Issue" (paper presented at the History of Education Society Meeting, Cambridge, Mass., October 1992).

73. See Jonathan P. Sher, ed., *Education in Rural America: A Reassessment of Conventional Wisdom* (Boulder: Westview Press, 1977). On efforts to preserve and reuse one-room schoolhouse buildings, see Andrew Gulliford, *America's Country Schools* (Washington, D.C.: Preservation Press, 1984).

74. Joseph Heavilon, "Good Roads," in Indiana State Board of Agriculture, *Report* (Indianapolis, 1900), pp. 1056–59.

CHAPTER THREE

1. Alva Agee, "Organization among Farmers," *Cultivator and Country Gentleman*, September 8, 1892, p. 665.

2. Chris Marti, "Should Farmers Organize?," in Iowa Department of Agriculture, *Fourth Annual Yearbook* (Des Moines, 1904), p. 524.

3. Grant McConnell, *The Decline of Agrarian Democracy* (New York: Atheneum, 1969); and Theodore Saloutos and John D. Hicks, *Twentieth-Century Populism: Agricul-*

tural Discontent in the Middle West, 1900–1939 (Lincoln: University of Nebraska Press, 1964).

4. Of all types of agriculture, dairying has been one of the most amenable to cooperation and organization. As early as the 1840s, Wisconsin dairy farmers established cheese rings in which they pooled their milk for the manufacture of cheese to reap the benefits of better quality control and economies of scale; their success led to imitators throughout the Midwest and Northeast. Some associations of neighborhood dairymen contracted with established cheesemakers at a fixed rate per hundred pounds for manufacture and storage and did the marketing themselves, while other groups actually owned their own factories and hired employees. Although these kinds of arrangements grew out of folk traditions of cooperation like swapping labor and threshing rings, they quickly became more formal and contractual as the levels of investment rose. See H. E. Erdman, "'Associated Dairies' of New York," *Agricultural History* 36 (1962): 82–90. A similar trend toward more formal arrangements and contracts as a result of greater capital investment occurred in threshing rings. See J. Sanford Rikoon, *Threshing in the Midwest, 1820–1940: A Study of Traditional Culture and Technological Change* (Bloomington: Indiana University Press, 1988).

5. In an 1853 study, John Mullaly estimated that two-thirds of the milk consumed in New York City was swill milk from distillery-fed cows. See John Mullaly, *The Milk Trade in New York City and Vicinity* (New York: Fowler and Wells, 1853), cited in Leland Spencer and Charles J. Blanford, *An Economic History of Milk Marketing and Pricing, 1800–1933* (Columbus, Ohio: Grid, Inc., 1977), vol. 1, p. 32. Much of the source material (but not the analysis or interpretation) for this chapter comes from the prodigious compilations of Leland Spencer, for many years professor of marketing at Cornell University. Spencer first published this work as a series of bulletins from the Cornell Agricultural Experiment Station, but later, with the help of Charles J. Blanford, amended it into a series of five volumes that was published in 1977. Volumes 1 and 2 are detailed histories from 1800 to the present; volumes 3 and 4 are sources and reference materials; volume 5 is a bibliography.

6. An earlier attempt to organize all milk producers failed. In 1870, milk producers in the New York area met in Croton Falls, where they urged a 25 percent increase in the price of milk and requested the prompt return of cans and daily marketing reports to avoid shipping a surplus. After the milk dealers' association rejected these suggestions (and was duly chastised in a *New York Times* editorial), dairymen tried their hand at direct marketing. These efforts quickly got bogged down because of the cost of buying wagons, worries about destructive competition between different farmers' organizations, and the middlemen's ability to buy milk from producers who were further out and eager to sell. See Spencer and Blanford, *Milk*, vol. 1, pp. 50–54.

7. Ibid., vol. 1, pp. 159–63; vol. 3, pp. 47–62.

8. Ibid., vol. 1, pp. 159–68.

9. *New York Times*, March 13, 1883, pp. 1–2; March 14, p. 2; March 16, p. 2, in Spencer and Blanford, *Milk*, vol. 3, pp. 67–78.

10. See especially *New York Times*, March 21, 1883, p. 5; March 22, p. 5; March 23, p. 8; and *New York Tribune*, March 17, 1883, in Spencer and Blanford, *Milk*, vol. 3, pp. 81–95, 165. The Orange County Milk Association was formed in 1844 and was the first organization of New York–area dairymen. It was not strictly a producers' organization, however, but a joint-stock company run for the profit of its ten owners, half of whom lived in New York City. Although the original country members were mostly producers of milk sold by the association, the group also bought milk to sell from neighboring farmers, employed a full-time collector, and ran twelve delivery routes. By the time of the strike, it was a leading dairy concern with plants throughout Orange County and upstate New York. See Spencer and Blanford, *Milk*, vol. 1, pp. 32, 94–95.

11. *New York Times*, March 23, 1883, in Spencer and Blanford, *Milk*, vol. 3, p. 92.

12. *New York Times*, March 23, 1883, p. 8; March 24, p. 5; March 25, p. 2, in Spencer and Blanford, *Milk*, vol. 3, pp. 86–103. See also ibid., vol. 1, pp. 163–68.

13. *Country Gentleman*, July 3, 1884, p. 564.

14. *New York Times*, March 11, 1883, p. 7, quoted in Spencer and Blanford, *Milk*, vol. 3, p. 65.

15. *American Agriculturalist*, December 8, 1894, p. 417; and *Milk Reporter*, February 1895; May 1899, in Spencer and Blanford, *Milk*, vol. 3, pp. 287–88, 757–59, 818–19. See also ibid., vol. 1, pp. 94–104.

16. *Rural New Yorker*, September 30, 1899, p. 697, April 25, 1903, p. 326; in Spencer and Blanford, *Milk*, vol. 3, pp. 502–7, 521.

17. *Rural New Yorker*, September 30, 1899, in Spencer and Blanford, *Milk*, vol. 3, pp. 502–5.

18. Eugene R. Milener, *Oneonta: The Development of a Railroad Town* (Oneonta, N.Y.: Author, 1983), pp. 491–95.

19. This message was delivered at a celebration of the tenth anniversary of the strike. As the speaker concluded, "If you had gained nothing else from the Strike besides relief from this humiliation, the struggle would have been worth it." Minutes of the Chenango County District of the Dairymen's League Co-operative Association, Inc., October 2, 1926, typescript, p. 4, Dairymen's League Papers, Accession no. 1820, Box 28, Division of Rare and Manuscript Collections, Cornell University Library.

20. William F. Seward, *Binghamton and Broome County, New York* (New York: Lewis Historical Publishing Co., 1924), vol. 1, p. 139.

21. Spencer and Blanford, *Milk*, vol. 3, pp. 1063–73; and Paula Baker, *The Moral*

Frameworks of Public Life: Gender, Politics, and the State in Rural New York, 1870–1930 (New York: Oxford University Press, 1991), pp. 131–32.

22. Spencer and Blanford, *Milk*, vol. 3, pp. 1063–73.

23. Mildred L. Bailey, *A History of the Town of Jefferson, 1771–1976* (N.p.: N.p., n.d.), pp. 8–13.

24. Spencer and Blanford, *Milk*, vol. 1, pp. 181–230.

25. From its inception, the Grange was involved in establishing cooperative stores and promoting the cooperative purchase of supplies, although not necessarily producers' cooperatives. Even though the importance of the Grange diminished in the Midwest after the 1880s, it experienced a revitalization in the Northeast during the late nineteenth and early twentieth centuries and became an important institution in many rural communities. See Joseph G. Knapp, *The Rise of American Cooperative Enterprise: 1620–1920* (Danville, Ill.: Interstate Publishers, 1969), pp. 194–212.

26. The recollections of O. W. Mapes are in the Dairymen's League Papers; also O. W. Mapes, "Dairymen's League Organized," *Rural New Yorker*, September 7, 1907, in Spencer and Blanford, *Milk*, vol. 3, pp. 528–29.

27. Mapes, "League," pp. 528–29. As Mapes's statement implies, government health regulations were an added source of discontent and expense, especially the requirement to pasteurize milk. This also helped to consolidate the dealers' power because they could afford the expensive machinery needed to process the milk.

28. Edgar L. Vincent, "Co-Operation among Farmers," *Ohio Farmer*, June 28, 1900, p. 537.

29. Mapes, "League," p. 529; Bartow W. Bull, interview, typescript, 1965, Division of Rare and Manuscript Collections, Cornell University Library, p. 2.

30. Dairymen's League Papers; and Spencer and Blanford, *Milk*, vol. 1, pp. 238–42.

31. Minutes of the Chenango County District, October 2, 1926, Dairymen's League Papers.

32. Letter from F. H. Thompson to H. J. Kershaw, May 18, 1916, J. D. Miller Papers in Dairymen's League Papers.

33. Letter from Mapes to Thompson, May 24, 1916, Miller Papers.

34. Letter, N. M. Congdon, n.d., Miller Papers. Chenango County farmers believed that the new cooperative creameries were being set up to cooperate with the dealers and would duplicate facilities already paid for by farmers. O. W. Mapes opposed the plan because he believed that league members would wind up absorbing the lower prices of manufactured milk, which was held off the market in order to raise prices, while nonleague members would benefit from the increase. See Mapes to Thompson, May 24, 1916, Miller Papers.

35. Minutes of the Chenango County District, Dairymen's League Papers.

36. Gould P. Colman, "Government and Agriculture in New York State," *Agricultural History* 39 (1965): 41–50.

37. *Milk Reporter*, August 1916, in Spencer and Blanford, *Milk*, vol. 3, p. 865.

38. *American Agriculturalist*, July 29, 1916, in Spencer and Blanford, *Milk*, vol. 3, p. 410.

39. R. B. Swift, "The Great Chicago Milk War," *Rural New Yorker*, June 10, 1916, in Spencer and Blanford, *Milk*, vol. 3, pp. 542–44.

40. In addition, they arranged for the New York State Department of Foods and Markets and its commissioner, John J. Dillon (on leave as editor of the *Rural New Yorker*), to serve as their marketing agent in order to avoid prosecution under the Donnelly Antimonopoly Law. Just like labor unions during the period, other farmers' organizations had been successfully prosecuted under the Sherman Act and other antitrust legislation. This worried the league's conservative leaders more than those demanding a strike, however. See the letter of July 20, 1916, from the Office of Markets and Rural Organization of the U.S. Dept. of Agriculture to F. H. Thompson, which discusses the legality of the Dairymen's League under the Sherman Act, in the Miller Papers.

41. Spencer and Blanford, *Milk*, vol. 1, pp. 245–56.

42. Ibid., pp. 257–73.

43. Minutes of the Chenango County District, Dairymen's League Papers.

44. John J. Dillon, *Seven Decades of Milk* (New York: Orange Judd Publishing Co., 1941), p. 100; William Stempfle, interviews, typescript, 1964, Division of Rare and Manuscript Collections, Cornell University Library, p. 14.

45. *Rural New Yorker*, November 25, 1916, cited in Spencer and Blanford, *Milk*, vol. 3, pp. 563–64; Helen B. Vandervort, interviews, typescript, 1964, Division of Rare and Manuscript Collections, Cornell University Library, p. 74.

46. Bull, interview, p. 34.

47. Mabel G. Feint, "Dairymen Continue to Organize," *American Agriculturalist*, November 4, 1916, cited in Spencer and Blanford, *Milk*, vol. 3, pp. 433–34.

48. *Rural New Yorker*, November 25, 1916, cited in Spencer and Blanford, *Milk*, vol. 3, pp. 563–64.

49. Bull, interview, p. 14.

50. Vandervort, interview, pp. 69–72.

51. Dillon, *Seven Decades*, p. 109.

52. See above, nn. 19 and 20.

53. Stempfle, interview, p. 10; Vandervort, interview, p. 74.

54. Fred Sexauer, interviews, typescript, 1963, Division of Rare and Manuscript Collections, Cornell University Library, p. 24. See also Gould P. Colman, "A Farmer Joins the Dairymen's League: An Interview with Fred Sexauer," *New York History* 48 (1967): 370–85, 383.

55. Spencer and Blanford, *Milk*, vol. 1, pp. 465–84.

56. Sexauer, interview, pp. 34–35.

57. Lowell K. Dyson, *Farmers' Organizations* (Westport, Conn.: Greenwood Press, 1986), pp. 71–76.

58. On the early history of the GLF, see Joseph G. Knapp, *Seeds That Grew: A History of the Cooperative Grange League Federation Exchange* (Hinsdale, N.Y.: Anderson House, 1960); and Thomas E. Milliman, *The GLF Story, 1920–1964, A History of the Cooperative Grange League Federation Exchange, Inc.* (Ithaca: Wilcox Press, 1965).

59. In 1925, Eastman published a novel entitled *The Trouble Maker*, which dealt with the 1916 milk strike. While not great literature, the novel is an extremely interesting depiction of conditions in the New York milkshed as well as a plea for the DLCA plan to solve long-term marketing issues. See E. R. Eastman, *The Trouble Maker* (New York: Macmillan Co., 1925).

60. Dillon, *Seven Decades*, pp. 182–83.

61. Ibid., pp. 200–208.

62. Dillon had played an important role in the success of the league's 1916 strike as commissioner of the New York State Department of Foods and Markets, but saw his influence diminish when he was later removed from that office.

63. John J. Dillon, *Organized Cooperatives* (New York: The Rural New Yorker, 1923), pp. 37, 47, 60–61; Edward S. Foster, interviews, typescript, 1963, Division of Rare and Manuscript Collections, Cornell University Library, p. 16.

64. Spencer and Blanford, *Milk*, vol. 1, pp. 438, 510–24, 603–8; Baker, *Moral Frameworks*, p. 220 n. 32. In 1926, at the initiative of John J. Dillon, the Non-Pooling Dairymen's Cooperative Association joined with several other similarly minded organizations and formed the Unity Dairymen's Cooperative Association.

65. Lowell K. Dyson, "The Milk Strike of 1939 and the Destruction of the Dairy Farmers' Union," *New York History* 51 (1970): 523–43.

66. Dillon, *Seven Decades*, pp. 181–82. On the Midwest, see Saloutos and Hicks, *Twentieth-Century Populism*; James Shideler, *Farm Crisis, 1919–1923* (Berkeley: University of California Press, 1957); and Joseph G. Knapp, *The Advance of American Cooperative Enterprise: 1920–1945* (Danville, Ill.: Interstate Publishers, 1973).

CHAPTER FOUR

1. *Federal Trade Commission Report on Cooperative Marketing*, S. Doc. 95, 70th Cong., 1st sess. (Washington, D.C.: Government Printing Office, 1928), p. xxi.

2. G. W. Schatzel, "Among the Wheat Fields of Minnesota," *Harper's Monthly* 36 (1869): 190–201.

3. For the best discussion of this, see Henrietta M. Larson, *The Wheat Market and the Farmer in Minnesota, 1858–1900*, Columbia University Studies in History, Eco-

nomics, and Public Law, vol. 122, no. 2, whole no. 269 (New York: Columbia University Press, 1926).

4. A few of these farmers' elevators actually preceded the rise of the new order. In Vasa Township, Goodhue County, Minnesota, a group of immigrants started the Scandinavian Transportation Company of Red Wing between 1866 and 1869; a similar, but nonethnic, organization was established in Blairstown, Iowa, in 1867 or 1868. See Larson, *Wheat Market*, pp. 104–5; and E. G. Nourse, "Fifty Years of Farmers' Elevators in Iowa," Iowa State University Agricultural Experiment Station *Bulletin* 211 (1923): 236–37. For the Grange period, the Proceedings of the Iowa State Grange for 1874 listed 53 elevators in Iowa, and about 200 in all; quoted in Herman Steen, *Cooperative Marketing: The Golden Rule in Agriculture* (Garden City, N.J.: Doubleday, Page, and Co., 1923), p. 199; see also Nourse, "Fifty Years," pp. 236–41; and Solon Justus Buck, *The Granger Movement: A Study of Agricultural Organization and Its Political, Economic, and Social Manifestations, 1870–1880* (1913; reprint, Lincoln: University of Nebraska Press, 1969), p. 243.

5. Nourse, "Fifty Years," p. 240.

6. Edward W. Martin, *History of the Grange Movement* (Philadelphia: National Publishing Co., 1873), pp. 318–19.

7. In western Kansas, the grain elevator was typically one of the first businesses established in town; in the newer wheat belt communities of the northern Great Plains, it was often the town's dominant structure, and, in some cases, its *only* structure, which contributed greatly to the physical uniformity of these settlements. See John C. Hudson, "The Plains Country Town," in *The Great Plains: Environment and Culture*, ed. Brian W. Blouet and Frederick C. Luebke (Lincoln: University of Nebraska Press, 1979), pp. 99–118; John C. Hudson, *Plains Country Towns* (Minneapolis: University of Minnesota Press, 1985), pp. 63–69; and Robert W. Schoeff, "The Grain Elevator," in *The Rise of the Wheat State: A History of Kansas Agriculture, 1861–1986*, ed. George E. Ham and Robin Higham (Manhattan, Kans.: Sunflower University Press, 1987), pp. 123–35.

8. The centralization of flour milling in the larger urban centers, which was also controlled by big businesses, also contributed to the increasing numbers of line grain elevators in the countryside during this period. Steen, *Cooperative Marketing*, p. 200; and Oscar N. Refsell, "The Farmers' Elevator Movement," *American Cooperative Journal* (September 1914): 20.

9. Larson, *Wheat Market*, pp. 165–219; Nourse, "Fifty Years," p. 242.

10. See Reuben A. Holman, *Forty Years of Co-operation: A History of the First Successful Co-operative Grain Elevator in the United States* (Rockwell, Iowa: Rockwell Farmers' Elevator Office, 1932), pp. 1–5, 52–53; and Philip J. Nelson, "The Rockwell Cooperative Society and the Iowa Farmers' Elevator Movement, 1870–1920," *Annals of Iowa* 54 (1995): 1–24.

11. Holman, *Forty Years*, pp. 1–5; and Nelson, "The Rockwell Co-operative Society," pp. 5–7.

12. Holman, *Forty Years*, pp. 6–9.

13. Thomas McManus, "Co-operation in Iowa," *American Cooperative Journal* (December 1911): 269; Holman, *Forty Years*, pp. 31–34.

14. Holman, *Forty Years*, pp. 14–15.

15. According to Reuben Holman's history, the society expanded into clothing almost accidentally. Campbell bought work clothes for the employees at wholesale, and when society members learned about this, they also bought their shoes and clothes at the elevator. In 1903, the society voted to expand shoes and clothing as a regular feature of its operations. See Holman, *Forty Years*, pp. 10–13, 21; McManus, "Co-operation in Iowa," p. 269.

16. Holman, *Forty Years*, p. 12.

17. Nourse, "Fifty Years," pp. 242–46; Lawrence Farlow, *The Farmers' Elevator Movement in Illinois* (N.p.: Farmers' Grain Dealers' Association of Illinois, 1928), pp. 41–42.

18. Similar tactics and pressures were also employed by retail dealers' associations in the most common elevator sidelines: coal, lumber, farm implements, and clothing. See Refsell, "Farmers' Elevator Movement," *American Cooperative Journal* (May 1915): 752–53; and Refsell, "The Farmers' Elevator Movement," *Journal of Political Economy* 22 (1914): 872–95, 969–91.

19. *Report of the Illinois Railroad and Warehouse Commission*, 1903, quoted in Refsell, "Farmers' Elevator Movement," *American Cooperative Journal* (November 1914): 210–11; Farlow, *Farmers' Elevator Movement*, pp. 27–32.

20. Refsell, "Farmers' Elevator Movement," *American Cooperative Journal* (November 1914): 210–11; Farlow, *Farmers' Elevator Movement*, pp. 27–32.

21. Farlow, *Farmers' Elevator Movement*, pp. 30–31.

22. *Interstate Commerce Commission Hearings on the Relations of Common Carriers to the Grain Trade*, S. Doc. 278, 59th Cong., 2d sess. (Washington, D.C.: Government Printing Office, 1907), pp. 605–12; and Tom Worrall, *The Grain Trust Exposed* (Lincoln, Neb.: Jacob North & Co., 1905).

23. *ICC Hearings*, pp. 644–55.

24. Refsell, "Farmers' Elevator Movement," *American Cooperative Journal* (December 1914): 291.

25. *ICC Hearings*, pp. 655–81.

26. Farlow, *Farmers' Elevator Movement*, pp. 21–34; and *ICC Hearings*, pp. 655–81.

27. Holman, *Forty Years*, pp. 52–53.

28. Nourse, "Fifty Years," pp. 247–50; Farlow, *Farmers' Elevator Movement*, pp. 41–42; and Joseph B. Kenkel, "The Cooperative Elevator Movement: A Study in Grain

Marketing at Country Points in the North Central States" (Ph.D. thesis, Catholic University, 1922), pp. 30–31.

29. Farlow, *Farmers' Elevator Movement*, pp. 38–39.

30. The absence of an organization in Wisconsin is due to the dominance of the Wisconsin Society of Equity during this period.

31. Refsell, "Farmers' Elevator Movement," *American Cooperative Journal* (December 1914): 289; Joseph G. Knapp, *The Rise of American Cooperative Enterprise: 1620–1920* (Danville, Ill.: Interstate Publishers, 1969), p. 225.

32. Refsell, "Farmers' Elevator Movement," *American Cooperative Journal* (December 1914): 288; *Federal Trade Commission Report on the Grain Trade*, vol. 1, *Country Grain Marketing* (Washington, D.C.: Government Printing Office, 1920), p. 91.

33. Knapp, *Rise of American Cooperative Enterprise*, pp. 143–75.

34. *Henry County, Ohio* (Napoleon, Ohio: Henry County Historical Society, 1976), vol. 2, pp. 358–59; *American Cooperative Journal* (October 1913): 111–12; (June 1910): 1690–91; (July 1910): 1759; and (August 1910): 1855–56; Richard G. Bremer, *Agricultural Change in an Urban Age: The Loup Country of Nebraska, 1910–1970* (Lincoln: University of Nebraska Studies, 1976), new series no. 51, pp. 41–42.

35. *American Cooperative Journal* (November 1917): 122.

36. F. E. Balmer, "The Cooperative Movement in the Minnesota Dairy Industry," typescript, collections of the Minnesota Historical Society, 1930, pp. 1–18; and Theophilus Hacker, "The Story of Clark's Grove," typescript, collections of the Minnesota Historical Society, 1913, pp. 1–5. The Danish connection was also a factor in the formation of cooperatives in Askov, Minnesota, which was founded in 1905 by the Danish Peoples Society on former timberlands that were opened to agricultural settlement. Askov was a dairying community and did not have a grain elevator, and while its cooperatives were predominantly Danish, they also had a few dozen non-Danish members. See Edmund deS. Brunner, *Immigrant Farmers and Their Children* (Garden City, N.Y.: Doubleday, Doran & Co., 1929), pp. 155–82; and Carle C. Zimmerman and John D. Black, "The Marketing Attitudes of Minnesota Farmers," University of Minnesota Agricultural Experiment Station *Technical Bulletin* 45 (1926): 9–16. Zimmerman and Black studied cooperatives in nine Minnesota farming communities, both ethnically homogeneous communities as well as ethnically diverse ones. In Faribault in Rice County, however, ethnic diversity was greater than elsewhere and included large numbers of French-Canadians, and this appears to have hindered cooperation. On Trempealeau County, see Jane M. Pederson, *Between Memory and Reality: Family and Community in Rural Wisconsin, 1870–1970* (Madison: University of Wisconsin Press, 1992), pp. 78–91. The cooperatives Pederson discusses were primarily dairy related and facilitated the transition from wheat to dairy production in the region, but she also cites the Pigeon Grain and Stock Cooperative, which was a marketing association. On Finns, see A. William Hoglund, "Flight from

Industry: Finns and Farming in America," *Finnish Americana* 1 (1978): 1–21; A. William Hoglund, *Finnish Immigrants in America: 1880–1920* (1960; reprint, New York: Arno Press, 1979), pp. 59–79; and John I. Kolehmainen and George W. Hill, *Haven in the Woods: The Story of Finns in Wisconsin* (1951; reprint, New York: Arno Press, 1979), pp. 70–105, 135–50. Finns tended to form cooperative creameries and stores more than other types of organizations, and they included significant numbers of non-Finnish members.

37. Refsell, "Farmers Elevator Movement," *Journal of Political Economy*, p. 990; Farmers' Elevator Company, Yorkville, Illinois, manuscript records, 1908–, Regional History Center, Northern Illinois University.

38. Nourse, "Fifty Years," pp. 250–51; Farlow, *Farmers' Elevator Movement*, pp. 41–42; Steen, *Cooperative Marketing*, pp. 196–209; James E. Boyle, "A General Survey of Present-day Farmers' Organizations," in *Readings in the Economic History of Agriculture*, ed. Louis Schmidt and Earle Ross (New York: Macmillan Co., 1925), p. 569; and *FTC Report on Cooperative Marketing*, p. 56.

39. Two years later, however, the Iowa Supreme Court found the penalty clause in restraint of trade in a case involving the Decorah Farmers' Cooperative Society, a livestock shipping association. By the end of the decade, though, farmers' elevators relied less and less on a penalty clause in order to ensure the loyalty of their patrons; they either did not adopt such a clause, repealed those that were on the books, or did not enforce them. In any event, penalty clauses were either protected or rendered unnecessary by the different cooperative laws that were passed during the 1910s and 1920s.

40. Refsell, "Farmers' Elevator Movement," *American Cooperative Journal* (December 1914): 290, and (May 1915): 749.

41. *American Cooperative Journal* (November 1909).

42. *American Cooperative Journal* (August 1918): 477; (March 1920): 2.

43. See Frank Robotka, "Membership Problems and Relationships in Iowa Farmers' Elevators," Iowa State University Agricultural Experiment Station, *Bulletin* 321 (1934).

44. W. F. Schilling, *Lest We Forget, or Eternal Vigilance Is the Price of Economic Liberty: A History of the Twin City Milk Producers' Association* (Northfield, Minn.: Mohn Printing Co., 1942), pp. 6–7; Zimmerman and Black, "Marketing Attitudes," pp. 35–36.

45. Alfred C. Nielsen, *Life in an American Denmark* (1962; reprint, New York: Arno Press, Inc., 1979), pp. 62–63; and Holman, *Forty Years*, p. 36.

46. *Prairie Farmer*, May 15, 1920, p. 1314. In a similar situation, another Illinois farmers' elevator that started in 1910 paid no dividends during its bitter struggle against the local line elevator. A few shrewd farmers gradually bought up the stock for a fraction of its value, and when its competitors finally went out of business, it was owned by a dozen well-to-do farmers. Instead of paying as close as possible to

Chicago prices, which had been the original policy, they instituted wide margins and paid themselves 100 percent annual cash dividends as well as occasional juicy divisions of stock. Local grain growers rebelled in 1919, however, and started a second farmer-owned elevator. See Steen, *Cooperative Marketing*, pp. 206–7.

47. *American Cooperative Journal* (November 1917): 91.

48. Ibid.

49. *FTC Report on Country Grain Marketing*, p. 92; Farlow, *Farmers' Elevator Movement*, pp. 110–23; and Robotka, "Membership Problems."

50. Holman, *Forty Years*, p. 40.

51. In 1907, James A. Everitt, the founder of the American Society of Equity, broke with the new direction of his organization and started a splinter group, the Farmers' Society of Equity, that adhered to his initial emphasis on centralized control. See the articles on the various factions in the Equity movement in Lowell K. Dyson, *Farmers' Organizations* (Westport, Conn.: Greenwood Press, 1986), pp. 24–30, 77–81, 102–4, 122–23.

52. Robert H. Bahmer, "The American Society of Equity," *Agricultural History* 14 (1940): 33–63; Theodore Saloutos and John D. Hicks, *Twentieth-Century Populism: Agricultural Discontent in the Middle West, 1900–1939* (Madison: University of Wisconsin Press, 1951), pp. 111–48; Theodore Saloutos, "The Wisconsin Society of Equity," *Agricultural History* 14 (1940): 78–95; Saloutos, "The Rise of the Equity Cooperative Exchange," *Mississippi Valley Historical Review* 32 (1945): 31–62; Saloutos, "The Decline of the Equity Cooperative Exchange," *Mississippi Valley Historical Review* 34 (1947): 405–26; Dyson, *Farmers' Organizations*, p. 103; and Carl C. Taylor, *The Farmers' Movement, 1620–1920* (New York: American Book Company, 1953), pp. 365–420, esp. 393–98.

53. *Prairie Farmer*, February 23, 1918, p. 185. The Griggsville, Pike County, Cooperative Company, which may have been the result of E.L.S.'s original interest, organized as a cooperative but not as an Equity elevator in 1921, according to Farlow's list.

54. Farlow, *Farmers' Elevator Movement*, pp. 110–23; Henry E. Erdman, "Organizations among Ohio Farmers," Ohio Agricultural Experiment Station *Bulletin* 342 (1920): 119–21.

55. Taylor, *The Farmers' Movement*, pp. 335–64; Dyson, *Farmers' Organizations*, pp. 214–32; Grant McConnell, *The Decline of Agrarian Democracy* (Berkeley: University of California Press, 1953), p. 38; Saloutos and Hicks, *Twentieth-Century Populism*, pp. 219–54; Knapp, *Rise of American Cooperative Enterprise*, pp. 176–82; Commodore B. Fisher, *The Farmers' Union*, University of Kentucky Studies in Economics and Sociology (Lexington: University of Kentucky Press, 1920), vol. 1, no. 2; and William P. Tucker, "Populism Up-to-Date: The Story of the Farmers' Union," *Agricultural History* 21 (1947): 198–208.

56. E. R. Eastman, *These Changing Times* (New York: Macmillan Co., 1927), pp. 94–96.

57. In 1912, Julius Rosenwald and Sears, Roebuck and Co., offered $1,000 to counties as a matching grant to support a full-time, salaried agricultural extension agent. This early effort was supplanted to some degree by the federal Smith-Lever Act, but Sears continued to support agricultural extension and organized its efforts as the Sears-Roebuck Agricultural Foundation in 1923. "Agricultural Foundation," typescript, Julius Rosenwald collection, Special Collections, University of Chicago Library.

58. *Milo Reno, Farmers' Union Pioneer* (Iowa City: Iowa Farmers' Union, 1941), p. 28. In Nobles County, Minnesota, for example, local farmers split 50–50 between the Farm Bureau and the Farmers' Union, a split that mirrored partisan divisions between Democrats and Republicans more than the ethnic distinctions that also characterized the area; in 1925, the union presented a petition of two hundred signatures opposing a county appropriation for extension work. In other Minnesota communities, the Nonpartisan League mounted similar campaigns. Al Goff, ed., *Nobles County History* (St. Paul, Minn.: Nobles County Historical Society, 1958), pp. 120–47.

59. Orville M. Kile, *The Farm Bureau Movement* (New York: Macmillan Co., 1921), pp. 116–17; Robert P. Howard, *James R. Howard and the Farm Bureau* (Ames: Iowa State University Press, 1983), pp. 140–41; and Dyson, *Farmers' Organizations*, pp. 14–23. Significantly, Howard also said frequently that if he had lived in North Dakota, he would have been a member of the league, and, according to his biographer, "He admired the spirit of the men who refused to be subservient to business interests, but he did not approve socialistic programs" (Howard, *Howard*, pp. 93–94).

60. McConnell, *Decline*, p. 60; Saloutos and Hicks, *Twentieth-Century Populism*, pp. 255–85; Joseph G. Knapp, *The Advance of American Cooperative Enterprise: 1920–1945* (Danville, Ill.: Interstate Publishers, 1973), pp. 35–53.

61. W. N. Woods, "Sixty-Five Years with Farm Co-operatives," *Northwest Ohio Quarterly* 50 (1978): 75. Woods's memoirs continue in 51 (1979). John J. Lacey, *Farm Bureau in Illinois: History of Illinois Farm Bureau* (Bloomington: Illinois Agricultural Association, 1965), pp. 65–79; Kile, *Farm Bureau*, p. 125; and "The Ohio Farm Bureau Federation from the Farmers' Viewpoint," USDA mimeograph report, Washington, D.C., 1931, p. 15.

62. Lacey, *Farm Bureau in Illinois*, p. 29; Kile, *Farm Bureau*, pp. 126–27; Goff, *Nobles County*, p. 120.

63. *American Cooperative Journal* (May 1920): 5.

64. Clark L. Brody, *In the Service of the Farmer: My Life in the Michigan Farm Bureau* (East Lansing: Michigan State University Press, 1959), p. 35; Woods, "Sixty-Five Years," pp. 108–9. Mary Neth also discusses the tensions between the Farm Bureau and other, more locally based, agricultural organizations, especially Equity and the

Farmers' Union, in *Preserving the Family Farm: Women, Community, and the Foundations of Agribusiness in the Midwest, 1900–1940* (Baltimore: Johns Hopkins University Press, 1995), pp. 139–46.

65. *American Cooperative Journal* (February 1922): 6–7.

66. Woods, "Sixty-Five Years," p. 70; "The Ohio Farm Bureau Federation," pp. 18, 41.

67. Kile, *Farm Bureau*, pp. 137–38; Paul Turner, *They Did It in Indiana: The Story of the Indiana Farm Bureau Co-operatives* (New York: Dryden Press, 1947), pp. 18–34.

68. Kile, *Farm Bureau*, pp. 148–64.

69. Knapp, *Advance of American Cooperative Enterprise*, p. 14. The best recent analysis of the tensions between centralized and decentralized control in the agricultural cooperative movement is David E. Hamilton, *From New Day to New Deal: American Farm Policy from Hoover to Roosevelt, 1928–1933* (Chapel Hill: University of North Carolina Press, 1991). According to Hamilton, Sapiro's plan was an attempt to overcome the problem of the "outsider," or noncooperator, who stood to benefit from the price increases gained by the cooperative without incurring any of the risks of participating in the organization. This "outsider" problem, according to a theory of economist Mancur Olson, limited the tangible incentives for collective action and consequently made it economically "irrational" for an individual to join. See Hamilton, *From New Day to New Deal*, pp. 8–25.

70. *American Cooperative Journal* (December 1921): 6–13; Knapp, *Advance of American Cooperative Enterprise*, p. 36; James H. Shideler, *Farm Crisis, 1919–1923* (Berkeley: University of California Press, 1957), pp. 104–17; and Hamilton, *From New Day to New Deal*, pp. 8–25.

71. H. Clyde Filley, *Cooperation in Agriculture* (New York: John Wiley & Sons, 1929), pp. 150–56; Saloutos and Hicks, *Twentieth-Century Populism*, pp. 296–97.

72. *American Cooperative Journal* (September 1921): 28–30.

73. Saloutos and Hicks, *Twentieth-Century Populism*, pp. 297–300; American Farm Bureau Federation, *Weekly Newsletter*, March 23, 1922; Earl Price, "In the Beginning," in *Fiftieth Anniversary Booklet* (Yorkville, Ill.: Kendall County Farm Bureau, n.d.).

74. From *We Kansas Farmers* (Topeka: F. M. Steves and Sons, 1953), p. 47, quoted in Knapp, *Advance of American Cooperative Enterprise*, pp. 38–39.

75. Alice A. O'Rourke, "Cooperative Marketing in McLean County," *Illinois State Historical Society Journal* 64 (1971): 173–91; Filley, *Cooperation*, pp. 156–59.

76. Dyson, *Farmers' Organizations*, p. 17; Woods, "Sixty-Five Years," p. 75; H. W. Mumford, R. C. Ross, and W. R. Tylor, "The Attitude of Illinois Farmers toward the County Farm Bureau," Illinois Agricultural Experiment Station, mimeograph report, University of Illinois, 1929, pp. 1–11; and "The Ohio Farm Bureau," p. 37.

77. Zimmerman and Black, "Marketing Attitudes," p. 24.

78. Filley, *Cooperation*, pp. 159–61.

79. Battles between centralized and local control continued to plague the federal farm policies of the Hoover administration during the late 1920s and early 1930s and compromised the Farmers National Grain Corporation and other marketing efforts of the Federal Farm Board that were established after the Agricultural Marketing Act of 1929. See Hamilton, *From New Day to New Deal*, pp. 130–47.

CHAPTER FIVE

1. This perspective parallels recent studies of urban society, which illustrate the efforts of the working class to negotiate consumer society on their own terms in order to minimize its unsettling effects. See Lizabeth Cohen, *Making a New Deal: Industrial Workers in Chicago, 1919–1939* (New York: Cambridge University Press, 1990); Kathy Peiss, *Cheap Amusements: Working Women and Leisure in Turn-of-the-Century New York* (Philadelphia: Temple University Press, 1986); and Roy Rosenzweig, *Eight Hours for What We Will: Workers and Leisure in an Industrial City, 1870–1920* (New York: Cambridge University Press, 1983).

2. Quoted in Christopher Clark, *The Roots of Rural Capitalism: Western Massachusetts, 1780–1860* (Ithaca: Cornell University Press, 1990), pp. 162–63.

3. Ibid., pp. 156–76.

4. Waldo R. Browne, compiler, *Barnum's Own Story: The Autobiography of P. T. Barnum* (1927; reprint, Gloucester, Mass.: Peter Smith, 1972), pp. 12–26.

5. Clark, *Roots of Rural Capitalism*, pp. 156–76.

6. For the best discussion of peddlers in the rural North, see David Jaffee, "Peddlers of Progress and the Transformation of the Rural North, 1760–1860," *Journal of American History* 78 (1991): 511–35. See also Gerald Carson, *The Old Country Store* (New York: Oxford University Press, 1954), pp. 37–63.

7. Richardson Wright, *Hawkers and Walkers in Early America* (Philadelphia: J. B. Lippincott Co., 1927), p. 28. These negative attitudes were exacerbated in the South, where Yankee peddlers operated in a context of growing regional tensions and suspicions. See Joseph T. Rainer, "Popular and Folkloric Images of the Peddler in the Old South" (paper presented at the Center for the Study of Southern Culture, University of Mississippi, March 1995). Dr. Rainer kindly provided the author with a copy of this paper.

8. Jaffee, "Peddlers of Progress"; and John Joseph Murphy, "Entrepreneurship in the Establishment of the American Clock Industry," *Journal of Economic History* 26 (1966): 169–86. The clock peddler was especially notorious for cheating rural customers, who, most probably, had never purchased such an item before and were therefore unable to judge either its quality or the fairness of its price. See Rainer,

"Popular and Folkloric Images," pp. 14–16. See also T. J. Jackson Lears, *Fables of Abundance: A Cultural History of Advertising in America* (New York: Basic Books, 1994), pp. 64–74.

9. Jaffee, "Peddlers of Progress," p. 532; Carson, *Old Country Store*, pp. 37–63.

10. Linda J. Borish, "Forsaking 'Clothes-Thumping' for 'Piano-Thumping': Farmers' Daughters Quitting the Homestead in Antebellum New England," unpublished manuscript, which Professor Borish generously provided to the author; Allan Kulikoff, "The Transition to Capitalism in Rural America," *William and Mary Quarterly*, 3d series, 46 (1989): 139.

11. While one scholar traces the beginnings of mail-order business back to Benjamin Franklin's 1744 list of books for sale, mail orders before the Civil War were typically only a small part of already established specialty businesses that advertised in trade catalogues. An example is the 1860 catalogue of the Cook Carriage Co. in New Haven, Connecticut, which carried notices from a wide range of other local businesses willing to take orders through the mail: J. Punderford, boots and shoes; Edward Harrison, flour and grain mills; Collins & Co., hatters and furriers; Elam Hull's Sons, candles; E. Whitney, improved firearms; Thompson & Co., fireproof safes, and more. See Lawrence B. Romaine, *A Guide to American Trade Catalogs, 1744–1900* (New York: R. R. Bowker Co., 1960), pp. ix–xv; Cecil C. Hoge Sr., *The First Hundred Years Are the Toughest: What We Can Learn from the Century of Competition between Sears and Wards* (Berkeley: Ten-Speed Press, 1988), pp. 2–11.

12. E. C. Allen & Co., *Descriptive Catalogue* (Augusta, Maine: E. C. Allen & Co., n.d.), pp. 2–16, in Romaine Trade Catalogue Collection, Special Collections, University of California–Santa Barbara. Allen's venture may have been modeled on a slightly earlier effort by a teenage Charles B. Thompson of Bridgewater, Connecticut. Thompson had his agents sell "Grandma's Wonder Healing and Complexion Cream," which he made at his home, in return for premiums like dolls, mandolins, lace curtains, watches, rifles, furs, and more. At his peak, Thompson employed over a hundred workers, but he later gave up the mail-order business and opened a country store. See Robert Hendrickson, *The Grand Emporiums: The Illustrated History of America's Great Department Stores* (New York: Stein and Day, 1979), pp. 206–7.

13. Frank Luther Mott, *A History of American Magazines*, vol. 3, *1865–1885* (Cambridge, Mass.: Harvard University Press, 1938), pp. 37–40. See also Robert W. Lovett, "Publisher and Advertiser Extraordinary: The E. C. Allen Collection," *Bulletin of the Business History Society* 24 (1950): 210–15.

14. P. O. Vickery, *Vickery's Latest Catalogue* (Augusta, Maine: P. O. Vickery, n.d.), in Romaine Collection, University of California–Santa Barbara.

15. W. H. Van Ornum & Co., *The "Ladies' Friend": Being a Catalogue and Price List of Goods Manufactured and Sold by W. H. Van Ornum & Co.* (Chicago: Van Ornum & Co., n.d.), in Romaine Collection, University of California–Santa Barbara.

16. Earl W. Hayter, *The Troubled Farmer, 1850–1900: Rural Adjustment to Industrialism* (Dekalb: Northern Illinois University Press, 1968), pp. 158–63.

17. Van Ornum & Co., *"Ladies' Friend."*

18. E. C. Allen & Co., *Descriptive Catalogue*, p. 2.

19. Hoge, *First Hundred Years*, pp. 7–17; Frank B. Latham, *1872–1972, A Century of Serving Consumers: The Story of Montgomery Ward* (Chicago: Montgomery Ward & Co., 1972), pp. 2–10. The Grange, or the Order of Patrons of Husbandry, consisted of over two thousand local chapters by 1873, with more than eight thousand new ones organized in the following year. See Thomas A. Woods, *Knights of the Plow: Oliver H. Kelley and the Origins of the Grange in Republican Ideology* (Ames: Iowa State University Press, 1991), pp. 147–64.

20. Montgomery Ward & Co., *Catalogue*, various issues (Chicago: Montgomery Ward & Co., 1872–1930). First hat picture in no. 12, Fall–Winter 1874–75; Grange regalia in no. 14, Fall–Winter 1875–76. Latham, *A Century of Serving Consumers*, p. 8. William Cronon also discusses the early history of Montgomery Ward and its connection to the Grange in *Nature's Metropolis: Chicago and the Great West* (New York: W. W. Norton & Co., 1991), pp. 333–40. The most recent study of the economic activities of the Grange as well as its relationship to Montgomery Ward is David Blanke, "Sowing the American Dream: Consumer Culture in the Rural Middle West, 1865–1900" (Ph.D. diss., Loyola University, 1996). Blanke attributes part of Ward's connection to the Grange to the fact that his wife's uncle, Jerome Cobb, was the purchasing agent for the Michigan State Grange, and that Ward employed two other Cobbs, his father-in-law and brother-in-law. The author thanks Dr. Blanke for sending him this manuscript.

21. Woods, *Knights of the Plow*, pp. 147–64. Song quoted in George Cerny, "Cooperation in the Midwest in the Granger Era, 1869–1875," *Agricultural History* 37 (1963): 187–205, 197.

22. Montgomery Ward, *Catalogue*, no. 11 (Spring–Summer 1874): 5; no. 14 (Fall–Winter 1875–76): 1–2.

23. *Chicago Tribune*, November 8, 1873; December 24, 1873; and Montgomery Ward, *Catalogue*, no. 10 (January 1874): 4.

24. *The Prairie Farmer*, November 1, 1873, p. 348.

25. In its early years, the Grange leadership divided over the issue of cooperative purchasing; Oliver H. Kelly, for example, favored it while others stressed the order's social, fraternal, and intellectual aspects. As a result, the National Grange made no constitutional provisions for economic cooperation and left it to the state and local organizations to make their own arrangements. See Solon J. Buck, *The Granger Movement: A Study of Agricultural Organization and Its Political, Economic, and Social Manifestations, 1870–1880* (1913; reprint, Lincoln: University of Nebraska Press, 1963), pp. 238–78.

26. See ibid.; D. Sven Nordin, *Rich Harvest: A History of the Grange, 1867–1900* (Jackson: University of Mississippi Press, 1974), pp. 131–67; Woods, *Knights of the Plow*, pp. 160–64; and Cerny, "Cooperation in the Midwest," pp. 187–205.

27. For example, there had been a Grange store in nearly every Ohio county, but by 1888, not one was in existence or retained cooperative features. See Amos G. Warner, "Three Phases of Cooperation in the West," in *History of Cooperation in the United States*, ed. Herbert B. Adams (Baltimore: Johns Hopkins University, Studies in Historical and Political Science, 1888); *American Cooperative Journal* (March 1920): 50; Buck, *The Granger Movement*, pp. 238–78; Nordin, *Rich Harvest*, pp. 131–67; Woods, *Knights of the Plow*, pp. 160–64; Cerny, "Cooperation in the Midwest," pp. 187–205; Cronon, *Nature's Metropolis*, pp. 362–64; and Blanke, "Sowing the American Dream," chap. 6.

28. Ward, *Catalogue*, no. 12 (Fall–Winter 1874–75): 41–42.

29. Ibid., no. 14 (Fall–Winter 1875–76): 5.

30. Ibid., no. 14 (Fall–Winter 1875–76).

31. Ibid., no. 12 (Fall–Winter 1874–75).

32. Carson, *Old Country Store*, pp. 34–35.

33. Ward, *Catalogue*, no. 1 (1872); no. 10 (January 1874).

34. Ibid., no. 10 (January 1874).

35. Ibid., various issues; Patrons of Husbandry, Wisconsin State Grange, *Price List* (Oshkosh, Wisc., 1874), pp. 3–5.

36. Floyd L. Vaughan, *The United States Patent System: Legal and Economic Conflict in American Patent History* (Norman: University of Oklahoma Press, 1956), p. 41.

37. Hayter, *Troubled Farmer*, pp. 158–63, 302 n. See also *Prairie Farmer*, March 29, 1873, p. 100; April 28, 1877, p. 132; and October 30, 1875, p. 348.

38. *Prairie Farmer*, December 2, 1876, p. 388.

39. Ward, *Catalogue*, no. 26 (Fall and Winter 1879): 57.

40. Ibid.

41. Margaret Walsh, "The Democratization of Fashion: The Emergence of the Women's Dress Pattern Industry," *Journal of American History* 66 (1979): 299–313. On sewing and rural wardrobes, see also Virginia McCormick, ed., *Farm Wife: A Self-Portrait, 1886–1896* (Ames: Iowa State University Press, 1990), pp. 99–105.

42. Ward, *Catalogue*, no. 45 (Spring–Summer 1889).

43. According to an 1899 questionnaire sent to subscribers of two farm magazines, ninety-eight mail-order houses solicited the rural trade. Cited in Blanke, "Sowing the American Dream," chap. 7.

44. Hoge, *First Hundred Years*, pp. 18–40. In contrast to the few histories of Montgomery Ward, the literature on Sears, Roebuck is large. See Boris Emmet and John E. Jeuck, *Catalogues and Counters: A History of Sears, Roebuck and Company* (Chicago: Uni-

versity of Chicago Press, 1950), esp. pp. 9–184; Louis E. Asher and Edith Heal, *Send No Money* (Chicago: Argus Books, 1942); Gordon L. Weil, *Sears, Roebuck, U.S.A.: The Great American Catalogue Store and How It Grew* (New York: Stein and Day, 1977); and Richard S. Tedlow, *New and Improved: The Story of Mass Marketing in America* (New York: Basic Books, 1990), pp. 259–343.

45. Emmet and Jeuck, *Catalogues and Counters*, pp. 150–64; Rae E. Rips, "An Introductory Study of the Role of the Mail Order Business in American History, 1872–1914" (master's thesis, University of Chicago, 1938), pp. 65–66, 76–111; and Hendrickson, *Grand Emporiums*, pp. 213–15.

46. Hendrickson, *Grand Emporiums*, p. 213.

47. *The Farmer's Guide*, November 16, 1907, p. 961.

48. Quoted in Emmet and Jeuck, *Catalogues and Counters*, pp. 161–62.

49. *Emporia Gazette*, June 17, 20, 22, 24, 29, 1905. On White more generally, see Sally Griffith, *Home Town News: William Allen White and the Emporia Gazette* (New York: Oxford University Press, 1989).

50. *The Farmer's Guide*, March 30, 1907, p. 297. For a similar example from Iowa, see Roy Alden Atwood, "Routes of Rural Discontent: Cultural Contradictions of Rural Free Delivery in Southeastern Iowa, 1899–1917," *Annals of Iowa* 48 (1986): 264–73.

51. *The Farmer's Guide*, August 12, 1905, p. 648; August 26, 1905, p. 669; September 30, 1905, p. 768; and December 14, 1907, p. 1038.

52. Ibid., November 16, 1907, p. 950; and April 18, 1908, p. 387.

53. Ibid., October 14, 1905, pp. 791–92. These sentiments were by no means confined to Indiana farmers. "Old Settler" makes many of the same points in his October 26, 1905, letter to *The Homestead* in Des Moines, Iowa.

54. *The Farmer's Guide*, November 4, 1905, p. 872; February 29, 1908, p. 228.

55. Ibid., August 26, 1905, p. 669; August 19, 1905, p. 653.

56. Ibid., August 19, 1905, p. 653; February 24, 1906, p. 160.

57. Ibid., June 10, 1905, p. 487; January 20, 1906, p. 49; and July 27, 1907, p. 622.

58. Ibid., July 27, 1907, p. 622; November 16, 1907, p. 961; and *Wallace's Farmer*, August 9, 1907, p. 881. The Gordon–Van Tine Company originally started in 1865 as the U. N. Roberts Company, a traditional wholesale supplier of millwork up and down the Mississippi, and merged with another firm and began a direct mail-order business in September 1906. In spite of the opposition of retail dealers, the company thrived during the 1910s and 1920s along with other firms that sold home kits through the mail. Known collectively as the Big Six, these included, in addition to Gordon–Van Tine, Sears and Ward in Chicago and Aladdin, Lewis, and Sterling, which were located at the mouth of the Saginaw River in Bay City, Michigan, a lumber and shipbuilding town. See Robert Schweitzer and Michael W. R. Davis, *America's*

Favorite Homes: Mail-Order Catalogues as a Guide to Popular Early 20th-Century Houses (Detroit: Wayne State University Press, 1990), pp. 61–80.

59. Wayne E. Fuller, *RFD: The Changing Face of Rural America* (Bloomington: Indiana University Press, 1964), pp. 199–227; Anthony H. Simon, "The Battle for Parcel Post: The Western Farmer vs. the Eastern Mercantile Interests," *Journal of the West* 13, no. 4 (1974): 79–89. See also Richard B. Kielbowicz, "Rural Ambivalence toward Mass Society: Evidence from the U.S. Parcel Post Debates, 1900–1913," *Rural History* 5 (1994): 81–102, which analyzes the congressional hearings on this legislation.

60. Fuller, *RFD*; Simon, "The Battle for Parcel Post"; and Rips, "An Introductory Study," pp. 76–111.

61. Fuller, *RFD*; Simon, "The Battle for Parcel Post"; and Rips, "An Introductory Study," pp. 76–111.

62. Rips, "An Introductory Study," pp. 76–111; House Committee on the Post-Office and Post-Roads, *Hearings: Parcels Post*, April 1910, p. 286.

63. Thomas J. Sullivan, *Merchants and Manufacturers on Trial* (Chicago: Thomas J. Sullivan Co., 1914).

64. *Lismore Leader*, February 12, 1909.

65. Richard F. Outcault himself came from a midwestern small-town background. Born in Lancaster, Ohio, in 1863, he was the first artist to achieve success with color comics in the big urban newspapers in the late nineteenth century, first with Pulitzer and then with Hearst. Early on, he organized the Outcault Advertising Company in Chicago and syndicated his efforts. He created Buster Brown in 1902, and in addition to comics and shoes, his most famous character was made into a toy doll and starred in a musical stage show and eight short films before the development of animated cartoons; he was also linked to watches, textiles, harmonicas, a soft drink, coffee, flour, bread, apples, suits, hosiery, and pianos. See Richard Marschall, "Masters of Comic Strip Art," *American History Illustrated* 25 (1990): 44–57; M. Thomas Inge, *Comics as Culture* (Jackson: University of Mississippi Press, 1990); and Arthur Asa Berger, *The Comic-Stripped American* (New York: Walker & Co., 1973), pp. 23–24. Ian Gordon discusses Outcault's advertising agency as well as his ties to different manufacturers in "Mass Market Modernism: Comic Strips and the Culture of Consumption," unpublished manuscript. Ironically, the 1908 Sears catalogue included an advertisement for a Buster Brown doll and described it as "a very fine imitation of the Buster Brown you read about." This was before he was used in the campaign against mail-order buying. The author thanks Professor Gordon for sending him this manuscript.

66. Susan Strasser, *Satisfaction Guaranteed: The Making of the American Mass Market* (New York: Pantheon, 1989), p. 219; Latham, *A Century of Serving Consumers*, p. 41; David L. Cohn, *The Good Old Days: A History of American Morals and Manners as Seen*

through the Sears, Roebuck Catalogs 1905 to the Present (New York: Simon and Schuster, 1940), pp. 510–17.

67. George Milburn, "The Catalogues," *Harper's Magazine* 167 (1933): 352–62. Milburn also published a novel, *Catalogue* (New York: Harcourt, Brace, and Co., 1936), which incorporates this story as well as several others about rural mail-order buying, particularly, "Uneasy Payments," *Harper's Magazine* 168 (1933–34): 26–37; and "The Wish Book," *Southern Review* 1 (1935–36): 253–70. The other fictional depiction of mail-order buying and small-town merchants is Edna Ferber's novel, *Fanny Herself* (1917; reprint, New York: Frederick A. Stokes Co., 1975). Drawn largely from Ferber's personal experiences as the daughter of a Jewish merchant family in Kalamazoo, Michigan, and Appleton, Wisconsin, the main character, Fanny Brandeis, is also the daughter of a midwestern small-town Jewish merchant. Although her mother, who runs the business, hated mail-order houses "like poison, the way every small-town merchant hates the mail-order houses" (114–15), Fanny sells the business and moves to the city after her death and becomes a very successful, if not completely fulfilled, executive with a big mail-order house. Interestingly, Ferber dedicated *Fanny Herself* to William Allen White.

68. Fuller, *RFD*, pp. 228–30; Emmet and Jeuck, *Catalogues and Counters*, pp. 293–310; Richard G. Bremer, *Agricultural Change in an Urban Age: The Loup Country of Nebraska, 1910–1970* (Lincoln: University of Nebraska Studies, 1976), new series no. 51, pp. 37–43.

69. See Frank Farrington, *Meeting Mail Order Competition* (Chicago: Byxbee Publishing Co., 1922). Examples of earlier articles include W. C. Holman, "Keeping Retail Trade at Home," *System* 23 (1913): 13–20; Joseph Mills, "How I Meet Mail-Order Competition," *System* 28 (1915): 642–44; John Allen Underwood, "What's the Matter with the Small-Town Store?," *Current Opinion* 59 (July 1915): 60–64; and "Seventy-Four American Towns Mobilize to Keep Trade at Home," *Current Opinion* 62 (April 1917): 288–89. On brand-name goods, see Strasser, *Satisfaction Guaranteed*.

70. Mills, "Mail-Order Competition," pp. 642–44.

71. *The Farmer's Guide*, March 12, 1921, p. 375.

CHAPTER SIX

1. On the efforts of agricultural professionals to promote rural consumption and the reactions of farm families, see Mary Neth, *Preserving the Family Farm: Women, Community, and the Foundations of Agribusiness in the Midwest, 1900–1940* (Baltimore: Johns Hopkins University Press, 1995), pp. 187–213. Neth refers to this ethos of rural practicality as "making do."

2. The best discussion of these conflicts is Michael L. Berger, *The Devil Wagon in*

God's Country: The Automobile and Social Change in Rural America, 1893–1929 (Hamden, Conn.: Archon Books, 1979). Joseph Interrante, "You Can't Go to Town in a Bathtub: Automobile Movement and the Reorganization of Rural American Space, 1900–1930," *Radical History Review*, no. 21 (1979): 152–53.

3. Berger, *Devil Wagon*, pp. 51–52.

4. Marianne Muse, "The Standard of Living on Specific Owner-Operated Vermont Farms," University of Vermont Agricultural Experiment Station *Bulletin* 340 (1932); Edward A. Taylor, "The Relationship of the Open-Country Population of Genesee County, New York, to Villages and Cities," Cornell University Agricultural Experiment Station *Bulletin* 583 (1934); Perry P. Denune, "The Social and Economic Relations of the Farmers with the Towns in Pickaway County, Ohio," Bureau of Business Research, Ohio State University (1927); George H. von Tungeln, J. E. Thaden, and E. L. Kirkpatrick, "Cost of Living on Iowa Farms," Iowa State University Agricultural Experiment Station *Bulletin* 237, pt. 1 (1926); J. H. Kolb and R. A. Polson, "Trends in Town-Country Relations," University of Wisconsin Agricultural Experiment Station *Research Bulletin* 117 (1933); and E. L. Kirkpatrick, J. H. Kolb, Creagh Inge, and A. F. Wileden, "Rural Organizations and the Farm Family," University of Wisconsin Agricultural Experiment Station *Research Bulletin* 96 (1929).

5. *Indiana Farmer's Guide*, August 17, 1918, p. 1022.

6. Reynold M. Wik, *Henry Ford and Grass-roots America* (Ann Arbor: University of Michigan Press, 1972), pp. 34–58. See also Michael Kammen, *Mystic Chords of Memory: The Transformation of Tradition in American Culture* (New York: Alfred A. Knopf, 1991), pp. 351–58.

7. Wik, *Henry Ford*, p. 33; Denune, "Pickaway County"; "Household Buying by Farm Families, 1929," Survey Records of Department of Household Economics and Management, Division of Rare and Manuscript Collections, Cornell University Library, accession no. 23/8/1648. This collection contains ten volumes of manuscript survey schedules, consisting of eighteen pages per family, from Allegany County, Chautauqua County, Niagara County, and Yates County. For the purposes of this study, 121 surveys from Jerusalem Township, Yates County, and from Royalton and Lockport Townships, Niagara County, were entered into a spreadsheet program. The aggregate results of the larger study were originally published in Marion Fish, "Buying for the Household as Practiced by 368 Farm Families in New York, 1928–1929," Cornell University Agricultural Experiment Station *Bulletin* 561 (1933).

8. *Indiana Farmers Guide*, May 18, 1918, p. 698.

9. "An Automobile Is a Good Investment for the Farmer, a Real Asset to His Business," *Indiana Farmers Guide*, May 18, 1918, p. 691.

10. *Indiana Farmers Guide*, May 18, 1918, pp. 717, 698.

11. Quoted in Berger, *Devil Wagon*, p. 134.

12. Eleanor Arnold, ed., *Buggies and Bad Times*, vol. 3 of *Memories of Hoosier Home-*

makers (Indianapolis: Indiana Extension Homemakers Association, 1985), pp. 41, 43. To a certain extent, rural men's control of the automobile continued patterns established in the earlier horse-drawn period. See Katherine Jellison, *Entitled to Power: Farm Women and Technology, 1913–1963* (Chapel Hill: University of North Carolina Press, 1993), p. 35; and Neth, *Preserving the Family Farm*, pp. 252, 325 n. 15.

13. New York survey data from "Household Buying by Farm Families, 1929."

14. In general, this picture of less than universal automobility for rural women contrasts somewhat with the portrayal of female empowerment in Virginia Scharff's book, *Taking the Wheel: Women and the Coming of the Motor Age* (New York: Free Press, 1991), pp. 142–45. New York survey data from "Household Buying by Farm Families, 1929." See also Carol K. Coburn, *Life at Four Corners: Religion, Gender, and Education in a German-Lutheran Community, 1868–1945* (Lawrence: University Press of Kansas, 1992), p. 118; and Arnold, *Buggies and Bad Times*, p. 39.

15. In Yates County, New York, for example, the number of blacksmiths in the county declined from 44 to 14 between 1900 and 1929, harness shops went from 12 to 2, and livery stables from 7 to 0, being superseded by 36 garages, 4 automobile dealerships, and 2 tire stores. See Harold F. Dorn, "The Social and Economic Areas of Yates County, New York," *Cornell University Agricultural Experiment Station Bulletin* 529 (1931).

16. Perry P. Denune, "Some Town-Country Relations in Union County, Ohio," *Ohio State University Studies, Sociology Series* 1 (1924); Harold C. Hoffsommer, "Relation of Cities and Larger Villages to Changes in Rural Trade and Social Areas in Wayne County, New York," *Cornell University Agricultural Experiment Station Bulletin* 582 (1934).

17. Hoffsommer, "Wayne County, New York"; Norman T. Moline, "Mobility and the Small Town, 1900–1930: Transportation Change in Oregon, Illinois," University of Chicago, Department of Geography, research paper 132, Chicago, 1971, pp. 94–121.

18. Committee on Business Research, College of Business Administration, "The Influence of Automobiles and Good Roads on Retail Trade Centers," University of Nebraska *Studies in Business* 18 (1927); Hoffsommer, "Wayne County," p. 40; and Dorn, "Yates County."

19. "The Automobile and the Village Merchant: The Influence of Automobiles and Paved Roads on the Business of Illinois Merchants," University of Illinois Bureau of Business Research *Bulletin* 19 (1928): 13. In part, rural consumers learned about these new styles from the advertisements of city stores in the daily papers, and one indirect consequence of the farmer's new mobility was a desire for more news from the larger centers that were now accessible. In Walworth County, Wisconsin, for example, 44 percent of the farmers surveyed subscribed to a daily newspaper in 1913. In 1929, however, 85 percent got dailies, and half got urban

dailies from Chicago and Milwaukee. See Kolb and Polson, "Trends."

20. "The Automobile and the Village Merchant"; Kolb and Polson, "Trends," p. 25; and "The Influence of Automobiles and Good Roads on Retail Trade Centers," p. 45.

21. "The Automobile and the Village Merchant"; Denune, "Pickaway County."

22. Dorn, "Yates County." On chain stores more generally, see Richard S. Tedlow, *New and Improved: The Story of Mass Marketing in America* (New York: Basic Books, 1990), pp. 182–258; and Jonathan J. Bean, "Beyond the Broker State: A History of the Federal Government's Policies Toward Small Business, 1936–1961," unpublished manuscript based on chapter 1 of Bean's Ph.D. dissertation. The author thanks Professor Bean for providing him with this study.

23. F. J. Harper, "'A new battle on evolution': The Anti-Chain Store Trade-at-Home Agitation of 1929–1930," *Journal of American Studies* 16 (1982): 407–26, esp. 408–13. See also Harper, "The Anti-Chain Store Movement in the U.S." (Ph.D. diss., University of Warwick, 1981); Carl G. Ryant, "The South and the Movement against Chain Stores," *Journal of Southern History* 39 (1973): 207–22; Ryant, "Kentucky and the Movement to Regulate Chain Stores, 1925–1945," *Filson Club Quarterly* 57 (1983): 270–85; David A. Horowitz, "The Crusade against Chain Stores: Portland's Independent Merchants, 1928–1935," *Oregon Historical Quarterly* 89 (1988): 341–68; and Thomas W. Ross, "Store Wars: The Chain Tax Movement," *Journal of Law and Economics* 29 (1986): 125–37. The Robinson-Patman Act limited the discounts that suppliers could give for purchases in large quantities and was an attempt to "level the playing field" between small retailers and the chain stores. See Bean, "Beyond the Broker State," chap. 1.

24. Taylor, "Genesee County, New York."

25. New York survey data from "Household Buying by Farm Families, 1929."

26. Moline, "Mobility and the Small Town," p. 104.

27. Coburn, *Life at Four Corners*, p. 114; Neth, *Preserving the Family Farm*, pp. 245–50; and W. V. Dennis, "Social Activities of the Families in the Unionville District, Chester County, Pennsylvania," Pennsylvania Agricultural Experiment Station *Bulletin* 286 (1933).

28. Moline, "Mobility and the Small Town"; and Edmund deS. Brunner, *Immigrant Farmers and Their Children* (Garden City, N.Y.: Doubleday, Doran & Co., 1929), pp. 170–71.

29. Brunner, *Immigrant Farmers and Their Children*, p. 171; Dorn, "Yates County"; "Household Buying by Farm Families, 1929."

30. Denune, "Pickaway County," pp. 25–26.

31. Everett Ludley, "The Growing-Up Years: Memories of Farm and Town Life," *The Palimpsest* 70 (1989): 144.

32. Horace Miner, *Culture and Agriculture: An Anthropological Study of a Corn Belt*

County, Occasional Contributions from the Museum of Anthropology, no. 14 (Ann Arbor: University of Michigan Press, 1949), pp. 70–71.

33. Denune, "Union County," p. 18; Eleanor Arnold, ed., *Girlhood Days*, vol. 4 of *Memories of Hoosier Homemakers* (Indianapolis: Indiana Extension Homemakers Association, 1987), p. 195.

34. C. F. Stevens, "The Pictures Talk," *Farm Journal* (January 1927).

35. Taylor, "Genesee County, New York"; Bruce L. Melvin, "The Sociology of a Village and the Surrounding Country," Cornell University Agricultural Experiment Station *Bulletin* 523 (1931); and Arnold, *Girlhood Days*, p. 194.

36. Melvin, "The Sociology of a Village"; Dennis, "Social Activities"; Kirkpatrick, Kolb, Inge, and Wileden, "Rural Organizations and the Farm Family." A 1914 survey of four Iowa cities, for example, shows that over half of the high school students went to the movies at least four times a month. See Daniel J. Czitrom, *Media and the American Mind: From Morse to McLuhan* (Chapel Hill: University of North Carolina Press, 1982), pp. 42–43.

37. Neth, *Preserving the Family Farm*, pp. 255–56; Thomas J. Morain, *Prairie Grass Roots: An Iowa Small Town in the Early Twentieth Century* (Ames: Iowa State University Press, 1988), p. 169; and Lary May, *Screening Out the Past: The Birth of Mass Culture and the Motion Picture Industry* (New York: Oxford University Press, 1980).

38. Randy Abbott Jr., "The Automobile Comes to Southwest Minnesota," Southwest State University Rural Studies Series (Marshall, Minn.: Society for the Study of Local and Regional History, 1993), p. 14.

39. Neth, *Preserving the Family Farm*, pp. 244–66; Coburn, *Life at Four Corners*, pp. 5, 133–35; and Miner, *Culture and Agriculture*, pp. 43–44. In Kansas and Iowa, this process of change and greater integration into the mainstream was accelerated by anti-German sentiment during World War I.

40. John O. Rankin, "Housing and House Operation Costs on Nebraska Farms," Nebraska Agricultural Experiment Station *Bulletin* 264 (1931); Eleanor Arnold, *Part Lines, Pumps, and Privies*, vol. 2 of *Memories of Hoosier Homemakers* (Indianapolis: Indiana Extension Homemakers Association, 1984), p. 44.

41. Carle C. Zimmerman and John D. Black, "How Minnesota Farm Family Incomes Are Spent," Minnesota Agricultural Experiment Station *Bulletin* 234 (1927); Melvin, "The Sociology of a Village"; and C. E. Lively, "Family Living Expenditures on Ohio Farms," Ohio Agricultural Experiment Station *Bulletin* 468 (1930). Zimmerman and Black do not test for ethnicity per se, but describe each of their sample communities in terms of its ethnic composition.

42. The following discussion summarizes Walter Prichard Eaton, "Everything Electrical," *The Farm Journal* (March 1929).

43. Arnold, *Party Lines, Pumps, and Privies*, pp. 125–26.

44. "Household Buying by Farm Families, 1929."

45. Ibid. Nonelectric stoves were a relatively common purchase for families without electricity, and eight families bought one during 1929. On installment buying, see Fish, "Buying for the Household," p. 74.

46. "Household Buying by Farm Families, 1929."

47. Ibid. In the larger survey of 368 farm families, which also included families in Chautauqua and Allegany Counties, 33 families, almost 10 percent, bought radios during 1929. Fish, "Buying for the Household," p. 74.

48. Von Tungeln, Thaden, and Kirkpatrick, "Cost of Living on Iowa Farms"; Glenn A. Bakkum and Bruce L. Melvin, "Social Relationships of Slaterville Springs– Brooktondale Area, Tompkins County, New York," Cornell University Agricultural Experiment Station *Bulletin* 501 (1930); Denune, "Pickaway County"; Rankin, "Housing and House Operation Costs"; and Kolb and Polson, "Trends."

49. Denune, "Pickaway County," p. 33.

50. Reynold M. Wik, "The Radio in Rural America During the 1920s," *Agricultural History* 55 (1981): 339–50.

51. E. L. Kirkpatrick, P. E. McNall, and May L. Cowles, "Farm Family Living in Wisconsin," Wisconsin Agricultural Experiment Station *Bulletin* 114 (1933); Melvin, "The Sociology of a Village."

52. Ethel Morrison-Marsden, "Mother and the Radio," *The Farm Journal* (March 1928); Jellison, *Entitled to Power*, p. 57.

53. In Wisconsin, farm wives spent 27 percent more time than their husbands listening to the radio. See Kirkpatrick, McNall, and Cowles, "Farm Family Living in Wisconsin."

54. Carl Hamilton, *In No Time At All* (Ames: Iowa State University Press, 1974), pp. 109–11; Wik, "Radio"; and Czitrom, *Media and the American Mind*, p. 74.

55. Quoted in Wik, "Radio."

56. Hamilton, *In No Time At All*, p. 109.

57. Wik, "Radio."

58. Edmund deS. Brunner, "Radio and the Farmer; and A Symposium on the Relation of Radio to Rural Life" (New York: The Radio Institute of the Audible Arts, 1935); Deemer Lee, *Esther's Town* (Ames: Iowa State University Press, 1980), pp. 6–7.

59. For the best history of WLS during this period, see James F. Evans, *Prairie Farmer and WLS: The Burridge D. Butler Years* (Urbana: University of Illinois Press, 1969).

60. For the best discussion of the importance of the WLS *Barn Dance*, see Bill C. Malone, *Country Music U.S.A.: A Fifty-Year History* (Austin: University of Texas Press, 1968), esp. pp. 33–78.

61. Ibid., pp. 68–70.

62. Evans, *Prairie Farmer and WLS*, p. 215.

63. Ibid., pp. 166–67, 184–87.

64. Ibid., pp. 185, 191–92.

65. Interestingly, some of radio's more mainstream stars also had connections with WLS. Charles J. Correll and Freeman F. Gosden were on the station briefly before they went on to create Amos and Andy on another station. Similarly, Marian and Jim Jordan played the Smith Family on WLS in 1927, and they later became Fibber McGee and Molly.

66. On radio and magazine advertising during this period, see Roland Marchand, *Advertising the American Dream: Making Way for Modernity, 1920–1940* (Berkeley: University of California Press, 1985). Much of the discussion in this section relies on the 1929 survey of household buying conducted by the Cornell University Department of Household Economics.

67. "The Automobile and the Village Merchant: The Influence of Automobiles and Paved Roads on the Business of Illinois Merchants," University of Illinois Bureau of Business Research *Bulletin* 19 (1928): 13.

68. Marchand, *Advertising the American Dream*; T. J. Jackson Lears, "From Salvation to Self-Realization: Advertising and the Therapeutic Roots of the Consumer Culture, 1880–1930," in *The Culture of Consumption: Critical Essays in American History, 1880–1980*, ed. T. J. Jackson Lears and Richard W. Fox (New York: Random House, 1983), pp. 1–38; and T. J. Jackson Lears, *Fables of Abundance: A Cultural History of Advertising in America* (New York: Basic Books, 1994). See also Sarah Larson, "'Just Like Homemade' vs. 'Looks Store-Bought': Marketing Modern Virtues to Rural Women" (paper presented at the Social Science History Association Annual Meeting, Baltimore, 1993). Dr. Larson kindly lent the author this paper.

69. George H. von Tungeln, E. L. Kirkpatrick, C. R. Hoffer, and J. F. Thaden, "The Social Aspects of Rural Life and Farm Tenantry in Cedar County, Iowa," Iowa Agricultural Experiment Station, Rural Sociology Section, *Bulletin* 217 (1923): 436–94; Von Tungeln, Thaden, and Kirkpatrick, "Cost of Living on Iowa Farms"; Melvin, "Sociology of a Village"; and E. L. Kirkpatrick, "The Standard of Life in a Typical Section of Diversified Farming," Cornell University Agricultural Experiment Station *Bulletin* 423 (1923).

70. These were the most popular women's magazines of the period. *Ladies' Home Journal* reached a circulation of 1 million in 1903, and was the first major magazine to do so. It was followed in achieving this milestone by *McCall's* in 1908, *Pictorial Review* in 1915, and *Woman's Home Companion* in 1916. Its circulation reached 2 million in 1927. In several cases, there was also considerable overlap between farm periodicals and women's magazines. The *Ladies' Home Journal* developed out of the "Woman and the Home" section of the *Tribune and Farmer* in 1883, and Barton Currie, who became editor in 1921, came from the *Country Gentleman*, which was also published by Curtis Publishing in Philadelphia, continuing a long-standing practice of editorial staff movement between the two publications. *Better Homes and Gardens* was started in

1922 by Edwin Thomas Meredith, who had been Secretary of Agriculture and had started the agricultural monthly, *Successful Farming* (seven subscribers in the survey), and he recruited his first editor from another farm journal, *Iowa Homestead*. See entries for the different magazines in Frank Luther Mott, *A History of American Magazines* (Cambridge, Mass.: Harvard University Press, 1938, 1957, 1968), vols. 2, 3, 4, and 5.

71. The survey did not give any direct information on wealth, but the reported value of home furnishings was used as a proxy. It ranged from $100 to $3,000, with an average of $1,200.

72. Marianne Muse and Isabelle Gillum, "Food Consumption of Fifty Vermont Farm Households," Vermont Agricultural Experiment Station *Bulletin* 327 (1931); Kirkpatrick, "Standard of Life"; Elizabeth E. Hoyt, "Value of Family Living on Iowa Farms," Iowa Agricultural Experiment Station *Bulletin* 281 (1931): 185–239; and John O. Rankin, "Cost of Feeding the Nebraska Farm Family," Nebraska Agricultural Experiment Station *Bulletin* 219 (1927).

73. This number actually understates the popularity of these two brands (as well as the brands of toothpaste discussed below) because the earliest survey forms, particularly some of those used near Lockport, did not ask for preferences for soap and toiletries. In some cases, the surveyor wrote in that information on the old form, anticipating the revised schedule of questions that was used for most of the interviews.

74. According to Sarah Larson's recent research, Lux soap flakes, as opposed to its bar soap, may have been more popular among rural consumers. The J. Walter Thompson advertising agency, which represented Lux, conducted a marketing survey of 355 rural consumers in Putnam County, New York, during 1923, and 78 percent said that they used the product. Larson sees this brand awareness as evidence of cultural continuity between urban and rural societies during the 1920s. Sarah Larson, "Lux for Chickens and Silks: Cultural Continuity in Progressive Era Rural Homes" (paper presented at the Duquesne History Conference, Pittsburgh, October 1993). The author would like to thank Dr. Larson for providing a copy of this paper.

75. On Listerine's advertising, see Marchand, *Advertising*, pp. 18–20.

76. Ibid., p. 20.

77. Eleanor Arnold, ed., *Feeding Our Families*, vol. 1 of *Memories of Hoosier Homemakers* (Indianapolis: Indiana Extension Homemakers Association, 1983), pp. 84–90.

78. Hoyt, "Value of Family Living on Iowa Farms"; J. O. Rankin, "The Cost of Clothing the Nebraska Farm Family," Nebraska Agricultural Experiment Station *Bulletin* 248 (1930); and Muse, "The Standard of Living."

NOTE ON SOURCES

A book that ranges as widely as this one relies on a variety of sources. Specific references to both primary and secondary sources are contained in the notes, and rather than repeating them in a separate bibliography, it is more profitable here to delineate the *types* of sources used, especially since some of them are obscure.

This study began by mining the Newberry Library's extensive collection of local histories and published reminiscences of rural and small-town life. Local histories, often home-grown endeavors that are published privately, vary widely in style, quality, and content, but they contain many valuable nuggets of information and specific examples of larger trends. In addition to written reminiscences, oral history projects that deal with agriculture and rural life are also useful sources, and two in particular were important to this study: the multivolume *Memories of Hoosier Homemakers*, edited by Eleanor Arnold and originally published in the 1980s by the Indiana Extension Homemakers Association; and the interviews conducted during the 1960s at Cornell University, which deal with the Dairymen's League, county agents and agricultural extension, and other farm organizations.

For any study of rural and agricultural history, the agricultural press is an invaluable source. For this project, I searched through a large number agricultural newspapers and periodicals, including national and regional publications as well as titles pertaining to different commodities or organizations. These include *Rural New Yorker, Prairie Farmer, Indiana Farmer's Guide, Wallace's Farmer, Farmer's Wife, American Agriculturalist, Country Gentleman,* and *American Cooperative Journal,* among others. In addition to the usual news items and editorials, letters from readers are an important way to recapture the voices of more ordinary rural folk. One agricultural economist with an interest in history compiled an extensive collection of newspaper articles pertaining to the dairy industry in the New York milkshed that proved to be particularly useful: see Leland Spencer and Charles J. Blanford, *An Economic History of Milk Marketing and Pricing, 1800–1933* (Columbus, Ohio: Grid, Inc., 1977), 5 vols.

A number of the issues dealt with in this book received attention from different government agencies, state and federal, which also generated many important sources. Speeches and discussions at local farmers' institutes, typically published in the reports of state agriculture departments, consider a variety of concerns in the countryside. Similarly, reports from state highway and education departments often give detailed examples of local reactions to attempts at reform. In one case, New

York's deputy commissioner of education was so frustrated by rural opposition to
school reform that he compiled a massive documentary history of the subject that
includes what appears to be every column and letter published in small-town newspapers and every local Grange resolution that discussed the issue. See Thomas E.
Finegan, "The Township System: A Documentary History," New York State Department of Education, *Report* (Albany, 1921), vol. 1, 1,693 pp. In a different vein,
congressional, federal, and state commission hearings shed light on controversies
surrounding mail-order buying and parcel post, the grain trade, and the formation of
farmers' cooperatives, among other issues.

Rural sociologists, agricultural economists, and home economists during the
1910s and 1920s were also deeply concerned with the transformation of rural life
during this period, and they conducted numerous surveys and studies of these
trends, which are also key sources for this book. Many of these studies appeared as
agricultural experiment station bulletins or as more preliminary mimeographed bulletins, and others, especially studies of the impact of the automobile on small-town
businesses, were conducted and published by university business schools. In addition to their quantitative and social scientific dimensions, these surveys are also useful for the less formal comments and observations that they contain. In addition,
manuscript schedules from a survey of farm families' household buying provide a
critical window on the consumption patterns and preferences of rural New York
families. See "Household Buying by Farm Families, 1929," Survey Records of the
Department of Household Economics and Management, Division of Rare and Manuscript Collections, Cornell University Library, accession no. 23/18/1648.

INDEX

Union County Law (New Jersey), 252 (nn. 33–34)

United Express Company, 182, 183

United States: in second great transformation, 19–20; Federal Aid Road Act of 1916, 35, 37–38; Bureau of Public Roads, 38, 39; Federal Highway Act (1921), 39; agricultural policies of, 41; Bureau of Education, 63; Interstate Commerce Commission, 90, 117–18; Capper-Volstead Act, 122; Federal Trade Commission, 137; Robinson-Patman Act, 202, 282 (n. 23); Sherman Act, 264 (n. 40); Smith-Lever Act, 271 (n. 57)

United States Department of Agriculture: Office of Road Inquiry, 37, 252 (n. 30); Office of Markets and Rural Organization, 122; and Farm Bureau, 142; in Committee of Seventeen, 145; radio broadcasting by, 217; surveys by, 222

U.S. Grain Growers, Inc. (USGG), 145–49; membership of, 147–48; failure of, 148, 149, 150

Unity Dairymen's Cooperative Association, 265 (n. 64)

Urban life: inferiority of, 14, 155, 163, 243; ambivalence toward, 16; and road reform, 28; consumerism in, 273 (n. 1)

Vandervort, Helen Bull, 9

Vickery, P. O., 162

Vickery's Fireside, 162

Wallace, Henry, 35, 36

Wallace's Farmer, 35, 182; on educational reform, 74; on radio, 220

Walpole (New Hampshire), 53

Walton, George A., 258 (n. 27)

Wanamaker, John, 182

Ward, Montgomery, 8, 164–74, 243, 277 (n. 58); agrarian values of, 156, 172, 173; market of, 157; career of, 164; and Grange organizations, 164, 166–68, 169, 170–71, 174, 181, 275 (n. 20); in *Prairie Farmer*, 166, 167–68; integrity of, 169–71, 173; catalogue of, 171–74; competitors of, 174–75; rumors circulated against, 175–

76; use of express mail, 183; effect on rural consumers, 190; radio sponsorship by, 225

Warren County, Iowa, 22

Warrick County, Ind., 60, 63

Watkin's liniment, 228

Wayne County, N.Y., 199

Wells, George A., 118, 119

Wells Fargo Express Company, 183

Welsh-Slater Physical Training Law (New York, 1916), 70

Western Grain Dealers' Association, 126

Wheat: price depression in, 111–12

Wheelmen. *See* Bicycling

Wherry, Elizabeth C., 217, 220

White, William Allen, 177, 184, 279 (n. 67)

White House coffee, 225, 229

Wholesale Dry Goods Association, 183

Wiebe, Robert, 10, 11

Wilson, Grace, 223

Wisconsin: road reform in, 34, 38; school construction in, 65–66; one-room schoolhouses in, 73; dairymen in, 104, 261 (n. 4); radio ownership in, 216

Wisconsin Society of Equity, 139, 141, 268 (n. 30)

WLS (radio station), 284 (n. 59); *Barn Dance*, 194, 222–23, 241, 243, 284 (n. 60); stars of, 222–23, 285 (n. 65); *RFD Dinnerbell*, 224, 241

Woman's Home Companion, 226; advertising in, 231; circulation of, 285 (n. 70)

Women: voting rights for, 50. *See also* Farm women

Woodbury's soap, 230

World War I: and road reform, 38–39, 255 (n. 53); effect on cooperatives, 138; anti-German sentiment during, 283 (n. 39)

Worrall, Thomas D., 118, 120

Yates County, N.Y., 201

Yorkville, Illinois, Farmers' Elevator Company, 124, 125

Young people: use of automobile, 208–10; movie viewing by, 283 (n. 36)

Zunz, Oliver, 10, 11